T0329863

THE NEW WHITE RACE

France Overseas
Studies in Empire and Decolonization

SERIES EDITORS
A. J. B. Johnston, James D. Le Sueur,
and Tyler Stovall

THE NEW WHITE RACE

Settler Colonialism and the Press

in French Algeria, 1860–1914

CHARLOTTE ANN LEGG

University of Nebraska Press

Lincoln

Chapter 4, "Pages without Borders: Local Publications in Global Networks," is derived in part from an article published in *Settler Colonial Studies* 8, no. 2 (2018), © Taylor & Francis, available online: https://www.tandfonline.com/doi/full/10.1080/2201473x .2016.1273868.

Publication of this volume was assisted by the University of London Institute in Paris.

All photographs courtesy of Bibliothèque Nationale de France.

Library of Congress Cataloging-in-Publication Data
Names: Legg, Charlotte Ann, author.
Title: The new white race: settler colonialism and the press in French Algeria, 1860–1914 / Charlotte Ann Legg.
Description: Lincoln: University of Nebraska Press, 2021. | Series: France overseas: studies in empire and decolonization | Includes bibliographical references and index.
Identifiers: LCCN 2020038247
ISBN 9781496208507 (hardback)
ISBN 9781496225214 (epub)
ISBN 9781496225221 (mobi)
ISBN 9781496225238 (pdf)
Subjects: LCSH: French newspapers—Algeria—History—19th century. | French newspapers—Algeria—History—20th century. | Press and politics—Algeria—History—19th century. | Press and politics—Algeria—History—20th century. | Journalism—Algeria—History—19th century. | Journalism—Algeria—History—20th century.
Classification: LCC PN5499.A4 L44 2021 |
DDC 079/.6509034—dc23
LC record available at https://lccn.loc.gov/2020038247

Set in Arno Pro by Laura Buis.

For my sisters, Joanna and Caroline

CONTENTS

FIGURES

ACKNOWLEDGMENTS

This book is the product of long friendships, chance encounters, well-laid plans, and fortuitous opportunities.

Part of the research that contributed to this book was undertaken when I was a graduate student at New York University, where I had the great fortune to receive the advice of Edward Berenson, Stéphane Gerson, Frederick Cooper, George R. Trumbull IV, and Christelle Taraud. It is doubtless thanks to their guidance that I was lucky enough to find a job at the University of London Institute in Paris, where I have benefited from the support of my colleagues, in particular Catriona MacLeod and Kate Averis, to whom I have frequently turned to discuss an idea or work through a quandary.

I am grateful to the University of London for awarding me a period of research leave in spring 2018, which allowed me to work on drafting sections of the manuscript. During that time I spent an incredibly productive month as a visiting fellow at the Moore Institute of the National University of Ireland in Galway. I am incredibly grateful to Niall Ó Ciosáin, Daniel Carey, Gearoid Barry, and Philip Dine for that opportunity and for their warm reception.

Just as things were going so well, the road unexpectedly got rocky. I will be forever grateful to my sisters, Joanna and Caroline, and to my friends—especially Claire Cornille and Emily Thomas—for keeping me going and enabling me to keep writing as I wandered between Ireland and Ibiza, Algeria, London, and Paris. Thank you to Grégoire (Jérémie Aureliano Arthur) for meeting me in Montreuil at the end of that particular road. What a wonderful surprise.

I have been spurred on by inspiring conversations and the excellent advice of other historians. I am grateful to Rebecca Scales and Tony Ballantyne, for pointing me toward some helpful readings, and to Briony Neilson, for lending me a friendly ear in the later stages of this project. I hope we will have other opportunities to take on and vanquish coffee machines in libraries and archives across the world. I am indebted to Jennifer Sessions for her very helpful advice about carrying out research in Algeria. Thanks to her suggestions and to the assistance of Karim Ouras and Robert Parks from the Centre d'études maghrebines en Algérie, I was able to spend some time in the archives in Algiers and Oran.

In Algeria I benefited from the kind hospitality of Père Guillaume Michel and Soeur Angélique Somda at the Centre d'études diocésain and Soeur Maisy at the Centre Pierre Claverie. I was touched by the kindness of the women of Algiers and Oran, who offered me their assistance every time I was lost in the streets, who led me to bus stops and metro stops, and who entrusted me to the care of other women to ensure I found my way around. I am especially grateful to Latifa Bouraba, for feeding me cake and teaching me about the infrastructure of Algiers during the Ottoman period, and to Assia and her family in El Madania, whose generous invitation to *iftar* I shall never forget.

Finally, I would like to thank the University of Nebraska Press and their external reviewers, whose insightful comments have exemplified academic community at its best.

All images are from the collections of the Bibliothèque nationale de France. All translations are my own. To consistently reflect the primary sources on which this book draws, I have used colonial-era names and added contemporary place names in brackets when they are first mentioned.

THE NEW WHITE RACE

Introduction

"Another newspaper?" joked the editor of *Le Progrès algérien* in 1900, announcing the arrival of the new publication.[1] It was a curious remark with which to launch a journalistic endeavor. The humor would not, however, have been lost on readers and observers of news in Algeria, who had witnessed a breathtaking increase in titles in the years following the establishment of civil rule under the French Third Republic in 1870 and the liberalization of the press across France and its empire in 1881. "And why not?" continued the editor of *Le Progrès algérien*, unruffled by the competition. "Although the press is much maligned, these days the newspaper is something nobody could do without."[2] His optimism was based not only on an ever-increasing number of publications but also on their diversification in terms of readership, language, and political affiliation. Across the three Algerian provinces, journalists devoted their attention to a wide variety of topics, from local news to national politics, from satire to sports. This burst of journalistic activity was sustained until the eve of the First World War, when the disruption of communications networks and the control of information temporarily calmed the debate. Until this time, however, enthusiasm for the press remained high; in the years before the war, editors could still quip with confidence, "Another newspaper? Aren't there enough already?"[3]

In an era of fast media and fake news, when reactions to events deemed newsworthy are livestreamed across the globe and rumors spread across the web in a matter of moments, print journalism may appear to some as a quaint relic of a bygone age of tranquility punctuated at intervals by leisurely perusal of the morning papers. The dismissal of print journalism, however, often rests on two misconceptions: that the current state of affairs somehow represents a democratization of access to information and that the previous state of affairs reserved this access to the privileged few. Certainly, the historical development of print capitalism in western Europe and its colonies of settlement linked the press to the social and political dominance of the bourgeoisie.[4] Certainly, in these regions and in other colonial settings, social and political hierarchies have been upheld by differential access to publication and self-expression.[5] And yet to reduce the newspaper to a tool of bourgeois colonizers would be to overlook the many and inventive ways in which people from a variety of backgrounds created and interacted with printed news. It would be to overlook, also, the sense of urgency, excitement, and self-investment of journalists, readers, and other recipients of news as they hastily produced their copy, fumbled for coins to buy newspapers from hawkers, or passed articles around groups of friends and colleagues, passing comment as they did so.

The development of the press in Algeria was necessarily shaped by the confluence of these repressive and creative forces. First introduced by the French invaders in 1830,[6] the newspaper was frequently used as a tool for the dissemination of an official narrative by a colonial regime anxious to defend and legitimize French authority. This anxiety was heightened by the particular demography of the conquered territory, where French residents were outnumbered by foreign European nationals for much of the century, and the European population as a whole—which grew from around two hundred thousand in the early 1860s to over seven hundred thousand on the eve of the First World War—never constituted more than a fraction of the Muslim populace, whose estimated numbers fluctuated between three million and five million.[7] To limit opportunities for the different inhabitants of Algeria to question French authority, the colonial government enthusiastically enacted restrictive measures that applied to the press in the French metropole for much of the nineteenth century, and it made use of considerable discretionary powers to quash undesirable publications and penalize errant publishers.[8]

While these measures applied to all inhabitants of the conquered territory, they did not apply equally; Algerian Muslims were policed with the greatest zeal.[9] If the liberalizing legislation of 1881 improved conditions for journalists of French origin—removing the need for official authorization of publications and relieving the tax burden under which French journalists had labored in previous decades—it confirmed the precarious status of those of other European national groups and adversely affected Algerian Muslims. Although the law of July 26, 1881, was hailed by French statesmen as "a law of freedom, such as was never heretofore known by the press," article 6 of the legislation explicitly required chief directors of newspapers to be French citizens in possession of full rights.[10] Amid a population of nearly four million, only some 262,000 individuals—settlers of French origin and Algerian Jews who had been collectively enfranchised by the Crémieux Decree of 1870—could claim such rights in Algeria in the early 1880s.[11] It was not until 1889 and the passage of legislation naturalizing children born of foreign parents on French soil that significant numbers of Europeans of non-French origin enjoyed these same rights.[12] Algerian Muslims did not enjoy these rights at all during this period. As *indigènes* of subordinate legal status, most Algerian Muslims found themselves excluded from newspaper publication, forcing them to rely on naturalized peers or sympathetic Europeans to advance their journalistic projects.

Despite the considerable restrictions generated by the colonial context, by the end of the nineteenth century the press in Algeria was growing faster than that of the French metropole.[13] Although the journalistic field was dominated by French male settlers, settlers of non-French origin were increasingly active in press production, and European women, Algerian Jews, and the first generation of Algerian Muslim journalists had also fought their way onto the pages of newspapers as writers, illustrators, and editors. Their efforts diversified journalistic perspectives and further increased the number of publications in Algeria. By 1897 the French-language press alone, estimates Didier Guignard, was producing one newspaper for every twenty-six inhabitants of the territory.[14] Added to these francophone titles were fluctuating numbers of newspapers in Spanish, Italian, Arabic, and Judeo-Arabic, as well as in bi- and multilingual formats.

While readership was limited by unequal access to education—Guignard estimates that only 11 percent of the population of Algeria at the time would have been able to read French, for example[15]—the influence of the newspaper spread beyond each title's narrow community of readers, as hawkers called out headlines on town squares and street vendors displayed front-page illustrations to curious passersby. In shops, parlors, and cafés, families, friends, associates, and acquaintances regularly crossed paths, discussing newspaper articles and *faits divers*, brief sensational news stories. By the early twentieth century local associations had also been created in a number of settlements, founded with the explicit intention of making newspapers and other publications more widely available to promote education within the family and other spaces beyond the formal confines of the classroom. Some of these associations, such as the Ligue de l'enseignement in Batna, made their resources available to Algerian Muslims as well as European settlers.[16] Such opportunities for Muslims to engage directly with French and colonial newspapers, however, remained rare in a context of state surveillance and severely restricted access to French education. Making effective use of collective reading practices and informal networks of communication, Muslims nevertheless sought to counter their marginalization within established circuits of information.[17]

Moreover, even before their dissemination, newspapers were embedded in dynamics of social exchange through processes of production. "Rather than approaching newspapers simply through the analytical problematic of representation," suggests Tony Ballantyne, "it is more useful to think about them as 'assemblages,' the complex product of a conjuncture of a particular set of material, skills, technologies, financial arrangements and cultural conventions."[18] Despite the growing influence of groups of wealthy investors in the early twentieth century and the resulting drive to use a more standardized format,[19] the press in this era was characterized by artisanal production methods and small, often ephemeral enterprises. Impassioned individuals of all backgrounds were forced to rely on the help of friends and associates to launch, compose, and advertise their papers and frequently called on readers to contribute articles, letters, or literary pieces. The line between journalist and reader was thus often blurred, especially in small and underresourced publications. Although the term *journalist* is used throughout this book, and although the period examined saw the increasing professionalization of journalism in France, newspaper writers and editors in Algeria rarely shared the same status as their metropolitan counterparts. Few, even among settlers, had prior experience in this professional milieu, and many—even the most well known, such as Ernest Mallebay and Omar Racim—supplemented their income with other activities at various stages of their career.

What drove these differently situated members of colonial society into journalistic activity, often against considerable odds? And what forces sustained readership and wider interest in newspapers? Theorists and historians of the press in a variety of contexts have pointed to the role played by newspapers in processes of cultural and political identification in the modern era, an era of rapid cultural and political transformation.[20] Newspapers, as Benedict Anderson has famously argued, were integral to the development of "imagined communities"—particularly that of the nation—as readers congregated around the repeated declaration of common values communicated in dominant languages. If, as in Anderson's analysis, the process of imagining national communities in print was sparked in Europe by the experience of European settlement in the Americas in the eighteenth and early nineteenth centuries, the models it produced were later appropriated by anticolonial nationalists in Asia and Africa.[21] While scholars have criticized the Eurocentrism of this analysis and pointed to other spaces in which the nation was imagined in Europe and in other contexts,[22] the contribution of the newspaper to this historical process of imagining is widely recognized. In a variety of places, therefore, newspapers acted to construct readers' sense of belonging to a given national community through providing imagined borders and stability in a rapidly changing world. Able at once to provoke change and provide reassurance, newspapers encapsulated the contradictory forces of hope and fear that characterized the birth of nations and even modernity itself.

As settings for extraordinary explosions of hope and fear in the form of nation-founding revolutions, both France and Algeria have interested historians of the press. In both cases, however, the enduring strength of national mythologies has often limited historians' ability to look beyond the nation to identify other forms of community proposed by journalists and their readers. While historians of the press in France have largely focused on the ways in which the press contributed to the "homogenization of the national body" in the wake of the revolution of 1789, those who have studied the press activity of the first generations of Muslim journalists in Algeria have often examined their place in a teleology of anticolonial nationalism.[23]

These histories, moreover, have largely developed in parallel. In reading the voluminous *Civilisation du journal*, for example, one might forget that Algeria was ever French.[24] And yet it was perhaps in Algeria, with its array of ethnolinguistic groups and religious communities, that the question of what it meant to be French was being posed by journalists with the most urgency. Although the Algerian provinces were integrated into French national territory in 1848, the separate legal regimes applied to different groups within the population and the lack of full administrative integration with the metropole made the status of the territory and its inhabitants perennially unclear to journalists and readers alike. The failure to integrate colonial Algeria into studies of the press in France risks replicating the historical failure of the state to recognize either the Muslim or European settler inhabitants of the territory as part of a French political or cultural community. The exclusion of settlers has sometimes provided a convenient means of disavowing the republic's responsibility for colonial violence, while the omission of Muslims continues to generate social tensions in French society today.[25] In treating Algeria as an exception, yet another risk emerges—that of overlooking the extent to which other parts of French territory also harbored ethnic and linguistic diversity and how other displaced and migrant populations contributed to the imagination of various forms of community on French soil.[26]

The current study, then, seeks both to resituate colonial Algeria within the history of the press in France and to look beyond the nation as the frame of journalistic imagination. It examines some of the ways in which the diverse ethnic, linguistic, and religious groups living in Algeria in the nineteenth and early twentieth centuries used the press to imagine their relationship with the French national community, to reimagine this community, and to imagine other forms of community entirely. In so doing, it complicates the argument that "from its inception, the colonial press directed the attention of its readers towards metropolitan horizons."[27] European, Jewish, and Muslim journalists in Algeria not only looked to France, but they also looked nearer to home and much farther afield in their efforts to resolve the many questions of settler colonial contest. The objective of this book therefore is to show how local, national, and transnational senses of attachment were simultaneous and interwoven, shaped by and shaping in turn the operation of colonial power in Algeria.

In seeking to think beyond the nation in this way, the book builds on recent scholarship that emphasizes the multidimensional nature of processes of identification among various groups within Algerian society.[28] This scholarship forms part of a wider development in historiographical approaches to North Africa and the space of the Mediterranean.[29] In French scholarship on Algeria, this multidimensionality has often been collapsed by what Sung-Eun Choi refers to as the "repatriation politics" that followed the trauma, for the French nation, of Algerian independence; the French state, Choi explains, sought to "negotiate a post-French-Algerian nationhood" by negating the settler colonial past and "ascribing an innate French identity to colonists and citizens whose national belonging had been otherwise contested if not rejected during the Algerian War."[30] This narrative, as Claire Eldridge demonstrates, proved both appealing and useful to many *pieds-noirs* (displaced European colonists) in the decades following their flight to the French metropole and has sustained a branch of historical writing that insists on the national assimilation, or francization, of the former settlers.[31] Such politically useful narratives have ultimately reified a binary model of colonial power, in which an undifferentiated group of "colonizers" is set against an equally undifferentiated group of "colonized."

In an effort to disrupt this binary model, historians have pointed to the ways in which the various inhabitants of Algeria identified with communities both within and beyond that of the French nation. Reacting against narratives of the straightforward francization of non-French settlers, they have noted that large migrant communities from Spain or Italy, for example, actively cultivated ties with their countries of origin, maintaining native languages and distinct regional and national traditions into the twentieth century.[32] The social interaction of settlers of different national origins—especially those of a lower socioeconomic status, who inhabited the mixed European neighborhoods of colonial cities—also produced, as David Prochaska argues, a strong sense of local belonging and a settler colonial culture that the Europeans of Algeria actively sought to distinguish from that of the French metropole.[33] As intermarriage between settlers of different national origins increased in the last decades of the nineteenth century, and the number of Europeans born in Algeria came to exceed that of first-generation settlers, expressions of "Algerian" settler identity were amplified.

Muslims similarly maintained personal, spiritual, and commercial connections beyond the occupied territory of French Algeria and sought to defend spaces of local autonomy and forms of indigenous cultural expression from the incursions of the colonial state. Despite the violence of these incursions, observes Julia Clancy-Smith, the French did not succeed in fully undoing the ties of the kinship networks and religious communities that had been established in the precolonial era.[34] Nor, James McDougall affirms, did patterns of exchange and circulation between Algeria and the world beyond cease with the arrival of the French.[35] This was also true of the circulation of news, which, as Arthur Asseraf demonstrates, assumed many forms, including rumor, song, and—later in the colonial era—radio broadcast, alongside print. In these forms, news was able to breach the controls and restrictions of the colonial state, link points of reference both near and far, and underpin the imagination of communities other that of the nation—either French or Algerian—by Muslims in the colonized territory.[36]

According to Asseraf, newspapers—as objects "associated with the overwhelming privileges of settlers"—ultimately had little direct influence on the Muslim population when they did not interact with other elements of the broader "news ecosystem." This ecosystem, moreover, polarized colonial society, leading European settlers to increasingly identify with France as the site of domestic news and Algerian Muslims to increasingly identify with other colonized peoples across the world.[37] Asseraf draws these conclusions based on a detailed analysis of the surveillance reports of the colonial authorities and the official correspondence between these authorities and government officials in Paris. While this book by no means rejects either of these conclusions—and indeed, it seeks to build on the arguments of Asseraf and other scholars regarding the multidimensional nature of processes of identification in colonial Algeria—it employs different analytical frameworks, sources, and methodologies to reassert the divergent perspectives of settlers and the metropolitan French in this era. Moreover, it affirms the significance of these divergent perspectives in framing the varied ways in which Algerian Muslims—as well as Algerian Jews and European settlers—engaged with printed news.

The analytical framework of the book is informed by settler colonial theory and takes account of the particular power dynamics of what Lorenzo Veracini terms the "settler colonial situation"—a triangular encounter among "settlers," "indigenous others," and "exogenous others."[38] In the Algerian case, these groups corresponded, respectively, to the mixed European population that had developed since the French conquest of Algiers in 1830; the Muslim and Jewish communities, whose presence in Algeria long predated this conquest; and the French of the metropole, who viewed Algeria from the other side of the Mediterranean.[39] In this struggle for control of the land, peoples, and resources of the occupied territory, settlers sought to differentiate themselves both from the indigenous population and from the metropolitan French. Their quest for distinction fractured the broad category of the colonizer, creating persistent structural tensions of empire.[40] While divisions between settlers and the metropolitan French at times could increase the obstacles for Algerian Muslims and Jews, at other times they could be strategically exploited.

This book traces these power relations as revealed in the construction and utilization of discourses of civilization, race, and gender by journalists from across colonial society. Tracing discourse formation in the press and evaluating the relative dominance of particular discourses in a dynamic field of power requires close analysis of the content and form of a large number of newspapers produced by a wide variety of journalists. The newspapers that form the primary corpus of this study were produced by French citizens of French origin, French citizens of foreign European origin, naturalized and unnaturalized Algerian Muslims, Algerian Jews writing before and after their emancipation, and Spanish and Italian nationals. Female journalists have been included where sources allow, though they remained a small minority in the groups they were able to infiltrate. Opinion is gleaned from across the political spectrum, which at the time accommodated growing populist currents on the left and right and left a shrinking middle ground to be fought over by moderate republican Opportunists and their Radical opponents.

In terms of types of publication, the corpus includes dailies with wide circulation figures, weekly titles with restricted local circulation, and ephemeral papers intended as urgent cries of alarm or discontent in the face of imminent danger or endless frustration. Given that the study seeks less to gauge the relative influence of one publication or another than to trace the production of discourse across the press as indicative of the possibilities of the journalistic imagination in settler colonial Algeria, this approach has seemed appropriate. It is not without its difficulties, however; faced with the impossibility of reading all available newspapers from 1860 to 1914, I have tried to cast as wide a net as possible while focusing the analysis around events that provoked journalists' explicit questioning of the settler colonial relationship, such as the visits of the French heads of state in 1860, 1865, and 1903; the anti-Jewish violence at the turn of the century; wars of independence in territories of foreign empires; and the proposed conscription of Muslims in the early twentieth century.

Through the discussion of these events and others, journalists with different perspectives on the settler colonial situation in Algeria sought to define certain populations in relation to others and to transform the nature of empire. Despite enjoying shared privileges as Europeans, settler journalists and their metropolitan counterparts did not readily agree on the definition of the colonial project. Under the Second Empire, Napoleon III's vision of an Arab kingdom in Algeria generated deep mistrust of the French authorities. Fears of French withdrawal from the territory were mixed with resentment toward the state and the army, as settlers were forced to confront their dependence on these institutions for the protection of their lives and privileges. Although the hopes of many settlers were revived by the reinstatement of the republic in 1870 and the concomitant transition to a civil regime in the Algerian provinces, the passage of the Crémieux Decree—collectively enfranchising the Jews of Algeria—sustained a sense of vulnerability that, in the decades that followed, was often expressed in the press in the violent rejection of Algerian Jews and the French political establishment. Expressions of vulnerability and isolation were further fueled in these decades by the elaboration of the discourse of the "civilizing mission" by metropolitan politicians and journalists.[41] Perceived as an arabophile threat to the primacy of the European population, this discourse was strongly criticized by settler journalists and local authorities.

Their rejection of the civilizing mission was also motivated by their perception of this mission's indiscriminate nature: like indigenous peoples, the mixed settler population of Algeria was often viewed by metropolitan observers as in need of moral improvement and cultural correction. Settlers' mixed origins and multiple allegiances posed a problem for the French state, especially after 1880, when the consolidated republican regime began a concerted program of cultural assimilation. It was this ideological objective, combined with anxiety surrounding the strength of a recently unified German nation, that finally led the state to approve the collective naturalization of foreign European nationals in Algeria in 1889, after decades of indecision.[42]

Far from allaying French fears, however, the sudden creation of new citizens generated further anxiety in the metropole as observers noted the obstinate cultural difference of the neo-French, a difference that threatened to "contaminate" the body politic.[43] Such fears reached a fever pitch at the turn of the century, as metropolitan journalists and politicians condemned the violent anti-Jewish protests led by their settler counterparts in reaction to what they saw as nefarious Jewish influence on colonial society. Despite the coincidence of these events with the Dreyfus Affair and the outpouring of antisemitic sentiment elsewhere on French soil, settlers' actions were taken by metropolitan onlookers as evidence of their uncivilized and "barely French" disposition.[44] Such violence temporarily abated after the settler colony gained financial autonomy in 1900, with the creation of the Délégations financières, a colonial assembly in which representatives of French citizens and Muslim French nationals debated the allocation of the colonial budget.[45] French authorities nevertheless remained wary of settlers, who used their dominance of the newly established assembly to renew pressure on the state. Foreign and naturalized settlers of foreign origin particularly drew the suspicion of the authorities and were closely surveilled in the tense decades around the turn of the century.[46]

Similarly operating within contemporary colonial discourses of race and civilization, settlers also employed this language to express notions of belonging and difference. In contrast to their metropolitan counterparts, however, settlers drew boundaries that were at once more stark, when dividing Europeans from Muslims and Jews, and more fluid, when accounting for differences among Europeans, particularly those from the Latin nations of the Mediterranean. From the 1860s settler journalists referred to a "Latin race" to which they believed the principal European groups in Algeria—French, Spanish, and Italian—belonged by virtue of their common classical heritage and shared destiny to "resurrect the granary of Rome" in a region left to stagnate under a supposedly moribund Arab rule.[47] This daring venture, settler journalists advanced, had the potential to restore a process of European civilization seen to have gone dangerously awry in the decadent, failed societies on the other side of the Mediterranean Sea. The notion of Latin heritage thus served to distinguish settlers from indigenous peoples while allowing for degrees of difference among settlers themselves. While the notion was flexible enough to allow settlers to claim the kinship of their community with the French people they were destined to regenerate, this very destiny set them apart from the rest of the French population, as the vanguard of a new form of civilization.[48]

This cultural definition of race, Ellen Amster notes, belied an increasingly prominent biological dimension in the last decades of the nineteenth century, as French doctors in North Africa came to understand culture as the outward expression of fixed internal characteristics.[49] The biological dimension of "Algerian" settler specificity was emphasized starting in the 1870s, as settler doctors and demographers studied the effects of intermarriage among French, Spanish, and Italian settlers, concluding that an acclimatized people had been produced, specially adapted to the local environment by their interactions and by the physical process of settlement itself. This people, noted local specialist Dr. René Ricoux, was also more robust and fertile than the French of the metropole,[50] whose apparent failure to increase the national birth rate had been a major cause of concern for the state since the devastating defeat at the hands of the Prussian army in 1870. Dynamic and full of youthful potential, the settler community constituted, in Ricoux's expert opinion, nothing short of a "new white race."[51] If differences between colonizer and colonized were henceforth drawn according to color, differences between settlers and the Europeans living over the sea were similarly racialized, according to sensibilities, behavior, and forms of cultural expression.

Those settlers whose comportments seemed dominated by Anglo-Germanic or Arab blood—the Swiss, Germans, or Maltese, for example—were thus entirely overlooked by most settler journalists, who wrote for a Latin majority whose cultural practices and forms of linguistic expression were seen to be compatible without being stultifyingly standardized.[52] It was this Latin majority that formed what journalists routinely referred to during this period as the "Algerian" people. Via the expansion of the settler press, this term—which settlers had employed from the 1830s and 1840s in defense of their shared political interests—was increasingly used to describe a community conscious of its cultural specificity.

The legitimate "Algerian" public as presented by settler journalists, therefore, was defined in racial and cultural terms. Widely understood as an expression of a people's true nature, and fundamental to the development of their race, gender codes were integral to the journalistic imagination of the "Algerian" community. The "Algerian" defended by settler journalists was male, aggressively masculine, favoring physical activity and a forthright manner over the ratiocination and niceties of European civilization. Settler journalists blamed such niceties, along with their inherent comforts, for contemporary Europe's state of decadence, and the true "Algerian" would eschew them in favor of a simple, honest existence. Honesty was to be the remedy to the stifling and emasculating etiquette of the French metropole, and the true "Algerian" was exhorted to speak his mind and to act on his thoughts through impulsive physical expression—often at the expense of settler women and Algerian Jews and Muslims, who would bear the brunt of this aggressive liberation.

The frontier masculinity promoted by settler journalists in Algeria echoed that identified by historians in other colonial settings.[53] In Algeria, however, the remaking of man had as much to do with the anticipated resurgence of the white Latin race as with the project of French national regeneration. Whether defending French interests or acting on behalf of a transnational Latin people, settler journalists embraced an aggressive, undisciplined form of manliness as an antidote to the restrictive self-discipline of the dominant codes of modern masculinity.[54] Though the fear of losing French favor after the violent excess of the turn of the century caused most journalists to recalibrate the measures of the "Algerian" manly ideal, they continued to define settler colonial masculinity in opposition to the codes of the metropole and to those of Muslim men. Although the perceived barbarity of Muslim masculinity fascinated settler journalists, intent on divesting themselves of the mollifying trappings of civilization, emulating the gendered behavior of the *indigène* ultimately represented too great a threat to the racial hierarchies of empire and was rejected.

Throughout the period, settler journalists sought to set a manly example for their readers, portraying themselves as frank, self-sacrificing, and ready to fight to defend their land and their privilege. As discussed in chapter 1, the gendered and racialized professional culture that developed among settler journalists strongly discouraged the participation of settler women, as well as Algerian Muslims and Jews. Making inventive use of the terms of "Algerian" identity as proposed by their male settler counterparts, however, these other groups of writers persisted, founding their own newspapers in which they explored other forms of community, both national and transnational.

The professional hierarchies established by male settler journalists were sustained by the particular mix of emotions created by the specificities of the settler colonial experience in Algeria. "Fear," writes Martin Evans, "was a constant emotional presence for Europeans in French Algeria"; if their fear stemmed primarily from their situation as a privileged demographic minority surrounded by a Muslim population whose customs and language they little understood, it was also nourished by their dependence on a French state and wider French public who appeared alternately uninterested in and disparaging toward settlers.[55] Mixed with this fear were feelings of pride in what they believed they had achieved in Algeria, excitement about the promise of new beginnings, and frustration at the seemingly slow pace of colonial development. These emotions contributed to the conceptualization of the settler colonial situation as a set of family dynamics, as examined in chapter 2.

Reacting to the prevalent metropolitan discourse of the "colonial family romance," in which France appeared as a benevolent parent to its blighted colonized children,[56] settler journalists rejected Algerian Muslims as their brothers and insisted on their own exclusive claim as heirs of France. Unwilling to submit to the same infantilizing discourses that were imposed on the indigenous population, however, they also asserted their claims as brothers and equals to their metropolitan counterparts. The gendered dynamics of this settler colonial family romance changed over time, between the visits of Napoleon III in the 1860s and that of French president Emile Loubet in 1903, as settler journalists presented colonists alternately as dutiful French daughters and rebellious "Algerian" sons. Once again turning settler journalistic discourses to their own ends, the first Muslim journalists in Algeria presented themselves as France's adopted children, thus underscoring their loyalty while defending their cultural differences.

The tensions between the competing claims of settler journalists—who wanted their readers to enjoy the protection due to children of France while claiming the independence of grown "Algerian" men—remained unresolved until the turn of the century, when a series of events forced settlers to confront the realities of losing their French guardian. The desire for greater autonomy from France had long been expressed in the settler press as antisemitism, as settlers reacted against the political enfranchisement of the Algerian Jews in 1870 and the perceived power of the Jewish electorate to block the creation of more autonomous administrative institutions. Chapter 3 examines the growth of the anti-Jewish press in Algeria and interrogates its relationship to the gendered and racialized terms of "Algerian" inclusion. Initially leading the charge of a growing anti-Jewish movement, and inciting a wave of popular violence against Algerian Jews in the last years of the nineteenth century, settler journalists were forced to reevaluate their position when the separatist undertones of the movement came to the fore. The attack on the settlement of Margueritte in 1901, led by Righa tribesmen left destitute by the confiscation of their lands, came as a painful reminder of the settler colony's dependence on French protection; the metropolitan press's assignation of blame for the attack to violent settler practices and attitudes served as an equally painful reminder of metropolitan observers' disregard for the settler community. By the time of President Loubet's visit in 1903, most settler journalists were prepared to submit to French sovereignty. This did not lessen their claims to local cultural specificity, however. As chapters 2 and 3 show, the anti-Jewish turbulence and subsequent presidential visit ultimately reinforced settler identification as part of a transnational Latin family, of which the French national community was but one branch.

The multiple affiliations of settler journalists and their readers were similarly strengthened by the development of telecommunications in the last decades of the nineteenth century. As described in chapter 4, the increasing integration of the settler colony into an expanding global network of telegraph cables neither effaced the sense of being a distinctive local community nor allowed a technically dominant French national community to impose itself, but instead provided settlers with multiple points of comparison to which they made ready reference in their imagination of an "Algerian" people. Comparisons with other settler colonies—particularly those in Cuba and Southern Africa, where contemporary rebellions against the imperial center were underway, and the United States, where independence had already been won—gave settler journalists perspective on their own aspirations to greater autonomy. Tempted by the success of the United States, and supportive of the efforts of the rebellious Boers, settler journalists nevertheless cautioned against rupture with their French protectors. This caution was exercised not only in the name of the French colonial empire but also in the interests of a transnational Latin race, whose energies were already being uselessly depleted in Cuba rather than conserved in preparation for the looming conflict with Germanic peoples in Europe.

Settler journalists' experiments in bi- and multilingual publication further demonstrated their belief in the significance of the "Algerian" people as a vanguard of a regenerated Latin civilization. While French imperialists believed firmly in the superiority of the French language as a vessel of a superior civilization, a number of publications in the settler colony placed French alongside Spanish and Italian as but one version of a shared Latin idiom. Chapter 5 examines the nature of the linguistic interaction in newspapers in Algeria, noting the different politics of translation evident in settler publications and in the bilingual Franco-Arabic, Franco-Hebraic, and Franco-Judeo-Arabic publications pioneered by Algerian Muslims and Jews.

The different approaches of the journalists from each of these groups reflected their different legal statuses, as well as their different reimaginings of community in French Algeria. Aiming to defend and consolidate the place of the Algerian Jews in the French nation after 1870, Jewish journalists promoted the French language as a vector of civilization, employing direct translation in an effort to francize their coreligionists. While some Muslim journalists used the same strategy to prove the potential for the cultural assimilation of the politically disenfranchised *indigènes*, others resorted to translation only to circumvent colonial surveillance—or eschewed text entirely in favor of images of Muslim resistance. Still others used the French language exclusively, turning the language of the colonizer to the defense of the cultural and religious differences of the colonized and thereby proving that differences could reside within the nation. Seeking to defend their cultural differences from within the political community of the nation, settlers, by contrast, did not have to choose between languages or subordinate other idioms to translation of a French original.

In diverse ways, therefore, settler journalists in Algeria contributed to the imagination of a "new white race." This race was born out of the interaction of the principal European groups of the settler colony—the French, Spanish, and Italians—in the specific conditions of struggle for land, privilege, and survival created by the settler colonial situation in Algeria. Operating within the same field of power relations, Algerian Muslims and Jews also influenced the discourses of the settler colonial press. Not only did their actions and political demands elicit hope and fear among settler journalists, but their incursions into the public space of the press affected the delicate relationship between settlers and the French authorities. Reappropriating notions of regeneration and of French and Algerian community, these journalists challenged the racial definition of the colonial public.

1

...

The New White Race

Journalism and Civilization in French Algeria

"A people's stage of development is reflected in the press," insisted Franco-Spanish newspaper *El Patuet* in 1883.[1] The link between the press and civilization was widely accepted by European journalists in Algeria, regardless of their different national origins, class backgrounds, and political persuasions. Their confidence echoed that of their forebears on the European continent, who had long cherished a belief in the capacity of newspapers to both generate and reflect the progress that defined the modern era. Whether one was liberal or conservative, asserted Catholic publication *La Croix*, one could not deny that in such an era, "the press forms public opinion; public opinion forms the legislator; the legislator forms the law."[2] And if the law proved too restrictive, noted the radical *Le Sans-culotte*—whose editorial board supposedly included "Robespierre, Danton, Marat, Saint-Just, [and] Mirabeau"—the press provided a popular forum within which a revolutionary "program of healthy purification" and "social regeneration" could be launched.[3]

As a measure and motivator of progress, the press held particular appeal in a settler colonial context where, journalists insisted, "all is yet to be created, all is yet to be imagined."[4] Newspapers, they believed, had an essential role to play in transforming nebulous ideas into material measures of development. "These days," mused the editor of *Le Progrès algérien*, "the newspaper is something that nobody could do without.

The ideas that float about in the atmosphere of our spirit, and vivify it, should they not be captured in order to become even more lively and productive?"[5] In this way *progress* became the watchword of the settler colonial press, particularly after the liberalizing republican legislation of 1881, which permitted European journalists in Algeria to freely express their visions of the colony's future after decades of restriction under previous regimes. The concept inspired numerous titles, from *Le Progrès algérien* and *Le Progrès de l'Algérie* to local newspapers of a more limited circulation, including *Le Progrès de Rouïba, Sétif, Jemmapes* (Azzaba), *Guelma, Mascara, and Orléansville* (Chlef). Editors and journalists also favored a hopeful allusion to the promise of progress yet to come, with titles such as *L'Avenir algérien* and its local variants, *L'Avenir de Jemmapes, La Calle* (El Kala), *Tlemcen, Bel Abbès, Mostagenem, Batna, Biskra,* and *Saïda.*[6]

The progress to which these newspapers referred, however, was not to be measured solely in social and political terms. Among the ideas "floating about in the atmosphere" of the settler colony during this period was that of the development of the "Algerian" people, a "new Latin race" deriving from the interaction of Frenchmen, Italians, and Spaniards on North African soil. This idea, first cautiously raised by writers working under the constraints of the Second Empire and then more fully interrogated by doctors and demographers in the last decades of the nineteenth century, was widely promoted by settler journalists working in the more liberal conditions created by the 1881 legislation. Using their publications to examine the character and composition of a "new white race," settler journalists sought to distinguish the principal groups of European residents in Algeria from Arabs, Berbers, and Jews and from the French of the metropole. Unlike these other peoples, they suggested, whose aged civilizations had succumbed to decadence and degeneracy, the "Algerian" people were young and powerful—a force for progress within North Africa, around the Mediterranean, and beyond.

Heir to the genius of the powerful "Latin race" of antiquity—"the race of art, of science, of generosity and heroism"—the "neo-Latins" were further strengthened by the physical trials of settlement in an inhospitable new land.[7] These antecedents and experiences were understood by journalists to have produced a racial formation predicated not only on an imagined communality of Latin blood but also on a shared set of cultural practices and gender ideals. In particular, the hypermasculine behaviors of undisciplined self-expression and physical force were lauded as antidotes to the feminizing effects of European modernity, as well as safeguards against "Oriental" decadence, and were consequently viewed as prerequisites for the health of the young "Algerian" people. Social and political progress, settler journalists submitted, was dependent on the growing strength of this people, which could be ensured only by the effective management of interactions among the various racial, ethnic, and religious communities living in Algeria.

Criticizing the French authorities for their failures in this regard—as evidenced in their perceived arabophilia and "Jewified" corruption—settler journalists increasingly took it upon themselves to police the boundaries between these various communities. As self-proclaimed representatives and defenders of the "Algerian" people, settler journalists presented themselves as the very embodiment of "Algerian" ideals, espousing a professional culture that emphasized aggressive physical engagement and a stubborn independence of character. Journalists, proclaimed *La France algérienne*, were to act in the settler colony as "legions of young, adventurous spirits," incarnations of Hope itself, "prettily defined by Aristotle as 'the fruition of the future.'"[8] Those who, like veteran journalist Augustin Castéran, were seen to use their "tough character and indomitable spirit" to "fight with vigor" in defense of their fellow "Algerians" earned the respect of their peers.[9]

Guarantor of progress, the press in Algeria thus became the preserve of the settler men who at once defined and incarnated the "Algerian" ideal. These men cultivated a professional culture that replicated and reinforced wider patterns of social and political exclusion in the colonial territory, managing press access and participation in journalistic activity according to their own ideals of race and gender. Incarnating what they saw as the legitimate colonial public, these journalists contributed to long-standing debates surrounding the administrative status of the colony, arguing with increasing frequency the need for a colonial body politic that reflected the emergence of a distinctive "Algerian" people.

Presumed incapable of the requisite independence of mind and combative physical engagement, Jews, Muslims, and European women were rejected from nascent professional networks and associations. Among these groups of writers, only European women gained a grudging acceptance in the pages of settler newspapers, as some editors saw female readers as a potential market. As both writers and readers, however, European women were constrained to adhere to the gendered stereotype of the "Algérienne." Straying beyond these confines, female authors were openly ridiculed by their male colleagues, as were indigenous writers, whose contributions to the field of press activity in Algeria were consistently mocked by their settler counterparts as contrary to the journalistic mission of progress and civilization.

Recognizing the power of the press to narrate and disseminate new forms of community, however, these marginalized groups persisted in their efforts to publicize alternative visions of Algeria's future. Their propositions necessarily differed according to their unique social and political situations, yet each group found ways to appropriate the dominant journalistic discourses of youth and progress in an attempt to mediate between the newly defined ideals of the "Algerian" people and the more established precepts of the French republic and its civilizing mission. Using wherever possible the particular power dynamics of settler colonialism to their advantage, these other journalists traced paths that deviated from those of their contemporaries in the metropole. While, for example, Marguerite Durand and the female journalists of Parisian publication *La Fronde* were performing femininity in an effort to destabilize dominant discourses of gender,[10] European women in Algeria were refashioning French femininity by enacting the perceived youth and dynamism of the "Algerian" people. For indigenous journalists, the two categories of French and Algerian far from exhausted the range of imagined possibilities, as writers turned a faith in youth and progress into the basis of transnational religious communities and political federations.

Embodying the New White Race in the Settler Press

"Do we not constantly try to popularize science and make it accessible to everyone, even the most modest among us?" asked *Le Petit fanal oranais* in 1900.[11] Journalists and their readers could not have but answered in the affirmative. Indeed, by the turn of the century settler journalists had spent several decades charting advances in scientific thought, advocating their application in the colony, and goading the general government and municipal authorities into action over questions of hygiene and sanitation.[12] The continual diffusion of medical and scientific information in the press served to write settler readers into modern narratives of progress. By tracing medical and technological developments within the colony, explained *Le Petit fanal oranais*, readers would come to appreciate "the transformations that have taken place before their eyes over a number of years."[13] Journalists juxtaposed these local developments with international news—such as British research into malaria in Sierra Leone or the American discovery of the curative properties of liquid air[14]—thereby situating "Algerians" alongside other supposedly civilized peoples and giving their readers a measure by which to evaluate colonial progress.

Despite widespread optimism in the onward march of civilization, journalists were conscious of its fragility, pointing to the supposed decline of a once-prosperous Arab race and the decadence of modern European societies as evidence of the degeneracy that inevitably befell peoples neglectful of their moral and physical health. Fears of degeneracy— understood by nineteenth-century scientists as a state of chronic moral, physical, and mental weakness, apt to be transmitted from generation to generation until the race eventually declined[15]—were heightened in the settler colonial context, where French hygienists identified exposure to the African climate and contact with indigenous peoples as threats to the health of the European. Well beyond the turn of the century and the rise of germ theory to paradigmatic status, French doctors held to climatic understandings of disease, believing that the incautious venturing of Europeans into the North African sun could enervate them and disrupt their constitution, leading to a loss of civilized propriety and the onset of physical weakness and mental instability.[16]

While metropolitan doctors sought to help settlers escape this fate through the prescription of strict sartorial and dietary regimes, moral codes, and hydrotherapy, settler doctors, by contrast, worked to recast the local environment as a source of racial regeneration.[17] According to self-proclaimed colonial "experts," both the local climate and the unique mix of European peoples contributed to the formation of a strong and fertile "Algerian" race, described by Dr. Edmond Vidal, general secretary of the Union des femmes de France (UFF) and champion of the "Algerian" people as a regenerative force for the French nation, as "a veritable fountain of youth, in which the tired and worn out elements of the most noble of nations will be rejuvenated by Algerian energy and youthful vigor."[18]

Informed by these competing currents of contemporary medical opinion, settler journalists made the defense of European health and the cultivation of an "Algerian" people central aspects of their wider campaign to ensure the growth and progress of the settler colony. Readers were offered a plethora of advice on how to maintain their health, gleaned from medical authorities on both sides of the Mediterranean, as well as from a number of well-meaning local amateurs, such as "Tio Fava" and "Tia Figarola," who offered remedies for hair loss or recipes for homemade insect repellent.[19] Although settler journalists gave credence to the anxieties of metropolitan hygienists, reprinting extracts from specialist publications that advised Europeans in Africa to maintain strict standards of behavior and "avoid excess of all kinds,"[20] they also excitedly reported the findings of colonial experts like Dr. René Ricoux, who had questioned the assumption that Algeria was an "insalubrious" land and demonstrated that the birth rate of the mixed settler population exceeded that of the French metropole. Such observations inspired great confidence in the potential of the "Algerian" people at a time when the French state and Académie de médecine were caught up in anxious discussions about national depopulation.[21] Metropolitan journalists who persisted in denouncing the Algerian climate as inhospitable, despite apparent evidence to the contrary, were taken to task by their settler counterparts, who compiled their own demographic statistics by way of argument.[22]

In publicizing these varying interpretations of the effects of settlement in North Africa on European bodies, journalists ultimately defended the emerging "Algerian" people as a new branch of the European race— "the new white race," as designated by Ricoux.[23] Of European descent, settler readers were enjoined to remain vigilant in the face of potential threats to their civilized constitution; as "Algerians," however, they were also reminded of their constitutional difference from Europeans on the other side of the Mediterranean. This difference, L'Algérie pointed out, was "a result of their *milieu*, and the fact of inhabiting a new country where all is yet to be created, all to be imagined—and of being in contact with diverse races." Such circumstances, journalists claimed, produced "a quicker temper, and a more resolute and more adventurous spirit than in the mother country." Most settler colonies were marked by these traits, journalists agreed, but by the end of the nineteenth century, these characteristics were "already visible" in the "Algerian" people, "despite the fact that Algeria [was] barely sixty years old, which is childhood for a colony."[24]

The particular characteristics of this forward-looking society were discussed in the press as journalists attempted to further define "Algerian" specificity. In addition to a quick temper and an adventurous nature, "Algerians" were said to be physically strong and to possess a heightened consciousness of their physicality, arising from their struggles against hostile surroundings. In contrast to the excessively refined sensibilities that doctors attributed to highly civilized Europeans,[25] the "Algerian" sense of physicality was linked to the more direct relationship between the body and the environment, which was believed to characterize "natures that are too strong or too primitive."[26] Far from decrying this perceived primitivism, however, most settler journalists celebrated the simplicity of the "Algerian," defending him from the critiques of observers from the other side of the Mediterranean. "You complain that the inhabitants of Algeria have no manners, are quick-tempered, even vulgar," noted a journalist at *L'Algérie*, addressing these critics. "Well, I'll admit that I prefer the brazen frankness of words and actions to a refined politeness of language and deceitful obsequiousness of manners."[27]

Settler journalists' emphasis on the transparent outward communication of inner thoughts and emotions recalled the sensibilities of the French revolutionaries who had, a century before, also attempted to make the world anew.[28] Just as the revolutionaries had sought to shore up the national community and transform the body politic through the policing of individual bodies, settler journalists promoted "Algerian" behaviors to strengthen the settler community and its basis for political negotiation with the metropole. And just as the "universal subject" of Enlightenment thought masked privileged male access to the public sphere,[29] the "Algerian" to whom settler journalists referred as representative of a distinct colonial public was necessarily male. More specifically, in recognition of the youth and dynamism of the new settler people, the "Algerian" of the journalistic imagination was a robust young man. Tracing the growth of the colony, suggested *Le Petit fanal oranais*, was like "looking through photos of dear children captured at various stages of their life," from "the chubby baby, the small child in a smock, the little boy in his school uniform, the student with his burgeoning moustache, the young soldier in military garb" up to the "finished man," portrayed as a fiancé on the brink of founding his own family.[30] Having arrived at reproductive maturity, the healthy "Algerian" man presaged the growth and success of the colony as a whole.

The "finished man" lauded by settler journalists, however, did not conform to the dominant model of manliness that emerged in the French metropole over the course of the long nineteenth century. This model, based on the bourgeois adaptation of prerevolutionary male codes of honor, privileged the manly control of emotions and their outward expression.[31] Even as journalists in the metropole came to favor an "embodied stereotype of masculinity" in the fin-de-siècle context of perceived depopulation and degeneration, self-control remained central to the dominant understanding of manly strength.[32] It was this capacity for self-discipline, French doctors and sensationalist reporters of the turn of the century affirmed, that distinguished manly men from effeminate deviants and criminals, as well as from women, whose inability to control their emotions explained their propensity for both hysteria and "crimes of passion."[33]

Such self-restraint, however, held little appeal for settler men, whose efforts to forge a new path for the French people and the white race depended on "a lack of self-control" and a "vivid and dynamic imagination that amplifies satisfaction and exaggerates disappointment." "Alongside great ambition," observed Dr. Vidal, the "Algerian" was prone to "sudden outbursts of anger followed by bitter periods of despondency."[34] Associating self-discipline with both age and inaction, settler doctors and journalists alike dismissed this trait as contrary to the desired march of progress in Algeria. "We are bored of ancestral doctrines," complained a writer for *La France algérienne*. "Gone is the seat by the fireside where, smothered in thick blankets, we would wait for imagined illnesses to be healed; we now need existence in the open air, powerful exercise that leaves us stronger and more handsome." By renouncing the comforts of their former homes and leaping into action in the colony, settlers, local journalists believed, would finally "become men" and thus ensure the development of "a new race."[35]

The vivifying effects of outdoor pursuits in the colonial environment were further emphasized in the sporting press, a sector that grew rapidly in the final decades of the nineteenth century. Sometimes linked to newly established sports clubs and associations,[36] such publications reported on local contests and displays of physical prowess, focusing on the popular activities of cycling, racing, gymnastics, and boxing. Journalists for these newspapers relied on breathless description of colors, textures, and sensations to emphasize the emotional dimension of "Algerian" masculinity and draw players and spectators alike into the same gendered physical culture. "It is for you, mister sportsmen, that we are primarily destined," explained *Algérie-Sports*, addressing the "drivers with enormous goggles, who travel the roads in their steel monsters, in the rain and in the dust," the "cyclists with powerful calves who ride for many kilometers," the "yachtsmen moved by love to tend a white sail to the azure sky," and the "footballers and walkers whose shirts brighten up the hippodromes of Mustapha and Saint-Eugène."[37]

The emphasis on temperamental instability, sensation, and the outward expression of emotion through action also led settler journalists to review dominant metropolitan attitudes toward youth. Often portrayed by French doctors and politicians as an ambiguous and unstable phase of life in which adolescents had yet to fully develop the manly traits of reason, independence, and self-discipline, youth became the unruly target of a range of state institutions.[38] For settler doctors and journalists, however, it was the very lack of refinement and respectability characterizing youth that made it a potent force for progress. In the last decades of the nineteenth century a number of youth publications were launched in which journalists used rousing language to mobilize young settler men and urge their physical investment in the colony's future.[39] Established by groups of "young, new men . . . whose only concern is the prosperity of Algeria, where most of us were born," such papers presented the passion and fervor of male youth as the driving force of colonial development. "Make way for the youth! Yes, make way for the youth!" proclaimed *La Bataille*. "Make way for those who are strengthened and driven by a fervent enthusiasm, their still-gleaming illusions, and a new and unbroken faith in the future." Unlike the men of old European civilizations, the paper suggested, these first generations of African-born "Algerians" could march onward unencumbered by the burdens of the past, "without trailing behind them anything that went before, anything that is worn out, outdated, and aged."[40]

Presenting themselves as the foremost defenders of the "Algerian" people, settler journalists across various sectors strove to embody the manly ideals of physical expression and youthful dynamism. Distancing themselves from any interpretation of journalism as an intellectual activity, settler writers cultivated a combative style in which words held weight, presaging direct physical engagement in social and political disputes. "We are not for noisy declarations, for empty and sonorous speeches," explained *L'Algérie nouvelle*. "We prefer things—which are as substantial as seed—to words, which are as insubstantial as straw."[41] "How we let ourselves be seduced and persuaded by the deceitful power of words!" echoed *L'Algérie*; symptomatic of the slow pace and indecision of metropolitan politics, words were perceived as an obstacle to progress in the colony. "So we wait," the paper continued, "but for heaven's sake, what are we waiting for? For Algeria to die of weakness . . . ? We believe the moment to act has come, and we must act quickly if we want the colony to experience a new burst of vitality."[42]

Settler journalists' sense of urgency was fueled by their frustration with long-standing and unresolved debates regarding the administrative status of the Algerian territory. The question had been under continual discussion in France since the last days of the Bourbon restoration and the first days of the July Monarchy.[43] Although three Algerian *départements* were created in 1848 and integrated into French national territory by the efforts of zealous republicans intent on creating a "one and indivisible nation," the supplementary structures of the Algerian general government were not dismantled, creating the basis for a complex, dualistic administrative system that survived both the Second Empire's brief experiment of a ministry for Algeria and the colonies and the Third Republic's drive to unification under the *sytème des rattachements* from 1881. This last reform, which placed various local administrative offices under the direct auspices of relevant ministries in Paris, had the potential to satisfy settler demands for closer assimilation to the metropole; inefficient and imperfectly realized, however, it ultimately spread further discontent.

Coinciding with the liberalization of the press, the creation of the *sytème des rattachements* prompted widespread public comment among settler journalists, who increasingly came to lament the French government's inability to impose administrative coherence across the Mediterranean. "We are strangely governed," asserted *La France africaine* in 1892. "A *colony*, with a civil governor; a *French département*, with departmental and communal administration; a *conquered land*, with areas under military command. . . . Laws, decrees, rulings, orders, decisions, circulars—all this comes and goes, passes through, arrives, collides, clashes, contradicts the others. . . . Try not to get lost in it all."[44] Two years later, the paper had still not unraveled the mystery: "Is Algeria a colony or not? It is a most complex question to which the most intelligent people are yet to find an answer."[45]

Faced with the circuitous discussions and unfulfilled promises of metropolitan politicians, settler journalists offered not words, but the embodied vow of the "Algerian," ready to invest physically in the struggle for colonial progress. "Having identified the halt in colonial development," promised journalists at *L'Algérie* in 1894, "we will not content ourselves with criticism—which is always easy—but we will show the remedies that must be applied and will solicit the judgment of public opinion."[46] Journalistic remedies included not only the provision of detailed plans for local infrastructure and colonial services but also the mobilization of young "Algerians" to ensure the execution of such schemes.[47] Newspapers launched campaigns ranging from local health-care initiatives, such as the drive to recruit nurses organized by *La Nouvelle France*, to grand projects designed to demonstrate the health of the colony and the empire at large, such as the scientific expedition to Lake Chad led by journalists and readers of *La France africaine* between 1891 and 1892.[48]

Such projects further emphasized the gendered and racialized dimension of settler colonial understandings of progress. Advertisements concerning the expedition to Lake Chad, for example, appealed unequivocally to settler men as the active agents of progress, calling for the participation of "all men of will, energy, and intelligence." The request for "ten young, robust citizens who are willing to promote the expedition" specifically restricted participation to men who were French by birth or naturalization, greatly reducing the scope for the involvement of Muslims, of whom few had renounced their particular civil status—as defined by their faith—in return for citizenship.[49] Alongside the French national community, the venture also affirmed a settler colonial community of distinct manly sensibilities and behaviors. Reinforcing this community, the paper reminded its readers that "it is Algeria that must claim the honor of conceiving of this great expedition, destined to peacefully conquer for herself all the lands that form her suburbs, so to speak, and which are so coveted by England and Germany, who are also preparing their own missions."[50] The strength and daring of the "Algerian" man was defined, in this case, not only by explicit comparison with rival imperialists in England and Germany but also by implicit comparison with the inaction of the French of the metropole.

Leading by example, settler journalists presented themselves as the archetypal colonial pioneers. They pointed to the suffering and self-sacrifice their work demanded, earning meager financial returns for their long hours of labor and running risks in criticizing the authorities for the common good, as evidence of their own physical engagement in the settler colony. Journalism in a colonial context, *L'Algérie française* proclaimed, was "above all a vocation."[51] Devoted to serving "the public interest," journalists readily overlooked their own comfort in the pursuit of colonial progress. To those skeptical administrators and politicians who did not appreciate the journalists' sacrifices, *L'Indépendant* of Constantine explained that "the journalist, of whom so much ill is spoken when he is considered unnecessary, is certainly the most generous beast ever created. He gives his labor, he gives the labor of his workers, whom he pays in full." The result of such generosity, the paper asserted, was often hardship and physical discomfort: "One would think that journalists are made of a special essence—that they lunch on sunbeams, dine on gusts of wind, and sup on moonlight."[52]

Such physical suffering, journalists claimed, was one of the defining conditions of the "Algerian" man, who, in bearing the responsibility for the survival of the colony's women and children, bore the greatest hardship. This connection between settler manliness and suffering dated to the first decades following the French invasion, when—as journalists regularly reminded their readers—brave pioneers had led their families into valiant battle against the land, the climate, and the indigenous peoples, thereby laying the foundations of the settler colony. In repeatedly emphasizing "the efforts of our ancestors," settler journalists promoted the narrative of colonial progress and encouraged their readers to continue to work for its realization. "We will study their work, their sacrifice, their patience," affirmed *Le Peuple algérien*, "and will give examples of admirable settler families who should be honored by everyone for having fought, worked, and done their duty." The lesson would be edifying: "Let us think of the future," the paper continued, "and come together as a courageous family in the work to be done and the most useful tasks for our prosperity."[53]

The emphasis on suffering and toil, moreover, allowed journalists to recognize migrants of foreign European origin within the "family" of the settler colony. "Those [Frenchmen] who came here full of enthusiasm and illusions returned to France, where they discredited Algeria with their tales of suffering," *L'Union latine* reminded its readers. "That's when precious assistance arrived from Spain and Italy. These serious men, these hardened workers, these vigorous pioneers . . . victoriously resisted illness and lent invaluable assistance to our French settlers."[54] Propagated by journalists at times of international crisis and inter-imperial rivalry, references to a shared experience of suffering helped mitigate recurring tensions among settlers of different national backgrounds and encourage mutual identification as "Algerian" in the face of attempts by certain journalists of French origin to stoke mistrust.[55]

In emphasizing their own manly suffering, therefore, journalists positioned themselves as heads of the settler colonial "family" and legitimized their claims to speak for the "Algerian" people as a whole. "Your neighbors will take you seriously when they see you taking up their interests," affirmed *L'Ami du peuple* in a call for its readers to get involved in journalism; despite the burdens created by the "social duty" of journalists, the paper explained, "it will be quite natural for you to exert an influence in your commune or canton."[56] The extent to which the "Algerian" male was perceived, or perceived himself, as the embodiment of public opinion in Algeria is reflected in the number of newspapers established by lone male authors after 1881. Evidence of the persistence of small-scale publication projects and artisanal production methods in the decades before the First World War, ephemeral titles such as *Le Sans-culotte*, *La Guerre aux Abus*, and *Mon journal* proclaimed social discontent in the first person singular, providing testimonies of individual settler men's identification with a social body perceived to be in distress.[57] As expressed in the complaints of Leon Bonnenfant, sole author of *La Guerre aux Abus*, disappointment with the French authorities could serve to reinforce a settler colonial community of manly suffering. "Nobody comes to my aid when I must fight not only locusts but hunger," lamented Bonnenfant; instead of offering support, the government had confiscated his printing press to prevent further publication of subversive complaint. The painstakingly lithographed text of his newspaper served as an additional reminder of Bonnenfant's physical investment in journalism as a force for colonial progress.[58]

Efforts to develop a professional culture based on the incarnation of an ideal of "Algerian" manliness extended to attempts to establish professional associations in the decades surrounding the turn of the century. Conscious of similar developments in the metropole, where the advent of the Third Republic had prompted republican journalists to organize into associations and unions at national and departmental levels,[59] settler journalists sought to define their own structures and codes of conduct. In addition to creating local branches of national professional bodies, such as the Syndicat de la presse périodique in 1895,[60] settler journalists established their own organizations, including the Syndicat de la presse algérienne and the Association des journalistes de l'Algérie. In a context in which, as *L'Africain* pointed out, the publication of false or inaccurate news risked inflaming tensions among ethnic groups and religious communities and thus jeopardizing the security of the European population, such organizations functioned to defend the dignity of the corporation.[61] They also served to combat perceived injustices—such as the exclusion of journalists in Algeria from the pension funds created by the establishment of a national press lottery in France in 1905—and to ingratiate their members with influential political and social elites through the organization of receptions and banquets.[62]

By 1907 the Algerian journalists' banquet had become an annual tradition, bringing together the men of the settler press. The cover of the May 18, 1907, issue of *Illustration algérienne, tunisienne et marocaine*

Deuxième Année — N° 25   50 Centimes   47   DÉPÔT LÉGAL   18 Mai 1907

LE BANQUET DES JOURNALISTES ALGÉRIENS

SOMMAIRE

ILLUSTRATIONS ET TEXTE : Le banquet des Journalistes algériens. A Corneille anniversaires, poésie de Georges Raffin. Contours, poésie de Gervais. Le Primus, par Magali Boisnard. Le Viaduc de l'oued Alaïr : l'ancevuent d'un pont de 110 metres, sur la ligne de Tlemcen à Marnia. Pour l'octre, poésie de Magali Boisnard. Le Théâtre du « oleil en Algérie : Les représentations de la tournée Silvain. Le Monde et la Mode. Les Sports. — Escrime : La Fête de l'Épée : Hippisme : La Réunion du Printemps à Alger ; Causerie de Michelin. Actualités théâtrales : Mlle Chombellau, du théâtre municipal de Tunis ; le chansonnier Aleïk. Revue financière de la semaine. Croquis humoristiques : Pour être élu député voici, par Ferré ; Nos faux mendiants, par J. Guerin. L'Algérie pittoresque.

DIRECTION & ADMINISTRATION : 6, Boulevard Laferrière, ALGER — Téléphone 3.99

1. "The Banquet of Algerian Journalists," *Illustration algérienne, tunisienne et marocaine,* May 18, 1907

(fig. 1) featured a photo of "Algerian journalists, united for their annual banquet at the Hôtel Excelsior, receiv[ing] the residents of the Sylvain theatre tour. In the center is M. Aumerat, the doyen of the journalists, on the arm of Mlle. Darlay, the youngest artist in the Sylvain troop."[63] Although by the early twentieth century a number of women—whose experience is discussed later in this chapter—were publishing articles and even founding newspapers in the settler colony, they remained notably absent from the depicted gathering of professionals, whose manly ethos was instead enhanced by the presence of young actresses. Even the oldest of the settler journalists, the report implied, exuded the youthful vigor that defined the true "Algerian" man.

Professional Bodies and the Body Politic

Like other professional groups whose claims to social and political influence were founded on the incarnation of an "Algerian" manly ideal, journalists defended the gendered and racialized frontiers of their professional community as necessary to the healthy growth of the settler colony.[64] The women and indigenous journalists who attempted to make incursions into the field of press activity in Algeria in the last decades of the nineteenth century were thus persistently ridiculed by male settler journalists, whose jokes and insults could not, however, fully disavow the threat they perceived to a public sphere dominated by "Algerian" men. In this settler journalists scarcely differed from their French colleagues on the other side of the Mediterranean, whose antifeminist diatribes and caricatures aimed to deter female journalists and protect the public sphere as a gendered space of male political expression.[65]

At the same time, however, journalistic assertions of an "Algerian" public fractured the public sphere of the colonizing power, establishing what Mrinalini Sinha has referred to in another context as a "colonial public sphere," in which the interests of settlers were distinguished from those of the metropolitan public and those of the emerging public of indigenous elites.[66] In creating a colonial public sphere that specifically defended the interests of "Algerian" settler men, these journalists raised the possibility of an autonomous body politic whose claims to sovereignty would be legitimized by the racial specificity of "Algerian" settlers. Thus, although not all settler journalists who joined the longstanding debate over the administrative status of the colonized territory openly supported "Algerian" autonomy, their active contribution to a colonial public sphere fueled wider perceptions of autonomy—or even independence—as a logical, perhaps even inevitable, step in the colony's development.

Journalistic assessment of the possible merits and disadvantages of autonomy or independence became explicit in the decades after 1881, as writers no longer found themselves constrained by the strict regulations of the Second Empire. Although, as explored more fully in chapter 2, the journalists of the Third Republic often maintained their predecessors' use of the metaphor of a parent-child relationship to describe the ties between France and Algeria, they were more direct in spelling out the implications of the "Algerian" people's arrival at maturity. "Arrived at adulthood," explained *L'Algérie*, "Algeria wishes to be freed from the bonds that—rather than helping her walk—now hold her back and force her to march on the spot."[67] Reacting against these perceived constraints, a growing number of settler journalists took up the cause for autonomy, with only the most socially elite writers of French origin rejecting the proposition outright. Indeed, support for administrative devolution was far from incompatible with a sense of renewed attachment to France, as many journalists anticipated the regeneration of the French national community through the actions of an "Algerian" vanguard. In the 1890s and early years of the twentieth century, therefore, settler journalists of diverse backgrounds proposed such varied projects as an "elected council" of "Algerian" representatives, an "Algerian assembly," or "a great colonial council."[68] Through these or other such institutions, journalists argued, "the heavy, old, outdated machines of the metropolitan administration" would give way to "a supple and lively regime," under which growth would be natural and inevitable.[69]

Aspirations to colonial autonomy inevitably raised the question of political representation, and journalists devoted considerable column space to outlining hypothetical plans for the regime best suited to the colony. Although most called for an "Algerian" electoral body whose gendered and racialized attributes matched those of the emerging "Algerian" people, they recognized the potential difficulties created by the dynamic instability at the heart of this imagined community. "If we take a look at the colonial population," observed former Oranais *député* Félix Dessoliers in *L'Algérie,* "we cannot help but be struck by its heterogeneous character. . . . From this primordial fact it can be immediately deduced that any constitutional organism destined to englobe these diverse masses—which the laws of naturalization themselves have been unable to unite—must be strong enough to include them all and simple enough to adapt to each."[70]

This left a not insignificant margin of error, which was exacerbated further by a plethora of alternative suggestions put forward by journalists who envisaged someday enlarging the "Algerian" body politic beyond the European residents of the colony, to include other groups who demonstrated their compatibility with "Algerian" values. Journalists at *La Nouvelle France,* for example, invoked the Kabyle myth, a colonial discourse elaborated by generations of French scholars and soldiers in North Africa, who made a politically expedient distinction between Kabyles and Arabs based on their cultural practices and perceived racial traits.[71] Maintaining that the Kabyles were "sympathetic to the most liberal tendencies of our time," journalists argued that their shared experience of poverty and hard work, as well as their greater racial proximity to Europeans, made them more capable than Arabs of appreciating the "political subtleties" of the colony and therefore becoming useful allies of the settlers.[72] *La France africaine* focused instead on Arab men and their "heroic devotion on the battlefield," which demonstrated not only their loyalty to the empire but also their manly strength; in recognition of these qualities, the paper argued, Arab men should be collectively naturalized and play an active role in the political life of both the colony and the French nation.[73]

Such calls, however, were most often predicated on the shifting allegiances of local politics and retained at their core Orientalist assumptions and racial distinctions. The enfranchisement of the Kabyle people, for example, was possible only because, according to *La Nouvelle France,* they were "less prone to *delusions of self-importance*" than the Arab population in Algeria and thus were unlikely to become too demanding or threaten the primacy of the Europeans.[74] Similarly, sporadic support for the political representation of Arab men correlated with peaks in anti-

Jewish sentiment, as settler journalists attempted to manipulate Muslim men into supporting their violent campaigns against the Algerian Jews.

Nevertheless, the discord among settler journalists over the most desirable form of an "Algerian" body politic, as well as the wider fracture between French and colonial publics, encouraged the journalistic activities of other groups, who sought to exploit these tensions in an effort to improve their own social and political circumstances. European women and indigenous Jews and Muslims thus established their own newspapers, reappropriating the dominant discourses of youth, dynamism, and regeneration to promote alternative imaginings of a path to progress.

European Women and the Settler Press

Purporting to reflect the general interests of the settler colony, newspapers in fact attempted to construct communities of readers according to gender. Although settler journalists increasingly recognized a market of female readers in the last decades of the nineteenth century, these readers were addressed as a specific group in separate columns and articles dedicated to "our dear female readers" or "our pretty and pleasant female readers."[75] In designating particular articles for the attention of women readers, settler journalists presented feminine concerns as supplementary to the essentially masculine project of the press, thus inadvertently revealing the extent to which the public sphere was a specifically masculine space.

Most articles appealing to women as a group, moreover, eschewed the dominant theme of progress, emphasizing instead the immutable nature of femininity, understood as primarily frivolous and sentimental. Rather than ask settler women to consider measures of colonial development or questions of administrative reform, newspapers enjoined them to turn their attention—such as it was—to sensational *faits divers*, society gossip, and advice on beauty and fashion. The popular literary character Cagayous neatly parodied the attitudes of most settler journalists in his own newspaper, *La Lanterne de Cagayous*. "To get women to buy the *Lanterne*," he explained, "we'll include the names of everyone who kicks the bucket, everyone who gets born, everyone who gets married, and everyone who f . . . s off to France. . . . We'll write about everything that happens in Algiers that will make old ladies die of fear and desire: stabbings, suicides, crashes, child theft, miserable people dying of hunger, 'strordinary catastrophes, drownings, sunstroke, and who knows what else!"[76]

Not all articles written explicitly for women, however, distanced them from issues related to colonial growth. Some sought to encourage their integration into the grand narrative of colonial progress by formulating appropriate gendered means of participation. Articles on fashion and beauty, for example, were not always mere confirmations of feminine coquetry but sometimes emphasized the particular contribution women could make to the healthy development of the settler colony as attentive wives and mothers. The fashion column of Le Petit fanal, for example, discussed at length the merits, in terms of hygiene, of various fabrics for tailoring and for dressing injuries.[77] Indeed, it was in focusing on health and hygiene, many journalists agreed, that women could make their principal active contribution to colonial progress. Their involvement in this domain was legitimized as an extension of their supposed maternal instinct, and newspapers sought to fashion their female readers into colonial medics, providing them with basic childcare advice and home remedies, as well as launching larger campaigns such as the recruitment drive for nurses led by La Nouvelle France.[78]

Developed in collaboration with the UFF, a charitable organization, this project proposed the rehabilitation of "poor, shameful women" by transforming them into useful servants of colonial society. In recruiting "miserable women who are interested in earning an honest living" alongside "decent women who are interested in making society less miserable and more dignified," and providing both groups with basic medical training and homes with respectable settler families, the scheme safely circumscribed European women's contribution to colonial progress within the norms of feminine domesticity and capacity to nurture.[79]

Few in number and in need of a way to legitimize their incursions into the field of the colonial press, women settler journalists in Algeria also

2. *Fémina journal*, June 25, 1911

invoked this feminine stereotype in their arguments for the inclusion of European women in the public life of the colony. In 1911 the front cover of the first issue of *Fémina journal*—later renamed *Fémitania* to avoid confusion with the contemporaneous metropolitan publication—featured a photograph of settler women trained as auxiliary medics by the UFF.[80]

Figure 2 shows Dr. Vidal seated in the center of the frame, checking the pulse of a young male patient standing to his right. Arranged around the men are three female auxiliaries—Mme. Domenech de Cellès, director of the clinic and training school; Mme. Falabère, a nurse; and Mme. Orsolini, the head nurse—holding medical paraphernalia. The position of the women clearly marks their subordination to the male doctor, who, at the center of the group, forms the focal point of the scene. Their almost theatrical offering of medical props—a towel, a bowl of water, and a blood pressure gauge—establishes them as mere attendants to the doctor, whose unmediated contact with the body of the patient suggests his greater authority and less nervous disposition.

The male patient stands in for the colony itself, overwhelmingly figured in the press as a young man of robust health. The patient is not visibly sick—he has no injuries and is able to stand—but the doctor is on hand to monitor his progress, checking the steady rhythm of his heart.

In a long accompanying article publicizing the work of the UFF in Algeria, Dr. Vidal spelled out the difference between the medical work of male doctors and the moral mission of most women auxiliaries, which drew on their natural feminine capacity for nurturing. If male doctors treated the physical injuries of a patient, female nurses tended to their moral health and well-being. "At his bedside, they know how to . . . stand in for his mother, his wife or his children," explained Vidal. "If he is sad, they will try to cheer him, if he is grieving they will console him, and when inexorable death comes to him, despite their efforts, they will endeavor to lighten his last moments and soften his pain." The long-suffering "Algerian" man, *Fémina* argued, required a female companion to witness and enable their expression of emotion.[81]

Fémina's presentation of an active but appropriately gendered form of women's participation in the growth of colonial society reflected the dominant approach of French feminists in the late nineteenth and early twentieth centuries. Understanding women to have essentially different qualities from men, yet believing in the complementarity of these qualities, bourgeois metropolitan feminists such as Marguerite Durand and contributors to her newspaper, *La Fronde*, campaigned sedately for improvements in women's social condition and their political emancipation on the basis of the necessity of feminine influence for the harmonious development of society.[82]

Although the colonial publication included articles from male contributors, whereas the metropolitan paper did not, *Fémina* addressed similar topics and followed the same political lines as *La Fronde*. Attempting to involve women in the major debates of the day, the paper proposed essays on "women and pacifism" or "women and the social movement," suggesting that their role in society and politics could and should be distinguished from that of men.[83] Without explicitly referring to the publication as feminist, contributors praised the wider feminist movement for its positive influence on the social condition of women and evinced guarded support for women's participation in politics. "We are very traditionalist," the publication assured its readers, "and we don't yet easily accept the idea of French women leaving their sitting-rooms to go out into the streets: but what possible objection could we have, I ask you, the day that they transform the streets into a sitting-room?"[84] If women could bring their domestic nature and concerns to bear on the colonial public, the paper implied, the colony, the nation, and the empire would be all the better for it.

Other newspapers created by settler women were less guarded in their demands for political participation. On the front page of the first edition, the writers of *L'Egalité* announced their affiliation with the Civic Society of the Defense of the Rights of Women and boldly declared, "The Society . . . DENOUNCES TO THE LEGISLATORS as contrary to the spirit of progress in a democratic and social republic ALL THE ARTICLES OF THE CIVIL CODE that exclude the female sex in favor of the male sex from the rights and advantages due to all *citoyens* and *citoyennes* of the same nation."[85] Demanding both equal pay and equal rights for women, *L'Egalité* was undoubtedly more radical than *Fémina*, yet it similarly sought to take advantage of the perceived youth of colonial society to transform the gender relations and political hierarchies of the French nation. At the same time, both papers relied on invocations of a French national community to argue for their place in a colonial project dominated by hypermasculine "Algerian" ideals.

Female journalists also devised other ways of incorporating settler women into the "Algerian" community. As the contributors to *Fémina* remarked, the very fact of establishing a newspaper "with the objective of bringing together all Algerian women's literature" represented an attempt to recognize settler women within the "Algerian" public. This initiative, the paper argued, would be fundamental to wider settler efforts to create the "Algerian Genre"—a distinctive local form of artistic expression inspired by the physical environment of the colony and the mix of ethnic groups therein. Surely, insisted *Fémina*, this "newly created" country already had poets and writers who were equal to those of the metropole and whose work pondered "our African sun, our ever-pure sky, our most picturesque sites, [and] the customs of our Bebers."[86]

Like their male counterparts, therefore, the female journalists of *Fémina* emphasized the youthful promise and dynamic diversity of the mixed population of Algeria and linked these traits to the creation of sensibilities specific to the "Algerian" people. Committed to gender difference, however, these women journalists saw men's and women's expressions of these shared sensibilities as necessarily distinct. Incarnating, first and foremost, her femininity, the "Algérienne" could not also embody the "Algerian" settler ideals of physical strength and endurance. The prioritization of gender difference over settler colonial difference was similarly evident in the newspaper's approach to sports and outdoor pursuits. Unlike settler men, who were encouraged by journalists to seek out new sensations and cultivate a competitive nature, settler women were advised to practice moderation. "A woman should not forget that—while it is necessary for her to know all sports—she must preserve her particular charms and grace. She must remain a woman above all else," cautioned *Fémina*. Being a woman, the paper explained, entailed tending to the suffering of male settlers, assuming the role of "the good angel who must calm quarrels and dress wounds." Taking on the same physical excess as the "Algerian" man would ultimately be detrimental to the population of the settler colony, as women would be rendered less attractive to men by their exertions. "The excess of animation that the body brings to sport is immediately visible," warned *Fémina*. "The delicate color of the face no longer has the same freshness, beads of sweat gather on the forehead, the hairstyle comes undone, clothes no longer have the same elegance."[87]

Even the female journalists of the militant *Antijuif*, or anti-Jewish, movement that emerged in the last decades of the nineteenth century renounced physical engagement as a basis for women's political and social participation, preferring instead to act as a reserve of moral support for their male collaborators. Male militants, as described in chapter 3, referred to the hypermasculine ideals of "Algerian" manliness to legitimize their violent verbal and physical attacks on Algerian Jews, whom they held responsible for the slow pace of colonial development since their collective emancipation in 1870. As the group of young women who set up *La Jeune France antijuive* in 1900 declared, however, their auxiliary role in the *Antijuif* movement did not imply their passivity: "We women are even more energetic than the men. Long live Algerian women, *Mesdames*! We must respond to the provocation of the Jews, and those who support them, while also encouraging our fathers, our brothers, and our fiancés to fight energetically against the many-tentacled yids." Although "the women who contribute to our paper have never taken part in a demonstration," confirmed *La Jeune France antijuive*, "they had vigorously supported the movement by boycotting Jewish shops" and encouraging other French and naturalized women to do likewise.[88]

Despite the publication's frequent assurances that its all-female staff maintained appropriately gendered forms of engagement in public debate, it could not escape the fact that the very existence of a newspaper that was founded by a group of women and remained independent of the official Parti antijuif ran counter to the gender codes of the movement's militants and of the settler colony more broadly. Although the journalists of *La Jeune France antijuive* established their paper with the stated ambition to "vigorously support the French workers' party, energetically lead the anti-Jewish struggle, [and] protect the indigenous Muslim by imposing a protective yoke that is benevolent but firm," they knew they could not achieve this without simultaneously establishing the right of women to participate in such activities. "The world is a vast field of action in which woman has her place beside man—whether he likes it or not," observed one female contributor to the paper. For the young women of *La Jeune France antijuive*, women's claim to a public role would be based not only on maternal instincts and "the great gentleness of her heart" but also on "the virile intelligence that is decisive in conquest."[89] Journalism itself, they implied, was further evidence of a woman's capacity for this last characteristic.

In advocating their right to work as journalists, the writers of *La Jeune France antijuive* reappropriated some of the ideals promoted by their male colleagues as central tenets of both the field of journalism and "Algerian" culture. In a long article simply titled "Women," the journalist Anza declared, "There is a terrain on which all women are sisters, where laws, convention, rank, fortune, honors have no meaning, and where only their mission remains. This terrain is suffering." Revising the imagined community of suffering posited in the settler press to unite a male readership, Anza invoked the greater suffering of women's social and biological condition as the foundation of a new community and new social order: "Suffering, in purifying each of our joys, each of our happinesses, will raise women above men."[90]

The promise of rebellion in this last phrase became all the more pronounced in later editions of the paper, as the female journalists were forced to defend themselves against the frequent derision of their male counterparts, expressed in jibes and derogatory articles. Faced with such insults, the women of *La Jeune France antijuive* explicitly likened patriarchal domination to despotism, undermining their male peers' claims to support the republic. Addressing an article "to the press," Anza demanded of her male colleagues, "Do you really believe that after 1789 an ordinary woman does not have the same worth as a princess? To refuse to her—not the right to think, which would be excessively autocratic—but the right to express herself in writing, that is absolute despotism."[91]

Despite their different political convictions, social backgrounds, and styles of journalism, the female journalists of *Fémina*, *L'Egalité*, and *La Jeune France antijuive* all viewed the youthful and ill-defined nature of the "Algerian" public as an opportunity to refashion social relations and political hierarchies. The act of writing in a newspaper asserted a demand for the incorporation of settler women into the colonial public sphere and allowed female journalists to elaborate their own ideal of colonial progress. In its own particular way, each publication represented the possibility of the alternative political and social organization of empire. Notably absent from the imaginaries of settler women journalists, however, were indigenous peoples, who appeared, if at all, as groups to be rejected or maintained under the protective guidance of a superior colonizing people.

Jewish Journalists and the Language of Regeneration

As dhimmis under the Ottoman regime, the Jews of Algeria had enjoyed relative liberty to maintain their own cultural codes and practices, despite the financial obligations and social exclusions linked to their status. Efforts by the Central Israelite Consistory of France to nationalize the Algerian Jews in the decades following the French conquest contributed, in the 1850s, to the creation of printing presses equipped with Hebrew and Judeo-Arabic characters.[92] These presses, however, ultimately reduced the local Jewish community's reliance on publishing houses in the metropole and did little to alter the community's distinctive codes and practices, which were maintained throughout the nineteenth century. Although the Algerian Jews were collectively naturalized in 1870, their cultural differences were not readily accepted by the settlers, who feared that colonial politics would be corrupted by Jewish influence and that colonial development would be stymied by sectional Jewish interests.

In an attempt to defend their community, a number of French-educated Jewish elites in Algeria turned to the press to encourage the cultural assimilation of their coreligionists, both in preparation for their political emancipation and, after 1870, to secure their newfound status as citizens. Yet while Jewish journalists promoted the use of the French language and an adherence to French cultural values, they also employed the language of youth and progress favored by their "Algerian" settler counterparts. Encouraging their readers to identify at once as Jewish, French, and "Algerian," these journalists sought to reform and regenerate local expressions of faith in order to better contribute to colonial growth and French national strength.

Bearing the motto "Reform, Emancipation, Progress," *L'Israélite algérien*—one of the first newspapers aimed at a Jewish readership—presented itself in 1870 as evidence of a process of French cultural assimilation already well underway. The paper, which published articles in both French and Judeo-Arabic, aimed to facilitate the assimilation of all indigenous Jews into French culture, which it considered the ultimate guarantor of progress and modernity. By habituating Algerian Jews to the practice of reading newspapers and by disseminating the French language, the paper's editor, Nessim Benisti, hoped "to activate the development of their natural disposition to progress, by making them understand that the time has come to unite behind liberal aspirations through ridding ourselves of certain prejudices that are incompatible with our sacred religion." The form of the newspaper, he explained, was key in bringing readers "to these aspirations through reason, good examples, and instruction."[93]

For Benisti, therefore, as for most Algerian Jewish journalists in the decades that followed, progress was to be defined as the standardization of religious practice across metropolitan and colonial Jewish communities and would be best achieved by both political and cultural integration into the French nation. In this their intentions explicitly converged with those of Jewish authorities in the metropole, who feared that the security of the wider population of French Jews could be jeopardized by the unregulated practices of their coreligionists in French Algeria. The "regeneration" and "civilization" of the Algerian Jews had been explicit objectives of the religious authorities in the metropole since at least the 1840s, when they advised the state to extend the consistory structure to the colonial territory.[94]

Jewish journalists in Algeria, therefore, measured the progress of their coreligionists along a trajectory defined by metropolitan standards. In articles such as "The Moral State of Algerian Israelites" and "The Algerian Jewess Faced with Progress and the Moral State of the Land," Jewish writers argued that although much remained to be done, their community had come a long way toward full cultural assimilation during the years of French presence in Algeria. They offered the Jewish press itself as an example of this progress: "What are forty years in the life of a people?" asked L'Israélite algérien. "Would truly old-fashioned men . . . have ever imagined creating or supporting a newspaper destined to defend interests of which they would not have understood the importance?"[95]

The program of cultural assimilation was maintained in the 1890s by La Jeunesse israélite and the 1900s by another iteration of L'Israélite *algérien* and by *Le Nouvelliste oranais*.[96] Despite the spread of French education following the application of the Ferry laws to Algeria in 1883, *Le Nouvelliste oranais* maintained that only the press could reach out to the most impoverished sectors of the Jewish community. In addition to familiarizing Algerian Jews with the French language, newspapers, *Le Nouvelliste oranais* argued, could educate local Jewish readers in science, history, and philosophy.[97] As in settler publications, therefore, articles disseminating scientific information or reviewing Algerian history encouraged readers to imagine themselves simultaneously in colonial, national, and transnational communities. Through such lessons, journalists proclaimed, they would at once "emancipate" and "francize" the Algerian Jews.[98]

Despite their primary emphasis on assimilation into the French nation, Jewish journalists in the colonial territory also invoked the "Algerian" discourses of colonial youth and dynamism in their attempts to regenerate the Jewish community. This was particularly true of the "secular" Jews, who privileged social and political questions over those of religious reform. Often linked to the commercial elite of the community, these journalists sometimes perceived more traditionalist factions within the consistory as an obstacle to the progress of both their coreligionists and the colonial territory as a whole. Convinced that "there are in our community two quite distinct categories . . . : the old and the young," *La Jeunesse israélite* aimed to encourage the preponderance of the latter.[99] Despite what they saw as the stubborn intransigence of the older generation, Jewish journalists felt that youth—synonymous with progress and exemplified by the press itself—would necessarily prevail. "To think that among the 'old turbans' there are still some who disapprove of the press, as a result of their retrograde spirit or their timidity," complained *La Jeunesse israélite*. "Nevertheless, the youth is alert," the paper reassured its readers, "and it is to the youth that we owe the future."[100]

If Jewish journalists referred to elements of "Algerian" colonial culture, they remained resolutely opposed to the creation of any separate "Algerian" body politic. Only recently recognized as French citizens,

Algerian Jews remained concerned with consolidating their place within the French nation by defending and reinforcing the national community. Jewish journalists in Algeria thus openly supported centralized administrative structures, rejecting calls for colonial autonomy. Established in 1884 by Henry Tubiana, a socialist militant and opponent of the "old turbans" of the community,[101] *La Gazette de l'Algérie* bore the subtitle "Republican and Assimilationist Newspaper." In the very first line of the first edition of his paper, Tubiana stated bluntly, "We are assimilators. We are neither separatists, nor protectionists; we simply declare ourselves assimilators. . . . This is patriotism as we understand it."[102]

For Tubiana, this was a matter that went beyond the interests of the Jewish community to touch Algeria as a whole, "its development and its glory." "Our ambition," he declared, "is to make Algeria great and prosperous; great in its ideas, and prosperous and rich through agriculture and commerce."[103] Antisemitism, in the form of the anti-Jewish movement, was dismissed by Tubiana as a distraction from these common goals, and he devoted considerable energy to exposing the falsehoods about Jews circulated in the settler press. His drive for complete administrative assimilation, moreover, led him to defend the political rights of Muslims, whose civil status, he argued, was no less compatible with citizenship than that of Jews.[104] The colonial regime's dispossession of Muslims, Tubiana noted, was not only detrimental to stability in Algeria but also incompatible with the French civilizing mission. "There is a lot of talk about propagating ideas of emancipation, reform and progress amongst the Arabs," he remarked, "but it is with notions and laws from another age that the francization and disciplining of the people is carried out!"[105] Using his position as simultaneously Jewish, French, and "Algerian," Tubiana held the French authorities to account, calling for a more inclusive and equitable national community.

Caught between the prejudice of settlers and the exigencies of Jewish authorities, who were keen to present the success of their drive to cultural assimilation, publications explicitly targeting Jewish readers appear to have declined and disappeared in the early twentieth century. Although Jewish journalists had affirmed the place of Algerian Jews within the

French nation and defended their readers from the attacks of settlers, anti-Semitic sentiment would cast a long shadow in the settler colony, returning with renewed vigor in the interwar era. This resurgence coincided with the destabilization of colonial rule, as Muslim journalists moved increasingly to support independence.[106] As an examination of early Muslim involvement in the press in Algeria reveals, however, journalists had long imagined possibilities beyond the nation.

Muslim Journalists beyond Reformism and Nationalism

The thought of Muslim expression in the press troubled settler journalists long before it became a reality at the end of the nineteenth century. Confident of their privileged, if heavily regulated, access to journalistic expression under the Second Empire, Europeans in Algeria were outraged to learn of the publication of articles by one Messaoud El Medani in Parisian daily *Le Siècle* in 1863. Presenting himself as a young man who had returned to Algeria after four years in Paris, El Medani exposed the injustice toward Muslims under the colonial regime, including the disproportionate tax burden placed on *indigènes* and their ill-treatment at the hands of settlers.[107] These articles, which scholars have attributed to Ismaÿl Urbain, Napoleon III's advisor and architect of the Arab kingdom policy,[108] were decried by journalists in Algeria, who remained as vexed by the uncertainty surrounding the author's identity as by the threat to colonial development posed by what they saw as the articles' unforgivable misinformation. The articles, claimed Albert Mercier of *L'Echo d'Oran*, were "anti-Algerian"; both French settlement and financial investment, he feared, would be deterred by "the hesitation and suspicion created by certain newspapers in the capital."[109]

Urbain's strategy was taken up by other writers across the nineteenth century, as metropolitan arabophiles and their settler detractors alike sought to fill the void of Muslim expression in the colonial press with voices that echoed their own particular interests. In 1882 journalists purporting to act on behalf of "a group of Muslims representing the notables of Constantine" established the bilingual Franco-Arabic newspaper *El Montakheb*. "Fervent friends of metropolitan and colonial

France," the journalists of this publication criticized the unjust nature of the *indigénat*—the repressive separate legal regime applied to Algerian Muslims—and drew attention to the vulnerability of a Muslim community deprived of its lands, but without questioning the fundamental necessity of French authority in Algeria.[110] Despite its unwavering support for "the benefits of French government," the paper was condemned by settler publications. "With some rare exceptions, each attacks us in turn, from the biggest to the smallest," complained one writer for *El Montakheb* just over a month after its launch.[111] Following further attacks, the paper was forced to reveal that its founders were in fact "of French race," motivated by support for the civilizing mission.[112]

Initially critical of arabophile initiatives to represent Algerian Muslim opinion in the press, settler journalists quickly took up the same strategy, turning the words of their imagined Muslim interlocutors to their own ends. Following Urbain's accusations against settlers in the early 1860s, journalists at *L'Echo d'Oran* claimed to have received correspondence from "an Arab in the neighborhood" seeking to relay an important message to the emperor. Their claims came in the context of settler discontent generated by 1863 legislation affirming tribal ownership of certain lands and a law of 1864 that abolished free concessions for corporations. The letter from a local Arab, these journalists insisted, showed that *indigènes* themselves were against these reforms: "We want the barriers that isolate us from Europeans to be removed. We are not insensible to progress, and we well understand that it can only be achieved by contact with them. Hence, far from banning settlers from our tribal territories, we call them to these lands with loud cries." The unlikely Muslim correspondent was at pains to point out that he was "neither a Kalif, nor an Agha, nor a Caïd," but "a poor fellah, tied to the land."[113] His letter thus served to uphold the accusations regularly leveled against Muslim elites by settler journalists, who blamed them for the impoverishment of their coreligionists, thereby obscuring the violence and the responsibility of settlers and the French state.

Settler journalists continued speaking for Muslims into the late nineteenth century, inventing indigenous writers whose observations and demands upheld settler interests and whose forms of expression reinforced reassuring Orientalist stereotypes of Muslim ignorance. Attentive in this way to both content and style, a settler journalist of French origin, E. Nicaise, launched *La Lanterne de Mohamed Biskri* in April 1898.[114] Posing as a naturalized Muslim who had decided to try his luck as a journalist—"'coz there's too much competition in the shoeshine business"—Nicaise incorporated errors of register and grammar in his text in an effort to imitate the voice of an Algerian Muslim speaking French. "So you thought Arabs couldn't be journalists?" asked Mohamed in the first edition of the newspaper. "Well, you'll never believe your eyes!" An absurd and comical figure, Mohamed joked with his settler readers, reassuring them that a Muslim "could never be a turncoat—he wears a *gandoura* and a *burnous!*"[115] In acting as ventriloquist to Mohamed, Nicaise aimed not only to affirm the civilizational inferiority of Muslims but also to render their difference as unthreatening to a settler readership.

Mohamed's lighthearted tone, poor French, and repeated affirmations of loyalty to the French conqueror all served to disavow the threat of Muslim insurgence. Try as he might, however, Nicaise could not fully dispel this menace. Mohamed Biskri also served as a warning to European readers and a reminder that their own behavior was constantly being observed and evaluated by the Muslim population. Commenting on the factionalism and public disorder caused by the anti-Jewish militancy in 1898, for example, Mohamed noted the atmosphere of "*kiffe* carnival" among settlers, particularly, in his view, those from Spain and Italy. If the French and the Muslims wanted to insult the Algerian Jews, reasoned Mohamed, that was their affair—"after all, everyone is free"—but as for foreigners, it was "not their business." "The French are even more stupid than I am," he surmised, suggesting that the foreign settlers were using antisemitism as a cover for their own exploitation of French resources. "They all have a good laugh at the French, thinking they are completely stupid. It's kind of my opinion, too, but I can't really say so because I'm an Arab, and Arabs shouldn't say anything," observed French nationalist Nicaise, via Mohamed, daring the colonizers to prove their intelligence and protect the territory from foreign influence before Muslims began to openly question French rule.[116]

In addition to speaking for Algerian Muslims, settler journalists maintained settler colonial hierarchies by speaking about them, albeit surprisingly infrequently. Settler journalists concerned themselves almost entirely with the affairs of the European community in Algeria, while also looking beyond the colonial territory to news from their readers' countries of origin and the current and former territories of European empires around the world.[117] Algerian Muslims entered their purview only when their actions were perceived to menace local development or when global affairs threatened to influence the behaviors or opinions of the local Muslim population. For the most part, however, settler journalists and readers were uninterested in Muslims, who were omitted from the columns of the newspapers in an expression of desire for their physical elimination from the territory. As the nineteenth century wore on, Muslims became increasingly absent from settler publications, until by the end of the century even the *faits divers* of the Second Empire— recounting accidents or minor misdemeanors in which Muslims had been involved—had disappeared.[118]

Instead, settler journalists in the decades around the turn of the century stuck rigidly to a script that, when it referred to Algerian Muslims at all, typecast them in one of two fixed roles: the loyal *indigène* or the unruly Arab. Thus in a single edition of *La Kabylie*, settler journalists were able to congratulate Bouscoura Larbi and Ismaïl for passing the exams at the Constantine *medersa*, a juridico-religious school established by the colonizers, thereby equipping themselves for a life of service to the colonial state, while also reporting on the verdict of the criminal court in Bougie (Béjaïa), which found Bachir, Mohand, and Abdelouab Benabdelouhab guilty of murder, parricide, and complicity.[119] In contrast to fictional characters like Mohamed Biskri, who were endowed with personalities and traits convenient to their creators, these Muslims were not attributed with any character beyond their crimes or achievements, as defined by the colonizers. Rare were the settler journalists who, like those of the Franco-Spanish publication *Fraternidad obrera*, regretted the absence of Muslim voices in the press and emphasized the need for a Muslim writer to "give his opinion without political or religious bias, with impartiality and frankness."[120]

For those Algerian Muslims who sought to give their opinion through the press, social and legal barriers added to the widespread opposition expressed by settler journalists. In a territory with no cultural tradition of press activity, indigenous interest in journalism largely coincided with increased exposure to French colonial education. Just as the first generations of French Muslims were emerging from the Franco-Arabic schools in the 1870s and early 1880s, however, republican legislation regulating the press came into force, stipulating that only French citizens could establish newspapers.[121] Without the status of French citizens, *indigènes* found their paths into the colonial public sphere curtailed.

Determined writers—such as Omar Samar, who helped found *El Hack* in Bône (Annaba) in 1893 and whom Samir Merdaci describes as "without doubt the first Algerian journalist," and Larbi Fekar, who established *El Misbah* in Oran in 1904—were forced to make difficult choices to find a way forward.[122] While Fekar opted to naturalize, and thus renounced his civil status as a Muslim, Samar turned to French collaborators for support. Once established, their publications remained at the mercy of the colonial authorities, who closely scrutinized newspapers produced by Muslims in Algeria, as well as those coming into the territory from elsewhere. Following complaints from settler journalists and local politicians, *El Hack* was suppressed in March 1894.[123] Muslim journalists were also closely surveilled; as a writer for *Le Croissant* in 1906 and again as director of *L'Islam* in 1913, Mohamed ben Ali Brizène found himself imprisoned for defamation.[124] The surveillance and oppression of Muslim journalists, as Zahir Ihaddaden notes, further increased at the beginning of the First World War, particularly for those writing in Arabic.[125]

Many Muslim journalists in this era, including Omar Samar, Khellil Caïd-Layoun, and Sliman Bengui of *El Hack* and Larbi Fekar of *El Misbah*, were products of Franco-Arab schools. Colonial education in Algeria, as Fanny Colonna explains, was geared toward producing a stratum of indigenous intermediaries among the Muslim elite to serve the needs of the colonial state.[126] These journalists' experiences of colonial education not only affected their career trajectories—Fekar, for example, was a schoolteacher, while Caïd-Layoun was a legal clerk—but also shaped their attitudes toward, and expectations of, their French rulers, as evident in their publications. Whereas some publications—such as *El Misbah*, *L'Algérie franco-arabe*, *L'Islam*, and *Le Rachidi*—sought to promote cultural assimilation and others, including both iterations of *El Hack*, *L'Eclair*, and *Le Croissant*, sought to defend cultural particularity, all aimed to defend the Muslim community while accepting the fact of French rule.[127]

These nuances aside, Muslim journalists in Algeria were attuned to the colonialist discourses of French civilizational superiority and found themselves "torn between two Frances": the France of enlightenment principles and democratic institutions, in which they wanted to believe, and the France they saw before them, a nation of colonial exclusion, land requisitions, and the *indigénat*.[128] Although, as a number of scholars point out, Muslim readership of newspapers remained limited before the interwar period, comprising a small number of educated elites,[129] the first publications produced by and for Muslims should not be dismissed as having no political significance. Indeed, Rabah Aissaoui argues that "the launch of a small number of Algerian newspapers had an impact on Algerian political activism that was more significant than the modest circulation figures would suggest."[130] Although such newspapers do not fit easily into a teleological view of nationalist mass mobilization, they provided an important space for Muslim journalists to confront and expose the paradox of French colonial rule and to propose solutions to this intolerable paradox. While some, such as Omar Racim of *Dou-el-fakar*, did come to imagine an independent Algerian nation, others sought to reimagine empire or alternative forms of political and cultural community.

In grappling with the unfulfilled promises of French rule, Muslim journalists were obliged to be more cautious than their settler counterparts, who freely expressed their own disappointment with the state. In its opening article in 1893, *El Hack* announced its "full acceptance of French domination."[131] Most subsequent publications founded by Muslim journalists followed suit, professing their gratitude to the French colonizers or expressing their intention to serve as a vector of communication and a symbol of concord between Algerian Muslims and their French rulers.[132] Although these papers explicitly pointed to the social divisions and political injustices of the colonial system, they did so in an effort to bring their colonial rulers back into line with their idealized image of France. In so doing they appropriated the discourse of regeneration, made popular by the colonial press, and turned it to their own ends: in fulfilling its "glorious destiny" of "raising, protecting and directing [Muslims] towards goodness and happiness," France would also find its own strength restored.[133] The regeneration of Islam as a form of "liberal and rational monotheism" was—for those assimilationist journalists who promoted it—but one dimension of this wider drive to regenerate France.[134]

As with settler journalists, who promoted new forms of expression as evidence of a regenerated racial formation capable of changing the balance of power within the French Empire, Muslim journalists also emphasized the politics of aesthetics. Writing in *El Hack* under the pseudonym Zeid ben Dieb, Samar conceded that—as settler detractors readily pointed out—Muslim journalists in Algeria "hardly had the talent of Rochefort or Drumont." "Yet, if they are not experts of rhetoric," he continued, "they do know how to reason and approach any subject with logic and a full knowledge of the facts. In this way, without using empty, conceited, fancy turns of phrase, seasoned with pompous words, the editors of this newspaper will develop all questions of public interest using a simple style and moderate tone, thus exposing the error of those who, in the future, would unjustly attack Arabs."[135] Transforming what settler journalists perceived as the essential intellectual weakness of Muslims into an expression of the blunt, dynamic style favored by these same writers, Samar argued for Muslim access to press expression in the name of regeneration of the French public sphere.

French regeneration, Samar pointed out in a later publication, *L'Eclair*, was not only a question of maintaining authority over the Algerian

Muslim population but also a key concern of contemporary geopolitics. "A closer Franco-Arab alliance would open up the path to central Africa for France," argued Samar, "and could be called upon to do its duty in case of war in Europe." It was to bolster the French nation, he insisted, that disparities in tax contributions between Muslims and settlers should be removed and that Muslims should be represented in both houses of parliament.[136] Such arguments were further developed and foregrounded by Muslim journalists in the years preceding the outbreak of war in Europe, when the contentious issue of Muslim conscription provided a platform for the negotiation of political rights by writers aligned with the Jeunes-Algériens movement.[137]

The question of conscription divided nascent Muslim public opinion, leading some journalists, like Omar Racim, to espouse more explicitly nationalist opinions. Leaving his post as editor of the Arabic-language section of the bilingual Algiers-based newspaper *El Hack* in 1912, Racim established his own exclusively arabophone publication, *Dou-el-fakar*.[138] Racim's rejection of the French language, as well as the militant content of his newspaper, challenged his contemporaries' adherence to the policy of assimilation. Relying on illustrations to further underscore his political message, Racim printed images in which the dominant figure of the settler colonial press—the young settler man—was replaced by the resurgent Muslim male. One such illustration depicted a young Muslim armed with a sword, flanked by a majestic lion, and crowned with a halo of sunlight, as a cowering European figure slunk away into the background.[139] Another image featured an indigenous youth brandishing a curved sword over the slain body of a monster whose head bore the caricatured traits of an Algerian Jew.[140] Echoing the settler journalists' discourses of youth and masculine aggression in support of an "Algerian" settler community, Racim redefined this community, founding it on the violent rebellion of Muslim men.

Motivated by a similar desire to overturn imperial authority, other journalists proposed alternative visions of Muslim community, focusing on transnational rather than national identifications. Such was the aspiration of *Tout ou Rien*, which appeared in Oran between 1912 and 1913.

The publication was founded and cowritten by a female journalist using the name of Sapho and edited by Aoued ould Ahmed ben Abdallah.[141] The origins of these journalists remain a mystery—one deliberately cultivated by Sapho, who declared that she was "not more from one country than another" and appears to have moved between Algeria and Tunisia, all the while keeping her eye on political developments in France, Britain, the Eastern Mediterranean, and the Arabian peninsula. Her primary allegiance, she explained, was to Islam and thus surpassed national borders.[142]

The community imagined in the pages of Tout ou Rien reflected both the religious and transnational preoccupations of the paper's founder. The newspaper, Sapho announced, would "defend Arabs from the persecution to which they are subjected, defend their interests, and advise their submission—unless France attacks Islam, which it is about to do."[143] In readiness for this attack, Sapho encouraged the development of a federation of Muslim territories, brought together in support of her "New Religion." This reinvigorated expression of Islam was based on "the obligation to keep the Quran intact—as it was recorded by the prophet Mohamed—the preservation of the Orient, as well as that of the standard Arabic idiom, and all that which makes up the beauty of the Orient." Acting as a political federation, the new religious community would be led by "Arabia, Persia, Palestine, Egypt [or] Turkey." "Other Muslim countries," proposed Sapho, envisaging an alternative imperial space and civilizing enterprise, "must be led by one of these five until they are capable of running their own affairs." Anticipating the cycles of civilizational growth and decline as described in French colonial discourse, Sapho suggested that "when one of the five enters into a period of degeneration, the nearest race from one of the other four countries will take up the reins."[144]

Before this new religious community could assume political form, however, many immediate concerns needed to be brought to the attention of the French authorities on behalf of Muslims in Algeria. Tout ou Rien presented its demands for the defense of cultural particularism, calling for funding for Islamic schools, promotion of the Arabic language, and extensive reform of indigenous infirmaries. In addition, the overall condition of the Muslim community should be improved, the paper argued, by introducing equal pay for Muslim workers and repealing the 1912 legislation forcing Muslims in the colony to perform French military service.[145] The reform of social and economic relations thus appeared as a necessary step in the protection of an Algerian Muslim community that could later be integrated into Sapho's "New Religion." Muslim press activity was also identified as central to this process. As Sapho explained, "Journalists must adopt another approach to their victors, as is necessary when the victor is a tyrant and a hypocrite; instead of studying French politics, which leads France into the abyss, they should study Oriental politics, which are better suited to their mentality."[146]

Part of this new journalistic approach, Sapho's own activity implied, included the recognition of the beneficial public influence of Arab women. In a number of articles, Sapho and contributor Magali Boisnard considered the nature of Arab women, valorizing their perceived sensuality and courage.[147] For Sapho, the Arab woman was "braver" than her male counterpart; "as a result," she observed pointedly, "the Arab man would do well not to wait to give her rights, lest she becomes a suffragette behind his back."[148] While Sapho expressed some admiration for British feminists, she found settler women's claims to political participation laughable. "When settler women get the right to vote," she joked, "Arabs—instead of rising up against such a humiliation—can sleep easy. Before these pretty dolls can be of use to the metropole and the colonies, they will have to resign themselves to banning pregnancy, or at least banning the high heeled shoes which they run about in, and which cause them to give birth to imbeciles who vote according to bribes, or the opinion of the alcohol merchant."[149] If given the right to vote, Sapho argued, these women would merely "continue to drink and take drugs, and hit, abandon, and kill their children more often than they already do."[150] Sapho's demands for the political rights of Arab women therefore were formulated not on the universalist models of contemporary European feminists, such as Hubertine Auclert, whose

Orientalist *Les femmes arabes en Algérie* had appeared a decade before the newspaper,[151] but on a belief in the particularity of a self-sacrificing Arab femininity and its utility to a reconfigured transnational Muslim community.

Concerned about colonial development, settler journalists in the nineteenth and early twentieth centuries pointed to the emergence of an "Algerian" people as a measure of progress and a guarantee of future success. Seen by doctors and journalists as a "new white race," born out of the union of French, Spanish, and Italian settlers in their common struggle against a hostile environment, "Algerians" were destined to bring civilization to North Africa, where other peoples, including the French of the metropole, had failed. With the intention of making the world anew, settler journalists promoted a new manly ideal, which they strove to embody though acts of suffering, sacrifice, and aggressive self-expression. For some, the "Algerian" man offered the possibility of regenerating the French nation; for others, the "Algerian" represented not only a distinct colonial public but also the possibility of a distinct body politic.

Settler journalists' defense of a community predicated on articulated discourses of race and gender motivated their rejection of female, Jewish, and Muslim journalists, whom they believed lacked the essential characteristics required to represent the "Algerian" public. In support of a professional culture that promoted the "Algerian" manly ideal, these journalists began to form networks and associations at the turn of the century. Before professional structures became well established, however, women, Jews, and Muslims made incursions into the colonial press, relying on the same combination of passion, luck, artisanal methods, and meager funding as many of their male counterparts. Further relying on the emphasis given to youth, dynamism, and regeneration in the settler colonial context, these marginalized journalists sought to reimagine both "Algerian" and French communities in novel ways and proposed new boundaries for the imagination.

The dominant community represented in the colonial press of the era nevertheless remained that of the "Algerian" male settlers. In lauding the advent of the "Algerian" man, settler journalists expressed their desire for colonial progress and autonomy. In seeking the approbation of a wider French public and the French state as affirmation of their achievements, however, these journalists displayed a deep sense of ambivalence. This ambivalence was frequently communicated by the narrative of the "settler colonial family romance," which served to discredit the political claims of indigenous peoples within the French national community, while maintaining an "Algerian" community as a competing source of sovereignty.

2

...

The Settler Colonial Family Romance

*Political Imaginaries under the Second
Empire and the Third Republic*

Disembarking in Algiers early on September 17, 1860, Emperor Napoleon III became the first French head of state to visit the French territory in North Africa. Accompanied by the Empress Eugenie and the young imperial prince, the emperor was greeted by French officials, including the minister of Algeria and the colonies and the mayor of Algiers, who drew His Majesty's attention to the assembled crowd of French soldiers and European settlers. "Together we form one large family whose unique strength is that of devotion and loyalty," declared the mayor, using the analogy of the family relationship to emphasize the bond between the French nation and the Algerian settler colony.[1] Looking beyond this crowd to the nearby Place Bresson, the emperor also saw "Arab chiefs, Jewish women, groups of Kabyles, the children of the Franco-Arab school, and indigenous apprentices." The groups gathered on the Place Bresson complicated the picture of the colonial family: standing separate from the European settlers, the indigenous people nevertheless represented, according to a journalist from the Parisian publication *Illustration*, "Algeria's past and future—the old generation, which we subdued by force, and the young generation, which we will win over with the benefits of science and civilization."[2]

The visit, which followed the emperor's triumphant procession through the newly annexed territories of Savoy and Nice, served to affirm French authority in Algeria and presaged a change in colonial policy. Under the auspices of the existing military regime, the emperor now sought ways to overcome divisions between Europeans and Muslims in Algeria and to ensure that the latter would be, as one administrator put it, "truly assimilated into the French family." Over the course of three hectic days, the emperor and his entourage toured the streets of Algiers, inaugurated a new boulevard, inspected the troops, and enjoyed the dancing, fighting, and feasting of an "Arab fantasia."[3] On returning from Algiers, Napoleon III began to ponder the creation of an Arab kingdom in Algeria, governed not by French administrators but by Muslim notables whose attachment to France would be based on gratitude, respect, and love.[4]

The emperor's voyage was hailed by Parisian journalists as the dawn of a new, more enlightened phase of French imperial domination. For the journalists of the European settler colony, however, the new direction in colonial policy heightened feelings of insecurity. That changes were needed in the government of Algeria they did not doubt. Indeed, journalists regularly tested the limits of the government's strict press controls to call for a definitive decision on the administrative status of the territory. Indecision, they complained, meant that "Algeria has been consistently subjected to all kinds of administrative experiments and abandoned to all kinds of systems."[5] Yet the solution, they believed, lay not so much in the fantasy of an Arab kingdom as in the real and insoluble ties of culture, race, and civilization that bound the Algerian settler colony to the French nation and the wider European continent.

Settlers consequently embraced the emperor's second visit to Algeria, in the spring of 1865, as an opportunity to set colonial policy back on the right path. This time, journalists decided, they would not allow the emperor to be distracted by "Oriental" exoticism; instead, they would impress him with a display of all that the European population had achieved in the thirty-five years of French presence. "As soon as the spectacle of the immense *fantasia* of 1860 . . . is replaced by a detailed review of the roots, branches and fruits of colonization across Algeria," predicted one settler journalist, "His Majesty will surely prefer to overcome all the difficulties of colonial development than to attempt the impossible by renegotiating the Treaty of Tafna."[6] This treaty, negotiated in 1837 between the French general Thomas-Robert Bugeaud and Abd al-Qadir, leader of the struggle against the French invaders, had long been invoked by settlers and French officials alike to uphold the principle of French sovereignty in the conquered territory.[7] By referring to the treaty in the context of shifts in French colonial policy, settler journalists reaffirmed their belief in the legitimacy of French rule and expressed their hopes for the permanence of European settlement in Algeria. Once again, journalists used the analogy of the family relationship to illustrate the immutability of the bond between France and the settler colony. The emperor's arrival, journalists enthused, had caused "the greatest animation—people greet each other with joy; it's like one big family celebrating a long-awaited Father."[8]

It would be almost forty years before another French head of state set foot in Algeria. In the time that elapsed between the voyage of Napoleon III in 1865 and the arrival of President Emile Loubet in 1903, the political context changed dramatically on both sides of the Mediterranean. As the Second Empire gave way to the Third Republic, colonial authority passed from military to civilian institutions. The press, which had been subject to strict controls under Napoleon III, enjoyed a period of ebullience as publications multiplied and diversified following the liberalizing legislation of 1881. Despite the different political regimes and conditions of press production, Loubet's voyage elicited a familiar set of images and metaphors from settler journalists, who continued to depict the head of state as an adored father. As Loubet toured the three departments of Algiers, Oran, and Constantine, journalists fixed on his benevolent paternal smile and fatherly bearing, affectionately referring to him as "Papa" Loubet.[9]

The persistent use of the analogy of the parent-child relationship in the colonial press indicates long-term continuity in settler journalists' understanding of the emotional dynamics of the settler colonial situation. Persistent anxieties that the settler colony was "unknown and unloved" by the French of the metropole, as Seth Graebner points out, were more than simple expressions of self-pity, instead providing "a stimulus to cultural production in the colony and a central argument for the recognition of a distinctive identity within the French Empire."[10] The recurring analogy of the family relationship, in particular, served as a framework for the political imaginary of settler journalists, who sought to redefine the dynamics of empire proposed by the dominant metropolitan narrative of the "colonial family romance."[11] This narrative of imperialist benevolence, explains Françoise Vergès, originated with the French Revolution and cast the enlightened French nation as the loving parent of indigenous and diasporic colonized peoples across the empire.[12] Fiona Barclay observes in her analysis of the evolution of *pied-noir* sentiments toward France and the patriarchal figure of Charles de Gaulle in the aftermath of the Algerian War that at times of heightened vulnerability, European Algerians appropriated this narrative in innovative ways to express feelings of hope and disappointment.[13]

This chapter traces the elaboration of a "settler colonial family romance" by settler journalists in the decades between the visits of Napoleon III and President Loubet. In this alternative narrative, journalists contested the legitimacy of France's indigenous "children" in order to proclaim settlers as the rightful heirs of the French nation. Rejecting infantilization by metropolitan observers, settler journalists also demanded that Europeans in Algeria be seen as brothers and equals of the French citizens on the other side of the Mediterranean. Although the notion of fraternity remained central to the family model proposed by journalists, the gender dynamics of the idealized settler colonial family evolved in reaction to the changing political context. While the violent autonomist movement of the 1890s favored representations of the settler colony as a grown man, ready to claim his independence from an overbearing French mother, an enduring sense of settler vulnerability—exacerbated by Muslim resistance at the turn of the century—caused journalists to revert to an older model in which the settler colony submitted as a dutiful daughter to the political authority of her metropolitan father.

If settler journalists in 1903 were ready to welcome Papa Loubet as the head of their political community, however, they were not prepared to relinquish affective and cultural ties to their diverse mother countries. By elaborating a further gendered division between political and cultural sovereignty, settler journalists claimed their place in the French nation while relating this nation to a larger transnational Latin family.

The Settler Colonial Family Romance

In welcoming both Napoleon III and President Loubet as figures of paternal authority, settler journalists conformed to a longer postrevolutionary narrative of the French national family. The trial and execution of Louis XVI enacted what Lynn Hunt describes as the ritual sacrifice of the political father, unleashing a torrent of fraternal violence that could only be stemmed by the rehabilitation of paternal authority in nineteenth-century political institutions and social structures.[14] This rehabilitation transformed cultural understandings of paternity and masculinity, reinforcing social expectations that men should act with reason and self-restraint, and strengthened the cultural association between masculinity and political authority. Women's potential for political action was limited, as their presence in public space was restricted in favor of feminine figures of allegory, including the increasingly respectable Marianne and the oft-naked Truth.[15] Settler journalists followed the tropes of this national narrative, welcoming the emperor and the president as embodiments of political and paternal authority.

In welcoming these heads of state as fathers, however, settler journalists were not merely playing out the family romance of the French Revolution. Indeed, settler identification with the French national family was increasingly called into question during these years by the growth of a local community of mixed European origins, with affiliation to multiple mother countries, and by mounting frustration with the discourse of the French civilizing mission. This mission, Vergès explains, refashioned the postrevolutionary political imaginary into a "colonial family romance" in which France played the role of parent to its colonized children, guiding them toward cultural and political maturity.[16] While the infantilization of indigenous peoples was a common feature of the discourse of European empire building,[17] in France it served to uphold a familial analogy of empire around which the nation could be reimagined during the political turbulence of the nineteenth century. The conquest of Algeria, as Jennifer Sessions demonstrates, was central to this process of national reimagination under the July Monarchy.[18] References to family relationships also served to extend French influence across North Africa and the Eastern Mediterranean, as the policy makers invoked affective ties between France and isolated Catholic communities in an effort to defend national interests from Ottoman expansion.[19] With the fall of the July Monarchy, a secular version of the colonial family romance came to the fore, as politicians, journalists, and artists emphasized at once the fraternity and the paternalism of Frenchmen bringing abolition and political reform to the French Caribbean.[20]

Relying on both secular and religious tropes to legitimize his personal authority under the Second Empire, Napoleon III maintained the narrative of the colonial family romance, emphasizing the role of France as parent to Catholic communities in rival empires, as well as to indigenous and diasporic peoples in French colonial territories. The emperor's attempts to reform French policy in Algeria contributed to the public conceptualization of the colonial empire as a set of familial bonds, as metropolitan journalists represented the French nation and its leader as benevolent parents providing moral uplift for the territory's Muslim and Jewish communities. By the time of President Loubet's visit to Algeria in 1903, the national civilizing mission, carried out by the male political agents of a beneficent mother country, had become a central tenet of French imperialist ideology and was widely popularized in the press.[21]

This particular family portrait, however, was painted from the perspective of the metropole. Settler journalists in Algeria reproduced it only insofar as it confirmed their own privileged status as colonizers over the politically and socially disenfranchised colonized. Certainly, for the more socially elite reading communities of the francophone colonial

3. Title banner of *La France algérienne*, April 7, 1907

press, the image of the colonial family romance could serve as a badge of distinction, linking them to the politically dominant French nation and distinguishing them from both foreign European migrants and indigenous peoples. The April 7, 1907, issue of the weekly publication *La France algérienne* bore a title banner proudly depicting Marianne, feminine allegory of the republic, offering comfort to an indigenous child (fig. 3).[22] The inclusion of Muslim and Jewish religious symbols in the upper right corner, in conjunction with the Gallic rooster in the upper left, emphasized the national mission to protect and guide all religious communities in Algeria, while the depiction of the tools of labor carried the promise of modernity and progress. In return, the republic received both material sustenance and adoration from its grateful colonial ward.

Alongside this ideal of imperial benevolence, journalists of the settler colony developed a distinct political imaginary: a specifically *settler colonial* family romance. Framed by the triangular dynamics of the settler colonial situation, this imaginary cast European settlers as the legitimate children of the French nation, delegitimizing any claim made by Muslim or Jewish populations. At the same time, however, settler journalists rejected the infantilization of the European colony by the French of the metropole, denouncing official attempts at cultural assimilation, which turned the apparatus of the state to the creation of a culturally and linguistically homogenous national community. Whereas the colonial family romance, as Vergès points out, invented a single French parent who alienated colonial subjects from their cultural heritage,[23] the *settler colonial* family romance allowed for settlers' multiple sources of filiation.

To defend their mixed heritage while ensuring that the French state continued to support and protect them, settler journalists proposed a gendered division of cultural and political sovereignty. While welcoming both Napoleon III and President Loubet as political fathers, settler journalists continued to cultivate their readers' affective and cultural ties to their diverse mother countries. These ties were maintained through references to settlers' local "Algerian" existence and common belonging to a transnational Latin community. As settler journalists gained greater freedom of expression in the last decades of the nineteenth century, the French colonial family became but one branch of an extended Latin family whose members were united by their cultural, linguistic, and racial heritage.

Napoleon III and the French Colonial Family

The emperor's first visit to Algeria, settler journalists generally agreed, had been something of a fiasco. Curtailed by news of the death of the empress's sister, the visit had been confined to the town of Algiers and the surrounding areas. The emperor, who had spent much of his time in the company of his guest, the bey of Tunis, had—like most metropolitan visitors—been distracted by the new and unfamiliar environment and consequently had not gotten to know the real Algeria. The authentic Algeria, these journalists intimated, was not to be glimpsed through the mesmerizing but superficial spectacle of the "Orient." Nor was it to be heard in conversation with Caïds and Aghas, whom settler journalists blamed for the destitution of the indigenous masses. Instead, they suggested, Algeria was to be known through the products of colonists' labor—the fruits of settler agriculture and the edifices of settler industry. This, they believed, was the real Algeria, resurrected by the hard work and ingenuity of Europeans after centuries of decline under the neglectful leadership of the Arabs.[24] Such claims to authenticity operated as attempts to indigenize, and thus legitimize, the settler colony.[25]

The consequences of the emperor's misplaced attention in 1860, settler journalists complained, had been serious. As a writer for *L'Echo d'Oran* summarized, "If, during his first visit to Algiers, the head of state could have inspected agricultural units instead of watching sumptuous fantasias in honor of the Arabs and their steeds . . . the idea of creating an Arab kingdom in a territory that had long been declared French would have never entered his mind."[26] The visit in 1860 had indeed helped Napoleon III clarify his new approach to Algeria, and it was during his trip to Algiers that the emperor first publicly articulated the notion of an Arab kingdom in which both European settlers and Algerian Muslims would enjoy an equal right to his protection.[27]

On returning from Algiers in 1860, the emperor had dissolved the Ministry of Algeria and the Colonies, an office that had ensured the territory's direct representation within the central government since 1858. The office was replaced with that of the military governor general, marking a return to the administrative structures of the years of conquest and reaffirming the uncertain status of Algeria, which was officially part of French national territory without being fully integrated into the national administration. Denied the same political representation as the citizens of the metropole, French settlers in Algeria rallied against these reforms. Settler privilege was further destabilized by the *sénatus-consulte* of April 22, 1863, which confirmed tribal ownership of areas of land not already requisitioned and designated for European settlement. Although settlers would ultimately benefit from this law, which imposed mechanisms of state intervention on the management of tribal land and facilitated the integration of land sales into a capitalist economy based on individual property rights,[28] the official presentation of the legislation as an attempt to protect tribal interests engendered anxiety in the settler press, and journalists nervously anticipated the catastrophic effects of a possible French withdrawal from the territory.

The decree of July 7, 1864—which brought the administration of the settler colony into line with that of the indigenous population by suppressing the office of the director general of civil affairs and making the prefect of each of the three departments answerable to that department's military commander—raised anxiety to a fever pitch.

Between 1860 and 1865, therefore, settler journalists regularly expressed fears of abandonment by the French government. As one reader of *L'Indépendant* of Constantine confessed in a letter written at the time of the emperor's second voyage, "Uncertainty about the future has been our greatest enemy."[29] The announcement of the emperor's return sparked a series of anxious rumors among local journalists, who feared that the head of state intended to announce French withdrawal from Algeria, revise the Treaty of Tafna, and perhaps even install the defeated resistance leader Abd al-Qadir as viceroy.[30] "The voyage itself," noted one journalist, "was but a rumor until it was confirmed by the reality of the fact. Many Algerian settlers doubted that it would come to pass and are still surprised by the event."[31]

Once these initial doubts had passed, settler journalists seized on the opportunity to counter the impression created by the voyage of 1860 and to present Algeria not as an exotic Arab kingdom, but as a European settlement to be integrated into the French nation. These expressions of patriotism were framed by the conditions of press production under the Second Empire, which constrained settler journalists' liberty of expression. Yet settler journalists also had their own reasons for encouraging readers to follow their lead and offer a heartfelt welcome to Napoleon III on his return to Algeria. In demonstrating the affective bonds that tied the colony to the metropole, journalists suggested, settlers could put an end to the vulnerability of the colony and attract the sympathies of the metropolitan public. As one writer for *L'Akhbar* explained, "If we let ourselves become preoccupied and suppress the joy in our hearts, critics of colonization will not hesitate to use our prevarication as a weapon against us."[32] Readers were therefore exhorted to turn out in great numbers for the emperor's arrival, to display all that they had achieved in the colony since the invasion of

1830, and to present these achievements as those of France. If all went well, their enthusiasm would ensure the favor of the emperor, the affirmation of French domination, the patronage of new investors, and the promise of future prosperity. "And even if the visit doesn't lead to any brilliant results," reasoned one journalist, "it will at least present a more favorable image of Algeria to French public opinion. Ignorant opinion that presumes us to be still, everywhere and always, threatened by the curved blades of Arabs and Kabyles and the teeth of lions, panthers, hyenas, and jackals, will perhaps be revised when nothing dramatic is relayed in the reports of official historiographers."[33]

Employing the political ideal of the French colonial family, settler journalists asked their readers to come and greet the emperor with their own families in tow. "Come along, we say again," encouraged writers from *L'Akhbar*, "bring your families, come and show the emperor the virile races who cover with crops an African land that barbarism long left sterile."[34] The healthy settler family embodied the success of the French colonial project, and robust settler children indicated its future security. To emphasize this point, journalists suggested organizing a display for the emperor, placing "a row of Muslim children opposite a row of European children!" This spectacle, insisted *L'Indépendant*, would allow the emperor to judge "on which side can be found the fecundity, vitality, health, faith, future—and, by consequence, the *providential nationality*—of Algeria."[35] The supposed achievements of settler families, in contrast to the supposed failures of Muslim families, were intended to mark the former as the legitimate children of France and delegitimize any possible claim by the latter.

To increase the affective value of their claims, journalists drew direct parallels between the children of the settler colony and the emperor's own child, the nine-year-old imperial prince. *L'Echo d'Oran* and *L'Akhbar* reported that a young boy of the same age as Louis-Napoleon had climbed onto the step of the emperor's carriage as he left Valmy and delivered the following message: "Sire, our parents talk every day about the imperial prince—they have taught us to love him. Would Your Majesty accept these few flowers on his behalf, as a gift and souvenir from the children of Valmy and Mangin[?]" According to local journalists, the emperor was "visibly moved" as he accepted the bouquet and tenderly caressed the young boy's cheek. The assembled crowd reacted with enthusiasm, and "everyone wished to thank the emperor for his paternal kindness."[36] The unusual level of detail given in the account suggests that it was, if not apocryphal, at least significantly embellished, reflecting journalists' own profound desire for the settler colony to be recognized by its French political father. Local administrators reiterated this desire in their correspondence with the emperor, drawing similar parallels between the settler colony and the young prince and expressing the wish that the heir to the imperial crown would return to Algeria one day.[37]

Journalists' appeals to the French colonial family not only were an expression of settlers' feelings of isolation and vulnerability but also constituted a strategic attempt to redeploy the language of the state to the colony's advantage. Since the voyage of 1860 the emperor himself had encouraged the depiction of the relationship between France and Algeria as a familial bond. To the chagrin of settler journalists, however, the emperor recognized Algerian Muslims and Jews as his colonial children. Arriving in 1860 amid unrest in Kabylia, where Muslims were reacting angrily to the nefarious local effects of the policies advanced by the new Ministry of Algeria and the Colonies,[38] the emperor had emphasized his own paternal role as a protector and moral guide of these communities. Napoleon III sought legitimacy through association with an established figure of North African political and religious authority, inviting the bey of Tunis to appear alongside him at the reception of local Caïds, Aghas, and Kabyle delegates. [39] Donning a red *burnous*, the emperor reviewed the colonial troops in the company of the bey and made the following declaration: "It is our first duty to provide for the happiness of the three million Arabs that the end of hostilities has placed under our domination. Providence has called us to this land to spread the benefits of civilization." Civilization, the emperor added, involved "well-being counting for something, the life of a man counting for much, and man's moral perfection counting for the greatest good." By providing a progressive education that would respect the Islamic faith, France, the emperor suggested, would surpass traditional forms of authority and "raise the Arabs to the dignity of free men."[40]

If the emperor was to play the benevolent patriarch, his wife, the empress, was to appear as a loving mother. While Napoleon III sought to bring the manly qualities of liberty and reason to the Muslim population, the empress would establish peace among the diverse communities. This was to be achieved by uniting the women of Algeria, whose differences of faith or ethnic origin could be overcome by their shared femininity. On her first day in Algiers, the empress received visits from groups of "Moorish and Jewish women."[41] A gift offered to the empress highlighted her maternal status via an inscription that read, "To the Empress Eugenie, 1830–1860." These dates were those of the territory, rather than those of the empress herself, to whom the birth of French Algeria had seemingly been attributed.

Despite her role in receiving delegations, the empress was divested of any political influence in metropolitan press reports, as journalists emphasized her emotional nature over her diplomatic activity. On hearing the news of her sister's death, the empress was said to have been overcome by emotion, withdrawing from a public ceremony and breaking down in tears behind the stage.[42] Journalists readily forgave her feminine sensibility, which corresponded perfectly to the gendered precepts of the civilization that the emperor hoped to establish in Algeria.

In 1865 the emperor returned to Algeria, this time without his wife and child. Unable to draw on the spectacle of his own family to impose his paternal authority, he instead relied on the local press to reinforce his image as a devoted father to his colonial subjects. The official newspaper of the colonial administration, *Le Moniteur algérien*, was all but requisitioned by officials who exercised "special surveillance" for the duration of the emperor's voyage. Publication rates accelerated as *Le Moniteur* was temporarily transformed from a weekly to a daily newspaper, and five special editions were printed. According to an administrative report, "Each issue necessitated extraordinary overtime from the typesetters, who worked until three o'clock in the morning."[43] Alongside *Le Moniteur*, the central government ensured the cooperation of other local publications by making official reports of the emperor's activities available to all local journalists.[44] This directive, issued within two weeks of the emperor's arrival, changed the character of local reporting on the voyage, as articles and opinion pieces gave way to a greater number of standardized descriptive summaries.

Summaries based on official accounts habitually featured scenes of interaction between the emperor and children of all communities. A typical article from the end of May described the emperor's procession through Batna, where "four young girls offered him a basket of flowers. The basket was held by a Catholic, a Protestant, an Israelite, and a Muslim. As they approached the imperial carriage, His Majesty lent over with great paternal kindness to receive the bouquet. This little group, which brought together the various religious communities of Algeria, was pleasing to the emperor."[45] The emperor was similarly greeted in Fort-Napoleon (Larbâa Nath Ithran), Philippeville (Skikda), Smendou (Zighoud Youcef),[46] and Algiers, where "all the children of the French, Israelite, and Muslim schools of Algiers and the suburbs were arranged along the length of the Chasseloup-Laubat ramp, and along the quay, each of them holding flags or flowers."[47]

Such descriptions of equality and cooperation among children of different communities served to reinforce the principal political message of the emperor, which was made explicit in the speeches he gave as he traversed the colonial territory. Local newspapers reproduced and extensively commented on these speeches. On May 3, shortly after his arrival in Algiers, the emperor issued his Proclamation to the Inhabitants of Algeria, addressing French settlers and publicly enjoining them to "treat the Arabs as [their] compatriots."[48] The Proclamation to the Arab People, issued two days later, called on Muslims to accept the French conquest and place their trust in their new sovereign.[49] Quoting liberally—and strategically—from the Quran, the emperor attempted to provide an example of the tolerance and cooperation that he hoped would flourish in Algeria.

According to settler journalists, however, such appeals were certain to be ineffectual—such, in their opinion, was the intransigent nature of Islam. Muslims, agreed *Le Sémaphore* and *L'Indépendant*, would not recognize the authority of those outside their faith, "whom they view as dogs and are commanded to treat as such by their religion." Although the emperor had clearly sought to "enlighten these enraged fanatics, who are always ready to kill and pillage," the journalists continued, "the *marabouts* will have no difficulty in rendering the imperial proclamation null and void." Resistance to French domination was thus reframed as "Muslim ingratitude to France," legitimizing settlers' own hesitancy to "extend their hands" and welcome Muslims into the French colonial family.[50] Hence while Jules Guérin, writing for *L'Akhbar*, affirmed that settlers would "follow the advice of the emperor and treat the Arabs as compatriots," he added that this could occur only "once they no longer trouble the peace of this land."[51]

That Muslims in Algeria had not yet earned their place in the French colonial family, settler journalists added, was amply evident in the uncivilized way the men treated the women of their own families. "The sad condition of the Arab woman is well enough known for it to be unnecessary to paint a picture," reported *L'Akhbar*. The journalist nevertheless went on to provide a description of this treatment, comparing the family lives of settlers and Muslims in such a way that ostensibly supported the emperor's call for moral uplift, yet ultimately cast doubt on its chances of success: "In penetrating our farms and seeing women together with their husbands, sharing their work not through fear but through devotion, the Arab will no doubt understand that man has other things to gain from the relations that nature has established between the sexes than brutal pleasures or imperious orders and low submissions."[52] Progress would not be made in Algeria, confirmed one reader of *L'Indépendant*, until Arabs stopped "buying and selling their own women like livestock."[53]

Settler journalists played on the stereotype of aggressive Muslim manliness to emphasize the dangers posed by admitting Arabs and Berbers into the French colonial family. *L'Indépendant* drew its readers' attention to an incident that was supposed to have taken place outside of Blida while settlers lined the road to catch a glimpse of the emperor.[54]

Unexpectedly stopping his carriage, the emperor began to converse with an orphaned settler girl, whom the local mayor presented as a victim of Muslim rebels. Encouraged by the emperor to recount her experiences, the girl described her fate at the hands of her parents' assassins:

> Arriving at a delicate passage of her narrative, the young girl blushed and said, "Sire, I cannot possibly tell you everything that they did to me." To which the emperor paternally replied, "Leave such things aside, my child." And the little victim of the brutalities continued, explaining how she had escaped. "Did you receive any help, my child?" asked His Majesty. "No Monsieur," replied the unhappy orphan, "but I now live here with these settlers who have taken me in by charity." "Well, I will not forget you," said the emperor, adding, "I knew nothing of these odious crimes; nobody ever told me."[55]

The incident was not widely reported, and the tone and style of the piece mark the tale as apocryphal. In a context in which reporting false news could lead to severe penalties for publications, the article reveals the inventive ways in which colonial journalists appropriated official narratives and used them as cover for the expression of their own concerns. Although the report likely did not recount an actual encounter between the emperor and a settler girl, it is nonetheless illuminating insofar as it reveals settler journalists' deep fear of the Muslim population and their strong desire for a political father who would acknowledge and protect the settler colony. The author of the tale was careful to preserve the emperor's paternal image by suggesting that any neglect had been the fault of obscurantist government advisors, rather than of the head of state himself.

Settler journalists' frustration with what they saw as metropolitan misinformation had grown in the early years of the 1860s. Following the emperor's first visit to Algeria and the corresponding shift in colonial policy, Parisian newspapers had featured regular articles exposing the vulnerability of Muslims and condemning both settlers and previous administrations for their disregard of indigenous property and customs.[56]

A number of these articles, suggests Michel Levallois, were penned by the emperor's advisor, Ismaÿl Urbain, posing as a young Algerian Muslim named Messaoud El Medani.[57] According to El Medani, "For us Arabs, the ambition is not to enter into the system of exceptional privileges afforded to the Europeans who inhabit our land, but to be adopted by France, by this great nation. We are ready to give her our blood, our money, all that she asks of her children."[58]

Such articles sparked outrage among settler journalists, who denounced "certain newspapers in the capital, which—for reasons beyond ignorance of our affairs—have besmirched Algerian colonization and represented it in a kind of false light." "If this tactic poses no danger for Algerian settlers or metropolitans who are familiar with Algeria," argued *L'Echo d'Oran*, "it could be deadly for those who know nothing of the country other than that which they read or have been told." These people might be dissuaded from emigrating or investing, worried journalist Albert Mercier, concerned about the negative effects on colonial development. More devastating still, he suggested, these people might decide to abandon settlers, convinced that "the Frenchman [in Algeria] is worth less than the Arab."[59]

Settlers' sensitivity to rejection by the wider French public was further tested by metropolitan press coverage of the emperor's voyage in 1865. Settler journalists' hopes that metropolitan readers would be disabused of their Orientalist fantasies by impartial and informative reports were not to be realized. Although local journalists declared themselves willing to make concessions to metropolitan readers' "love of the picturesque," they would not allow the settler community's actions or sentiments to be misrepresented by their colleagues on the other side of the Mediterranean.[60] Such misrepresentation occurred all too frequently, claimed *L'Akhbar*, denouncing "the errors peddled by *La Presse*, *L'Epoque*, and other big 'arabophile' titles."[61] Parisian paper *L'Illustration* provoked particular ire with an image of the emperor and his aides crossing the main square in Algiers (fig. 4).[62]

The image, observed an incredulous writer for *L'Akhbar*, showed the head of state "traversing a crowd *entirely composed of Arabs*."[63] This depic-

4. "The Emperor on the Place du Gouvernement in Algiers on the Evening of May 3—Based on a Sketch by Our Special Illustrator," *L'Illustration*, May 13, 1865

tion was contested by several settler journalists, who insisted that the crowd surrounding the emperor had been composed of Europeans.[63] In misrepresenting the occasion, these journalists suggested, *L'Illustration* had not only overstated indigenous attachment to France but also left settlers' affective ties unacknowledged. "The [European] population of Algiers" was profoundly hurt by this illustration, claimed the writer for *L'Akhbar*. "How could it not be?" In omitting settlers from the picture, the controversial image enacted the abandonment many settlers had long feared: "*L'Illustration* has eliminated this population at the stroke of a pencil," observed the journalist, "leaving only Arabs."[65]

While settler journalists sought to dismiss affective ties between Muslims and France, they emphasized the equality of sentiment shown by migrants of diverse European origins. Not only had there been so many Europeans on the square that night that it was impossible to move through the crowd, claimed *L'Akhbar*, but this crowd had included Spaniards and Maltese alongside Frenchmen.[66] Made in the context of an ongoing debate about the desirability of the collective naturalization of Europeans of non-French origin in Algeria, such claims articulated a specific local vision of the French colonial family—a settler colonial family in which a sense of French national belonging coexisted with a sense of local particularism and transnational community.

Although the French government had long recognized the importance of non-French Europeans' contribution to economic growth in Algeria, the question of naturalization had floundered amid uncertainty over the administrative status of the colonial territory. In the 1840s, Jennifer Sessions explains, proposals for extending political rights to non-French Europeans were rejected on the grounds that "a special naturalization law for Algeria would create a disjunction between colonial and metropolitan law that was inconsistent with the long-term goal of assimilation."[67] These aspirations to achieve administrative assimilation remained unrealized in the decades that followed, leaving the question of naturalization unresolved until the end of the 1880s, when the government of the Third Republic conceded the strategic advantage of such a measure in the context of growing imperial rivalry.

Writing for *L'Indépendant* in 1865, journalist Ferdinand Guillon presented the benefits to be gained by both the colony and the French nation from the naturalization of non-French Europeans. The government had only to look, he claimed, at the United States for an example of the positive effects of including diverse European immigrants in a cohesive political community. While Guillon acknowledged many differences between the two settler colonies—including "the contrasting temperaments of the races," their different "religious traditions and political customs," and what he saw as a less aggressive attitude toward indigenous peoples in Algeria—he felt it was nevertheless important to ask whether "Algeria might have something to learn, to emulate in the prodigious rise of this colonial and political, social, and continental Hercules?" In particular, it would be useful to consider "adopting the measures used in America concerning naturalization." The extension of political rights to non-French Europeans in Algeria would naturally be accompanied, in Guillon's opinion, by the restoration of full political rights to all settlers.[68]

In a second article, Guillon based his argument for the naturalization of non-French Europeans and the full enfranchisement of settlers on what he saw as a natural propensity for democratic practice among settlers in North Africa. This propensity was a legacy of the Roman Empire and had been inherited by nineteenth-century settlers through the special bond they had created with the local land and environment. "The previous five centuries of roman and Christian civilization cannot be taken from us," Guillon argued. "They must be counted in our record of service."[69] If this heritage were taken into account, pressed Guillon, then the extension of political rights to Europeans in Algeria could no longer be opposed on the grounds of the local settler population being less prepared for political participation than settlers elsewhere in the world. "When we bring up the example of North America or Australia, people counter that there is a difference in temperament between the Anglo-Saxon race and the Latin race," the journalist contended, "but what would they say if we reminded them that the supremacy of a civil regime over a military regime was established here, in this province [of Constantine], by the first shoots of Latin civilization?"[70]

Guillon's reference to a "Latin race" whose existence transcended national borders and whose claim to sovereignty in Algeria long predated that of France challenged the idea that Algeria was simply an extension of French national space. Although Guillon, like other journalists at the time, was arguing for settlers' inclusion in the French political community, he was also proposing a broader vision of cultural community—one in which the French nation represented but one parent in a larger, extended family. "We only claim these rights in order to share them with our young sisters, the provinces of Algiers and Oran," announced Guillon on behalf of the settlers of the province of Constantine, which he viewed as the true historical birthplace of settlers' political consciousness. "We sacrifice our privilege as the eldest to our solidarity in suffering and our common hopes, upon the altar of our triple patriotism: Roman, French, and Algerian."[71] The political community of the French nation was thus articulated with a local community based on "Algerian" experience and a transnational community based on Latin heritage. If France was still acknowledged as a parent to the three sister provinces in Algeria, it was not the only parent and would have to make room for the influence of multiple mother countries.

Even outspoken journalists like Guillon, however, recognized that overstating the differences between settlers and the French of the metropole could prove counterproductive to their quest for political equality. Although local journalists hoped to take advantage of the emperor's presence to press for reform, they were wary of appearing too demanding for fear of living up to the reputation that settlers had acquired in the metropole for being "overly impressionable and *demonstrative*."[72] "Settlers do perhaps go from one extreme to the other!" admitted Guillon, downplaying local specificity by adding, "But who doesn't in France?"[73]

Fears of overstating settler difference and thereby jeopardizing their chances of obtaining political equality, material support, or protection constrained journalists' efforts to influence the emperor's view of the colony. Attempts to formulate an "address to be communicated to the head of state . . . to make known to him the many and varied needs of Algeria" floundered, as a call from the editors of *L'Akhbar* went unanswered by journalists at other publications.[74] "We must assume that our colleagues either see things differently from us," reflected the editors of *L'Akhbar*, "or else perceive danger there where we perceive opportunity."[75] The danger, countered *L'Indépendant*, lay in being mistaken for "an electoral committee intent on agitating the country and contesting the government's decision regarding universal suffrage in Algeria."[76] This not only would be disastrous for the journalists and editors, who would face official sanctions, but also could harm the prospects of the colony as a whole. Direct appeals to the emperor were thus left to the initiative of municipal councils, who wrote to plead for the development of local roads or ports but were never so bold as to publish their demands in the press.[77]

Settler journalists came to regret their caution in the wake of the emperor's visit. They had set out to win the acknowledgment and affection of both the emperor and the metropolitan public in the hope of securing the prosperity of the settler colony. Their vision of the future had depended, in particular, on overturning the notion of an Arab kingdom and ensuring the recognition of European settlers as the legitimate children of France. Just one month after the emperor's departure from Algeria, however, the proclamation of the *sénatus-consulte* of July 14 dashed their hopes. Not only did the law stop far short of the collective naturalization of European settlers of non-French origin, but it also established the legal premise for the naturalization of Algerian Muslims and Jews. Individuals from these communities would henceforth have access to French citizenship in exchange for the renunciation of the particular legal status defined by their faith.[78] The direct intervention of members of the imperial family in favor of individuals who sought naturalization, such as the soldier Mohammed Ben Driss, who received the financial and personal support of the Empress Eugenie, framed naturalization as a form of adoption.[79] Although the condition attached to citizenship ensured that few Muslims and Jews in Algeria availed themselves of this new opportunity for political representation, settler journalists nevertheless received the legislation as a slight, a sign that the settler community was neither acknowledged by its political father nor understood by its metropolitan brothers.

Growing Pains and the Question of Independence

Feelings of rejection grew in the years that followed, which were marked by a series of environmental crises, epidemics, and famine. Although the effects of these disasters were felt by all colonial communities, the impact on the Muslim population—already made vulnerable by land requisition and the burdens of disproportionate taxation—was catastrophic. The consequences of poor harvests exacerbated by a colonial export economy were most keenly felt by this population, which suffered a devastating demographic decline of one-tenth to one-third, according to the different estimates of French administrators and Algerian historians. Campaigns for charitable relief organized by church officials from Algeria caught the attention of the metropolitan public, creating what Bertrand Taithe describes as "a fund of compassion" for

Algerian Muslims. Although this fund was much depleted following the insurrection of Muhammad al-Hajj al-Muqrani in 1871, the arabophile discourses it sponsored were still in evidence in the metropole in the 1890s and early 1900s. The charity campaigns of the late 1860s, moreover, helped reinforce the image of a French colonial family composed of a nurturing French parent and a grateful indigenous child. The fundraising initiatives relied on emphasizing the suffering of Muslim orphans, some of whom were even brought to France and paraded before a shocked metropolitan public.[80]

The relationship between the settler community and Napoleon III's regime deteriorated rapidly during these years. The refusal to apply the liberalizing legislation of 1868 to the press in Algeria created consternation among settler journalists, who nevertheless circumvented restrictions on their expression by reprinting extracts from opposition newspapers in the metropole.[81] By May 1870 colonial public opinion was overwhelmingly against the regime, and members of the municipal council in Algiers were openly questioning the emperor's authority and accusing him of manipulating the French electorate.[82] Disillusionment with the regime revived the republican sympathies of a settler population that owed its existence in part to the presence of political radicals exiled and dispersed by the conflicts of nineteenth-century Europe. The fall of the Second Empire brought republican sentiment out into the streets and onto the pages of local newspapers, as settlers founded their own revolutionary commune in Algiers and launched new publications. "What form of government would Algerian settlers logically like to see definitively adopted by the metropole?" asked the editor of one such publication, *La France algérienne*. "The republic, and the republic alone."[83]

Many local journalists believed that the arrival of the Third Republic and the transition to civil authority would finally give settlers the opportunity that Napoleon III had repeatedly denied them: the chance to convince the French of the metropole of the settler colony's attachment to France. Newspapers were expected to take a leading role in this campaign. "We are founding *La France algérienne*," explained the editor of the

Oranais newspaper, "to defend the interests of our great colony, make known its needs and aspirations, [and] reveal it to the metropole, which knows almost nothing about it." Once the French of the metropole had been enlightened, they would help ensure that "this land that has long been watered with our blood will bear glorious fruit, becoming the granary of France as it was once the granary of Rome." Its value definitively proven, the colony would "become completely assimilated with the metropole, or rather it would end up being a simple extension, a continuation of France on the other side of the Mediterranean."[84]

Such hopes once again proved illusory. Although an attempt at greater administrative assimilation was initiated in 1881 with the system of *rattachements*, it served only to render government more inefficient as ministers in Paris found themselves responsible for the direct provision of services of health, education, and justice in territories with diverse populations about which they knew little. Despite the apparent assimilation of governmental structures, moreover, the colonial general government was not abolished. The dispersed sources of political authority led to administrative chaos, which was ably exploited by opportunistic local politicians.[85] This system, complained a disillusioned revolutionary from *Le Sans-culotte*, was "completely paralyzing colonization and creating numerous obstacles to the development of wealth." Faced with the French government's continued failure to attend to local problems, journalists were left questioning the settler colony's parentage: "Are we Frenchmen here, or are we bastards?" continued *Le Sans-culotte*. "In the first case we should be completely assimilated and ruled by the Metropole. . . . In the second case we should be given a special constitution and proclaim our autonomy forthwith."[86]

Although the author of the article in *Le Sans-culotte* declared that he was in favor of the former option, his allusion to settler autonomy indicated that such an outcome had become imaginable for journalists in the last decade of the nineteenth century. This possibility was sustained by the notion that the settler colony had finally arrived at the age of maturity. Journalists' descriptions of a colony on the brink of adulthood echoed the work of local doctors and demographers, also cited in the press, who wrote with confidence of a French settler population whose intermarriage with Spaniards and Italians had produced a robust and acclimatized people with a birth rate surpassing that of the metropole.[87] "Algeria today seems to have come through the convulsions of its childhood," observed demographers Mandeville and Demontès, noting the "ethnic fusion" between Europeans in the settler colony and the consequent "constitution of a new people: the Algerian people."[88] Were settlers now in a position to become founding fathers of their own independent nation? local commentators began to wonder.

In contrast to the respected French political father lauded by settler journalists during the official visits of Napoleon III, representations of the family dynamics of French colonialism in the 1890s began to depict the metropole as a weak and irrational mother. The transformation of French political authority from a paternal to a maternal figure emphasized the supposedly transgressive and illegitimate nature of the metropole's continued hold over a settler colony that many journalists now perceived to be capable of running its own affairs. Imagining a dialogue between the French mother country and her settler children, journalists ascribed the masculine qualities of reason and strength to the "Algerians", who spoke as a united community, and the feminine flaw of hysteria to their mother, France:

> Algerians: "Good mother, we love you dearly and do not wish to be separated from you. But we are grown boys now, and wish you wouldn't keep us so close to you. . . ."
> France: "Ungrateful children! You want to break with me! . . . Have I not given you everything, my gold and my blood? And you dream of treating me like the United States once treated their mother, England."[89]

Developing from the analogy used by Guillon in the 1860s, such journalistic references to the United States now carried a more explicit threat of rupture between the mother country and the settler colony. Calls for settler autonomy gained momentum in the last years of the

1890s, as frustration with administrative inefficiency coalesced with other fears and recriminations. Settler anger at the collective enfranchisement of the Algerian Jews and their perceived influence on local politics had grown steadily from 1870, gaining in strength with the liberalization of the press and reaching its violent apogee in the final years of the century.[90] Feelings of betrayal and abandonment by the French government and the wider French public resulted in a short-lived but violent movement for the independence of the settler colony. "Algerian settlers are too proud and aware of their own dignity to allow themselves to be held on a leash and subjected to a family council," pronounced *L'Antijuif algérien*, publication of the antisemitic militant and separatist agitator Max Régis. "They came of age some time ago, and if they're pushed too far, they won't hesitate to push back. When the metropole stops being a mother to her colonies and instead becomes the evil stepmother, she risks losing hold of them."[91]

Despite a series of violent settler demonstrations in the years surrounding the turn of the century, the separatist movement rapidly lost ground. By 1903 settler journalists were once again announcing their submission to a French political father, complimenting President Emile Loubet on his "simple, patriarchal bearing."[92] What had happened to bring settlers back into the French national family?

Papa Loubet and the Great Latin Family

President Émile Loubet disembarked in Algiers on April 15, 1903. Unlike Napoleon III, Loubet was not the head of an imperial regime that depended on his personal authority—he was simply the "first citizen of the republic."[93] Yet his welcome in Algeria echoed that first offered to the emperor over forty years earlier. Met by local officials, assembled troops, and a large, enthusiastic crowd, the president was escorted through the streets to the Palais d'hiver along almost the same route the emperor had taken—albeit without stopping to observe mass at the cathedral. The highly choreographed arrival ceremony set the tone for the rest of the voyage, which was to last twelve days and would take the president across the three provinces of Algiers, Oran, and Constantine and onward to Tunisia, where the French had established a protectorate in 1881. "Over twelve days," observes Olivier Ihl, "the voyage would have but one aim: to affirm the happy enlightenment of colonial domination" to observers on both sides of the Mediterranean.[94]

The press, notes Ihl, was to play a fundamental role in this process of affirmation, disseminating to the French public an image of empire based on the colonizers' legitimate domination of a racially and culturally inferior people. In publicizing this image, Ihl suggests, metropolitan journalists conformed to the wishes of settlers, who had seized on the visit as a new opportunity to communicate their demands.[95] While it is clear that settlers did indeed seek to benefit from the president's visit, and indisputable that the occasion served to mobilize the mass press in defense of the colonial empire, the extent to which metropolitan and settler attitudes to the voyage coincided must be questioned. Such assumptions underpin a French historiographic tradition that has typically absolved the republic of responsibility for colonial violence by displacing blame onto a settler population perceived, in imperialist fashion, as insufficiently French.[96] Rather than suggesting entente with their metropolitan colleagues and unqualified support for a binary model of colonial hierarchy, settler journalists' reactions to President Loubet's voyage reveal a more complex set of professional dynamics and an ambivalent attitude toward French domination, in which submission to French political authority existed alongside a sense of local cultural sovereignty sustained by settlers' continued attachment to their diverse nations of origin. Their ambivalence was reflected in the discursive reconfiguration of the settler colonial family dynamic: if Papa Loubet were acknowledged as a political father, he could not displace settlers' multiple mother countries, to whom local journalists continued to attribute a role in the formation of a transnational Latin family.

Settler journalists greeted the news that the president would be visiting Algeria in much the same way as they had welcomed the announcement of the emperor's voyages in the 1860s—as an opportunity to display the progress of the colony and win over the government and the metropolitan public. By 1903, however, settler journalists enjoyed greater freedom of expression and rapidity of communication, and they used these tools to their advantage in their campaign to win the hearts, minds, and resources of their compatriots on the other side of the Mediterranean. "The voyage in Algeria is taking on the dimensions of a national event," declared *La Dépêche algérienne* two weeks before the president was due to arrive. In preparation for the voyage, the correspondent reported, the authorities had designated seventeen journalists from various Parisian and provincial newspapers for official inclusion in the presidential caravan—but would seventeen journalists be enough? "In reducing to the bare minimum the number of journalists allowed to accompany the president," the correspondent complained, "the colony is deprived of a significant and largely free form of publicity. New lands should never spurn such a resource." Were other Parisian and regional publications to content themselves with the dry summaries provided by press agencies? Were foreign reporters to find themselves excluded from the proceedings? This missed opportunity, *La Dépêche* feared, could frustrate the settler colony's ambitions.[97]

As it turned out, these anxieties proved unfounded. More generous than anticipated, the authorities allowed no fewer than thirty "representatives of the Parisian, departmental, and African press" to accompany the president on the official train and attend all scheduled engagements. Further provision was made for a number of other journalists to access alternative means of transportation and observe official ceremonies.[98] In addition, colonial authorities issued special instructions to facilitate the circulation of press reports around Algeria and across the Mediterranean, increasing the number of telegraph machines available to journalists, installing new phone lines, and creating special composition rooms for newspaper correspondents.[99] If some settler journalists continued to fret that these measures would prove insufficient, this only indicated the magnitude of their aspirations. The eyes of the world would soon be focused on Algeria. What would people see now that they were finally looking?

In the weeks preceding Loubet's arrival, local journalists and administrators considered the image they wanted to create. News of the voyage precipitated an immense stocktaking effort, as municipal officials compiled detailed descriptions of individual towns and villages, searching for suitable sights to present to the head of state. Like the reports produced at the time of Napoleon III's visits and those subsequently prepared for the governor general's colonial tours in the 1870s, these accounts aimed to communicate the immediate needs of each locality in terms of infrastructural development.[100] Much more detailed than the previous reports, however, the documents compiled in 1903 also served to underscore the achievements made by settlers over decades of colonial presence, imposing a narrative of progress and lending weight to local claims for recognition and investment.

In dividing their reports into subsections representing their town's past, present, and future, administrators depicted colonial development as being on an inevitable upward trajectory.[101] A description of Bône, for example, proudly gave the date of first settlement as 1848, then measured the town's growth according to a range of criteria: surface area, total population, transport and communication links, centers of sociability, access to drinking water, and number of public buildings. Among the projects yet to be completed, the report noted, was the redevelopment of the port.[102]

The narrative of local and colonial progress offered by administrators, moreover, was clearly inscribed within a larger narrative of French national triumph. Working together under the auspices of the French administration, some writers averred, settlers of all origins had ensured the stability of French rule and the pursuit of the civilizing mission. A typical report described the transformation of Philippeville from "a ravine and a wooded scrubland" into "a normal town, enjoying a very healthy climate and sufficient springs to aliment its population, which now surpasses 20,000 inhabitants," concluding "that French and foreign elements have made progress and that Philippeville is a very French and prosperous town."[103] Passed back and forth between administrative offices, such reports acquired additions and annotations or suffered revisions and redactions, as administrators sought to present the colony in its best light. A second report on Bône was supplemented with a handwritten expression of gratitude for the state's long-standing contribution to local development, while the writer of a particularly florid piece comparing the gardens of Biskra to those of *One Thousand and One Nights* was admonished by a superior with the annotation "Insufficiently developed!"[104]

These descriptions of European settlement contrasted sharply with the reports on sites perceived to be of importance to the Muslim community, which were conspicuously few in number and failed to adhere to the central narrative of colonial progress. Brief descriptions of saintly burial grounds and other ancient sites museumified Islamic culture, emphasizing its supposedly immutable and mystical nature.[105] The perceived opposition between European—specifically, French republican—progress and Muslim stasis was captured in a report on another proposed site of interest: the Sidi-bel-hassen mosque. The thirteenth-century edifice, "which had suffered considerably from the negligence of the Turkish administration and the vandalism of the first French occupiers," had been subjected to literal museumification at the end of the nineteenth century, when it was repurposed for the display of local archaeological discoveries.[106]

Settler journalists applauded the efforts of local administrators in ensuring that "the numerous parliamentary notables and metropolitan journalists accompanying the head of state will return well informed, despite the short duration of their visit." Such "positive propaganda," intimated Constantinois journalist Paul Salmon, was all the more necessary given that "Algeria has been the object of many inaccurate stories put about by those who speak without knowing the territory."[107] Presenting themselves as local experts, settler journalists joined colonial administrators in their "positive propaganda" campaign for the duration of the president's voyage. Their reports, they hoped, would be noticed by the visitors from the metropole and would serve to "dissipate the errors that circulate about our beautiful country, combat prejudice, awaken interest, and ensure that we finally receive greater justice."[108] A banquet for the visiting newspaper correspondents, organized by the Association of Journalists of Algiers, likewise presented an excellent opportunity.[109]

As part of their efforts to present settlers as agents of the French civilizing mission, most local journalists were at pains to show that the European residents of Algeria were perfectly civilized. Before the president's arrival and during his voyage, local journalists entreated their readers to demonstrate their best behavior.[110] The widely read *La Dépêche algérienne* reproduced official notices from the mayors of Algiers and El-Biar, instructing local residents to clean and decorate the facades of their houses and to provide "a warm welcome" motivated by both the "esteem" in which they should hold the man "who embodies the soul of the nation" and the gratitude they should feel toward "the first president of the republic to show, by his presence, sympathy and benevolence for hardworking Algeria and our hardy settlers."[111]

The repetition of such entreaties suggests that local journalists harbored some doubt as to the type of welcome the president might in fact receive. Indeed, in the weeks before his arrival, a series of articles indicated that a few journalists, as well as some of their readers, were opposed to the visit from the head of state. For some, the principal objection was the financial burden the voyage would place on the colony.[112] For others, it was the emotional cost to settlers of having their hopes of administrative reform once again raised and once again dashed.[113] The timing of the voyage, observed a writer for *Le Tell*, left much to be desired; not only were troubles on the Moroccan border creating anxiety among settlers, but public discontent with the metropolitan government was running high in the wake of financial reforms that had adversely affected Algerian viticulturists and the unpopular decision to extend military service for inhabitants of the colony from one year to two.[114]

In addition, settler journalists and their readers were still reeling from the verdict in the recent trial in Montpellier of over one hundred Muslims accused of attacking the settlement of Margueritte in April 1901.[115] The attack on the settlement, carried out by members of the Righa tribe, had profoundly shaken a settler community that had grown comfortable in the decades since the last major rebellion, led by Cheikh al-Muqrani in 1871. Although the events of 1871 cast a long shadow over the settlers, who increasingly took advantage of the new regime of press freedom to mark their cultural difference from Muslims and denounce the perceived arabophilia of the republican government, their fear of imminent attack had been somewhat attenuated by the reinforced segregation of ethnic communities in the rapidly developing urban centers of the colony.[116] The Margueritte Affair reignited long-standing fears among settlers, who felt that the metropolitan press, in blaming settlers for the deprivation of indigenous communities, had added insult to injury.[117] It seemed, lamented a writer for Le Tell, that during the legal proceedings that took place in Montpellier from November 1902 to February 1903, the notion of settlement itself—rather than the alleged attackers—had been put on trial.[118] If the settlers had been found guilty in the court of metropolitan public opinion, the jury in Montpellier was seen by local journalists as having been unduly lenient toward the accused Muslims, of whom none would face the guillotine. The settler press widely denounced the verdict as one that "excuses the murder of several settlers and innocent French workers" and "cannot bring satisfaction to Algerian settlers, who see themselves abandoned by the mother country."[119]

The Margueritte Affair reopened old wounds, reinvigorating settlers' suspicion of both Muslims and a metropolitan government that was seen to favor them. The Muslims, settler journalists generally concurred, were essentially still the "ignorant, weakling, cannibalistic, . . . half-savage hordes" they had been before European arrival—hordes who threatened to absorb the settler community by sheer force of numbers.[120] The French of the metropole, who had been duped by their colonial subjects' pathetic performance both inside and outside the courtroom, were not to be relied on. "French [settlers] in Algeria and Tunisia can only take one lesson from this," stated La Revue nord-africaine: "that is to always have a revolver in our pockets and an automatic rifle in the house, and to count on the French of France for nothing except for demanding our hard-earned money."[121] For a few journalists in Algeria, like Garnier of Le Tell or the aptly named O. Tonome of Le Réveil de Bougie, anger and disappointment fueled renewed demands for settler autonomy or even independence.[122]

For most settler journalists, however, the fear of further indigenous uprising pushed them closer to the French authorities. Indeed, if settlers had learned anything from the events in Margueritte, argued Sampiero of *L'Avenir de Tebessa*, it was how dangerous fractures in the colonial relationship could be: "A strange current of opinion has emerged on the other side of the Mediterranean," he observed, "that threatens to deviate the march of progress in Algeria from its normal course and compromise colonization itself. . . . Generous but ill-informed cries have been raised accusing Algerian settlers of subjugating the Arab, of spoiling him and making him the victim of revolting injustices—the habitual cliché presented by publications that only know Algeria through fantastical descriptions and the Arab through the tales of *One Thousand and One Nights*. Yet it is a cliché that leads to the horrors of Margueritte." Loubet's presence in the colony, Sampiero suggested, provided the ideal opportunity to disabuse the metropolitan public of their erroneous ideas and to reaffirm the affective bonds of the settler colonial family. In visiting "the so-called oppressors," the president "wanted to show his sympathy for those who, by agriculture, industry or commerce, have given France a magnificent colonial empire." It was therefore imperative that settlers respond in kind.[123]

Most local journalists agreed. Even *Le Tell*, which had led the charge against Loubet's visit, abandoned its skeptical tone as the president and his entourage disembarked in Algiers, enjoining its readers to "demonstrate their sentiments of sympathy and profound gratitude to the eminent citizen, the venerated head of state, with cries of 'Long live President LOUBET! Long live the republic! Long live France!'"[124] This mutual exchange of sympathy and respect, the paper hoped, would "tighten the patriotic bonds that unite us with our Mother Country," signaling "the long-lasting and durable reconciliation of all the children of this country!"[125]

Throughout Loubet's tour of Algeria, colonial journalists relied on the analogy of the parent-child relationship to represent their desired bond with the French nation. Like the emperor before him, the president was explicitly welcomed as a father. His arrival generated an outpouring of affection and sentimental poetry. More spontaneous exclamations of relief than refined pieces of literary expression, poems printed in local newspapers revealed journalists' and readers' desire for a benevolent paternal figure.[126] The following ode appeared in *La Dépêche algérienne* and *La Revue nord-africaine*:

> Be welcome in this faraway land,
> You who bring Peace, and dissolve all hatred!
> You who yesterday were master, today be the father!
> Be a guide to our proud settlers . . . be the one,
> Whose hand knows how to heal and whose voice knows
>   how to console![127]

This image of a father figure who tempered discipline with affection corresponded to the rehabilitated paternal authority of postrevolutionary France, particularly of the Third Republic, when broader understandings of masculinity were reconfigured in reaction to the patriarchal authoritarianism of preceding regimes.[128] It also reflected the settler community's desire for understanding and protection. Hence while the 1860s analogy of the parent-child relationship once again served as a model for settler journalists in 1903, reporters endowed President Loubet with considerably more warmth and joviality than they had Napoleon III. The president was "good, simple, and humane," said *La Dépêche algérienne*, "with a spontaneity that unsettles the restrictive stiffness of protocol."[129] His "bonhomie," observed *Le Tell*, balanced "the firmness of his principles" with "the gentleness and amenability of his character."[130] These qualities, a Parisian correspondent explained, had earned the president the nickname Papa Loubet in the capital.[131] In Algeria, the nickname was quickly taken up by settler journalists, who portrayed the president as the benevolent father for whom the colony had longed these many decades past.

Loubet's benevolent paternalism was further emphasized in the many articles that evoked his interactions with the children he encountered during his tour. These articles echoed those of the 1860s but focused exclusively on settler children, reflecting colonial journalists' explicit prioritization of the settler colony in these new conditions of press freedom. If, as one settler journalist noted, his Parisian colleagues were captivated by the sight of indigenous pupils in front of the school in Blida, his own attention was caught by a young settler girl, Jeanne Malaval, reciting a poem on the steps of the town hall.[132] According to the local journalist, it was the girl and the poem—which spoke of the "growth of the race of the future, yet more French than Algerian"[133]— that drew the attention of the president. The "kind smile" and "fatherly words" he offered to Jeanne further offered hope to the journalist and his readers that they had found the understanding and protection they sought: "I myself have grandchildren and will remember this poem to teach to them," the president was reported to have said. "I am happy. I will never forget the little Algerian settlers."[134] The representation of Loubet as a grandfather, as well as a father, reinforced the notion that his paternalism was more benevolent than authoritarian.

That the reports of meetings between Loubet and settler children overwhelmingly featured girls is undoubtedly significant. While settler girls had appeared in the local press reports surrounding Napoleon III's visits in the 1860s, they had done so alongside the boys of the settler colony, as well as Jewish and Muslim children. In 1903, however, settler girls came to dominate such reports. Their presence indicated a dramatic reconfiguration of the dynamics of the settler colonial family in the imaginaries of local journalists: the hysterical metropolitan mother and nonchalant settler son of the 1890s had been replaced by a kindly French father and his dutiful settler daughter. "In short," *L'Union latine* asserted, "Algeria wants to prove that she really is the eldest daughter of France, and she will stop at nothing, while her much-loved father is here, to show him her sincere affection and unassailable devotion."[135] This inversion of the gendered roles of the metropolitan parent and the settler child signaled the submission of the settler colony to the political authority of the French nation in the wake of years of anti-Jewish violence, separatist agitation, and the Margueritte Affair. Having been disgraced and exposed by metropolitan journalists and politicians, the settler colony had found itself isolated and vulnerable; settler journalists now sought to bring security to the European community by hailing the president "as a humbled daughter receives her father."[136]

The submission of the settler colony to the political authority of the French nation was also evidenced in the active choice made by journalists to acknowledge Loubet, rather than Governor General Paul Révoil, as their political father. Journalists had been forced into choosing between the two men on the eve of the president's visit, when Révoil suddenly resigned. The resignation—which journalists on both sides of the Mediterranean attributed to a personal feud with Prime Minister Émile Combes[137]—was also a result of lingering suspicion regarding the recriminatory actions taken by the colonial administration in the wake of the attack on Margueritte.[138] A telegram announcing the governor general's departure arrived in Algiers on April 11, just four days before Loubet was due to disembark, surprising colonial journalists and their readers.[139] "Emotions are running high," noted La Dépêche algérienne, for the first time in many days devoting the front page to something other than the president's impending arrival.[140]

The news divided the settler press, exposing long-standing differences of opinion regarding administrative integration. For some journalists, Révoil and his political ambitions had constituted an obstacle to administrative union with the metropole; his resignation therefore presented an opportunity.[141] For others, Révoil's forced departure was just more proof of the metropolitan government's contempt for the settler colony.[142] Local news reports had represented the governor general—who had been widely praised by settler journalists for his repressive reorganization of the indigenous justice system following the Margueritte uprising[143]—as a protective figure of paternal authority.[144] His departure provoked the resignation of at least one municipal councilor and generated angry letters from the readers of several publications.[145] Writing to La Dépêche algérienne, Maurice Aubert, the general secretary of the Syndicat commercial algérien, encouraged other disgruntled settlers to make their sentiments known to the metropolitan public by greeting Loubet with cries of, "Long live Révoil!"[146]

Ultimately, although such cries were reported as the president arrived in Algiers, they were dismissed by journalists as the actions of a small number of anti-Jewish militants whose views were not shared by the wider colonial public. An article in *Le Tell* insisted that cries in support of the former governor general had been "timidly voiced" and were "immediately covered by those of 'Long live the republic! Long live Loubet!'" Journalists sought to distance the settler community from what they saw as disobedient and childish behavior, reminding their readers that "Algeria is a big girl now. . . . She is capable of speaking calmly and is no longer reduced to seeking attention with simple cries." It would be more suitable, journalists suggested, to make requests of the metropole via the established institutions, including the newly created Délégations financières.[147]

This assembly, established at the turn of the century in an effort to calm unrest in the settler colony,[148] had been welcomed by settler journalists. Although it did not put an end to the debate over the comparative merits of assimilation and autonomy, it did change the tenor of these discussions, as most journalists endeavored to put the virulent discourse of the 1890s behind them and be "courteous, loyal, and nonpartisan in order to fulfill the noble mission of the press, which is to illuminate and not to insult."[149] It was in this spirit that settler journalists sought to reestablish the relationships of the settler colonial family and welcome Loubet as a political father. Reports contrasted the "respectful and enthusiastic" behavior of settlers during Loubet's voyage with the unruly "masquerades" that had greeted the *Antijuif* publicist and politician Édouard Drumont a few years earlier.[150] "It wasn't delirious," explained one report. "There was none of that ridiculous and shameful enthusiasm that transforms free citizens into drunken slaves, or men into animals who harness themselves to a chariot or a carriage, to pull a Roman victor or the idol of the day, who has emerged—heaven only knows how—from the murky depths of society." It was instead the display of a "respectful and enthusiastic people," which would help transform a reputation marred by the recent antisemitic violence.[151]

Local journalists' efforts to welcome Loubet as a respected political father formed part of a wider campaign to refashion settler colonial masculinity following the ructions of the turn of the century. In tempering their violence, journalists and administrators reasoned, settlers would not only rebuild bridges with the French of the metropole but also further differentiate themselves from indigenous peoples, whose violence could be seen in the recent attack on Margueritte. In preparing for the president's arrival, colonial administrators struggled to express new codes of manliness, which required ardent political conviction without violent engagement. Candidates to meet the president were those who, like Charles Beun, director of *L'Echo du Sahara*, had "relentlessly fought for republican ideas, without being a violent militant."[152] Descriptions of other candidates, such as Dr. Auguste Sanrey, the deputy mayor of Batna, were carefully edited by local administrators to ensure that the newfound emphasis on discipline did not imply feminine passivity; while administrators considered it appropriate to note that "he has never taken an active role in political struggles," the assertion that "he has never been personally involved in any important event" was judged to be taking caution too far and was carefully redacted.[153]

Loubet, settler journalists suggested, incarnated these new codes. Dignified but never pompous, patriarchal but never strict, Loubet was presented as a man of balance, an "enemy of all exaggeration and all violence."[154] *Le Petit oranais* noted with approval that the president was not excessively keen on revelry—as his unfortunate predecessor, Félix Faure, had been—nor was he averse to festivity like the former head of state, Jules Grévy.[155] Above all, settler journalists emphasized, Loubet was a simple man, a husband and father, who tried to live a simple life despite his exalted position.[156] In the eyes of local journalists, this simplicity, a legacy of his rural origins, created a bond of empathy between the president and the settlers, who also understood the sacrifices and simple pleasures of working on the land. "As he enjoyed telling us himself," reported Kabous in *Le Tell*, "M. Loubet—despite having pursued studies that distanced him from the land—remained a peasant in the deepest fibers of his being; he loved the land, he loved and admired those that work on it, that make it fertile, that sometimes live from it and very often, alas, die on it!"[157]

In this way, the president's character was admired not as an imposed metropolitan model, but as a reminder of an older form of settler manliness that had become obscured in the urban furor of recent years. In restating the mythology of the colonization and domination of the land, settler journalists reattached a form of masculinity still defined by physical strength and emotional endurance to a narrative of collaborative enterprise, providing the basis for calmer relations with the metropole and among the disparate European migrant communities of the settler colony.

It was in the context of this revision of the dominant codes of settler masculinity that colonial journalists were able to represent the settler colony as the dutiful daughter of a benevolent metropolitan father. This representation not only signaled a journalistic call for the settler colony's political submission but also signified journalists' recognition of the colony's cultural specificity in relation to the French nation. Female figures have been used as symbols of cultural specificity in a variety of European, colonial, and postcolonial contexts. As part of the modern worldview that associates femininity with passivity, women have been cast by colonizers and colonized alike as repositories of cultural authenticity, of the "truth" of a given people. In an effort to either uncover or protect this truth, colonizers and colonized have policed, surveilled, and strategically exploited women's bodies—whether indigenous, settler, or metropolitan.[158]

In colonial Algeria, the association between women and cultural authenticity motivated Orientalist fantasies about the harem and the veil, underpinned repeated conflict between French officials and Muslim elites, and inspired twentieth-century nationalists to use the image of the Muslim woman—as well as to mobilize actual Muslim women—in their anti-imperialist struggle.[159] It also underpinned the regulation of sexual contact between members of different colonial communities and limited the public role of settler women.[160] In the French metropole, comparisons between French women and Muslim women were employed by opponents of the nascent feminist movement and served to enforce dominant discourses of femininity.[161]

In colonial contexts, the utilization of women as symbols of cultural specificity by groups within the colonized population has often been accompanied by claims to political sovereignty. Such was the case with the Front de libération nationale (FLN) in Algeria and Hindu nationalists in British India.[162] Yet for settler journalists in Algeria, who sought the continued protection and support of the French state, using the figure of a young girl was more expedient. Unlike the adult *mujahidat* (women who participated in the FLN) or the imagined Mother India, the immature settler girl could neither physically nor discursively reproduce the nation and thus confirmed the presence of a mother country external to the settler colony. Although she carried the potential of future independence—and hence maintained press debate about the future evolution of the colony—in the immediate present she served to affirm the political authority of the French nation and validate settlers' cultural and affective ties to their countries of origin.

Settlers in Algeria, however, were tied to multiple mother countries. In their depictions of the settler colonial family, therefore, many colonial journalists acknowledged other sources of parental authority alongside that of France. For some, France remained the sole parent, assuming both political and cultural sovereignty in the colony. One report in *La Dépêche algérienne* declared that "forever and for everyone, M. Loubet is France, the true mother."[163] For others, France was just one of a number of nations with whom settlers felt an affective bond. The president's arrival in Algeria, noted a number of papers approvingly, had been marked by Spanish and Italian naval vessels sent in recognition of the "union of Latin nations" that had taken place in Algeria and could provide a model for the rest of Europe at a time of political crisis.[164] In these reports, the president featured less as the head of a French colonial family than as arbiter of a transnational Latin family composed of "sister races" who had found their shared home on the Algerian land.[165]

Napoleon III had also been welcomed by settlers of Spanish and Italian origin, but those celebrations had sometimes marked their separation from their French counterparts, such as with separate triumphal arches with dedications in Spanish and Italian.[166] By the time of Loubet's arrival, by contrast, the only separate festivities were those organized by small groups of American and English migrants, whose language and customs excluded them from expressions of Latin community.[167] Settlers of French, Spanish, Italian, and mixed origin, however, greeted the president's voyage as an opportunity to seek recognition for the Latin community that had developed in Algeria and linked the French nation to a larger transnational family. The launch of *L'Union latine*, the settler colony's first multilingual newspaper, featuring articles in French, Spanish, and Italian, coincided with the presidential tour. The multilingual format of the publication, which created a diverse community of readers, echoed its ambition to bring together settlers of Latin origin, "preserving our own unique character all the while."[168] In this paper, Loubet appeared as but one source of authority among others, and journalists supplemented the standard expressions of French fraternity with exclamations of "Long live France! Long live Loubet! Long live Italy!" and "Long live the republic! Long live France! Long live Loubet! Long live Algeria!"[169] Multilingual settler publications continued to flourish in the early twentieth century, reinforcing the image of a "great Latin family" of which the French nation was but a single branch.[170]

Long excluded from the colonial press, and further marginalized by settler journalists' emphasis on the Latin sensibilities required for true affiliation with France, Muslim writers were nevertheless also inspired by Loubet's voyage to advance a more inclusive vision of the French colonial family. Launching the Franco-Arabic newspaper *El Misbah* in June 1904, former schoolteacher Larbi Fekar made direct reference to the president's visit of the previous year and noted the "fraternal sentiment of respect" that he felt had united Muslims and Frenchmen at that time. "The echo of those festivities still resonates in our ears," he proclaimed. "The perfect union that presided over those events—a union to which we were little accustomed—gave me the idea to create a Franco-Arabic paper that could strengthen the bonds between the inhabitants of French Africa."[171] Throughout the seven-month run of the publication, Fekar and his colleagues made repeated and strategic use of the familial analogy, acknowledging "the many benefits for which we are grateful to the mother country" and presenting the Muslim population as a "submissive son."[172]

Combined with a detailed exposition of the loyalty of the French-educated Muslim elite and support for French interests in Tunisia and Morocco, this line of thought was designed to encourage the French government to invest further in the material progress of the indigenous population. "We wholeheartedly call for such uplift," explained the journalist Abdallah, "and loudly repeat that it is from France that we want it; a son cannot wish to be raised, protected, guided toward good and happiness by anyone other than his mother, and France is now the mother of all those in North Africa who shelter under her noble flag."[173] As French subjects, Abdallah continued in another article, Muslims in Algeria were indeed more entitled to "benefits from the mother country" than the non-naturalized Spanish and Italian migrants, whom European journalists defended.[174]

Although the journalists of *El Misbah* reached out to their "European brothers" in Algeria to encourage them to similarly express the "sincere desire to form but one and the same family," the settler journalists rarely acknowledged them as kin. Larbi Fekar was repeatedly obliged to defend the publication from the disparaging remarks of settler journalists and even fought—and won—a duel against Emile Pinguet of *L'Union républicaine*.[175] In the years that followed, Muslim journalists became increasingly disillusioned with the ideal of the French colonial family, all but denouncing it as a mirage, as settler journalists continued to reject their professional incursions and the French government failed to provide the material support they had hoped for. By the time *El Hack* appeared in Oran in 1911, Muslim journalists were systematically referring to France not as the mother country, but as their "adoptive mother"—when they invoked the familial analogy at all.[176]

Unlike *El Misbah*, *El Hack* openly broached questions of political inequality, arguing for the political emancipation of all, or groups of, Muslims in Algeria, especially following the introduction of obligatory military service for Muslim subjects. In a letter suggestively titled "A Place in the Family," a correspondent from Tangiers noted the "rights given to the immigrants of foreign nations," including "Israelites, Moroccans, Spanish, Italians, [and] Maltese." The Muslim of Algeria, however, had been forced "outside of society. For him, special laws, separate courts, and distinct administrations have been created. He is not human like the others."[177] The narrative of the French colonial family—once Muslim journalists' shield against the Latin family of the settler colony—had been exposed as a fiction. Rejected by settlers and the metropole alike, Muslim journalists saw their community cast out from the wider family of man.

Throughout the nineteenth century successive French governments framed the colonial relationship as a bond between parent and child, portraying the French nation as the benevolent parent to its colonial subjects in an attempt to legitimize its domination of colonial territories and subjugation of their inhabitants. The family analogy appealed to settler journalists and readers in Algeria, who felt vulnerable and iso-lated as a result of the demographic situation of European residents, the inconsistencies of French colonial policy, and the widespread misun-derstanding and fear of indigenous peoples and Islam. Representations of the colonial family thus came to characterize settler press coverage of the visits to Algeria of both Napoleon III and President Loubet, despite the very different conditions of press production under the Second Empire and the Third Republic.

Rather than accept colonial subjects as their brothers, however, set-tler journalists insisted that alien mentalities and cultural practices prevented Muslims from feeling true affection for the French nation. This affection, some argued, could be understood only by other Latins, who shared sensibilities and values compatible with those of the French. In presenting settlers of French and foreign European origin as the only legitimate children of France, settler journalists sought to change the attitudes of distant metropolitan observers at moments of perceived arabophile sentiment and to promote the access of the settler colony's various migrant groups to the rights and privileges of the colonizer.

Settler journalists, however, found that they were repeatedly frus-trated in their attempts to make themselves understood to metropol-itan officials and the wider French public. Taking advantage of their greater freedom of expression after 1881, these journalists reacted angrily against what they saw as metropolitan disdain for the settler colony. Developing ideas tentatively advanced by reporters in the 1860s, settler journalists discussed the Latin origins of a population matured by successive generations of intermarriage. Convinced that the settler colony had come of age, settler journalists evaluated the benefits of greater autonomy, leading some to advocate cutting ties with their overbearing French mother.

Faced with the rebellion of the Righa tribe in 1901, however, most settler journalists sought both sympathy and protection from metropolitan authority. The gendered dynamics of the settler colonial family were once again reconfigured, as the colonial press emphasized the youth and feminine obedience of the settler colonial child and the strength and benevolence of the French father. This reconfiguration reflected a larger shift in the ideals of settler colonial manliness expressed by the press, as readers were encouraged to value the simplicity and sacrifice of settler existence over exaggerated displays of violence. Placing the emphasis on this form of masculinity, settler journalists laid the foundations for rapprochement between settlers of all origins and the French of the metropole, as allies in the quest for colonial progress.

The notion of Latin identity served these efforts at rapprochement, linking settlers of French, Spanish, and Italian origin with each other and with the French on the other side of the Mediterranean. As a transnational form of identification, however, Latinness reaffirmed the colony's bonds with diverse countries of origin, while reinforcing its political ties to France. It also supported settlers' cultural identification as "Algerian," while limiting the extent to which this identity could serve as the basis of a national community. By the time of President Loubet's visit in 1903, therefore, settler journalists were able to proclaim the colonial public as at once French, Latin, and "Algerian" without fear of contradiction. In the portrait of the settler colonial family that they painted to mark the auspicious occasion, the political authority of the French father was not challenged but complemented by the cultural influence of multiple mother countries.

Although settlers would continue to negotiate their autonomy within the French nation in the decades to follow, never again would they spurn their French protectors with the same violence as in the late 1890s. Indeed, in the twentieth century violence ultimately became the means by which settlers fought to keep Algeria French. If the settler violence of the 1890s proved to be a turning point in the narrative of the settler colonial family romance, the submission to metropolitan authority was not accompanied by an acceptance of the precepts of the civilizing mission. The anti-Jewish movement in fact served to crystallize local journalists' conception of Latin identity, reinforcing barriers of race, sensibility, culture, and language between the settler community and indigenous populations. Despite the strategic attempts of Muslim journalists to appeal to metropolitan narratives of a more inclusive French colonial family, the notion of a benevolent mother country was exposed as a fiction.

3

...

Foreigners into Frenchmen?

The Press and the Algerian Antijuif *Movement*

"The Jewish peril revealed to us the double peril of foreigners and Arabs," declared journalist Augustin Castéran in 1900.[1] A contributor to several colonial publications in the 1890s, and founder of both the militant *Le Télégramme algérien* (1898) and the more moderate *Le Sémaphore algérien* (1890), Castéran was well placed to chart the development of the Algerian *Antijuif* (anti-Jewish) movement.[2] Eschewing designation as anti-Semitic, anti-Jewish colonial militants distinguished the Jews, as the primary target of their prejudice, from other ethnoreligious groups in Algeria. "The term anti-Semite," explained Castéran, "is an inadequate one that has, quite wrongly, passed into common parlance. Arabs, Phoenicians, and Syrians are just as much Semites as the Jews. We felt it was important to make this distinction so that *antisemitism* would not be understood as hostility toward indigenous Muslims."[3] The term *Antijuif* was not unknown in the metropole—furnishing, for example, the title of a publication launched by French nationalist Jules Guérin in 1898[4]—but it was in Algeria, in the context of ethnic and religious diversity, that the term found its full expression in a transnational discourse of racial exclusion.

The true *Antijuif*, suggested the militant settler journalists of the 1890s, was defined neither by his nationality nor by his faith, but by his belonging to a community of sensibilities best exemplified by the youthful "Algerian" people. "Instinctively, the Algerian hates the Jew," claimed Castéran in 1898. "This sentiment innate to the child accentuates itself in the adult and flourishes at the age at which reason and intelligence flourish in their turn."[5] The strength of the "Algerian" settler community, like that of the individual "Algerian" man, implied Castéran, could be measured by the vitality of its anti-Jewish prejudice. The riots that swept through the colonial territory in the last years of the nineteenth century thus represented for Castéran, as for many of his fellow militants, the arrival of this community at maturity. They were, Castéran insisted, "the greatest measure of Algerian patriotism."[6] Giving a triumphalist account of the riots, which targeted Algerian Jews and the metropolitan government that was seen to protect them, Castéran emphasized the "Algerian" participants' unity of purpose, sensibility, and behavior: "A breeze of independence was felt upon our faces," he recalled. "A surge of revolt freed the Algerian from the ties that bound him, and unimpeded, with head held high and fist raised, he readied himself for the task of righting wrongs."[7] These objectives and sensibilities were understood to be shared by settlers of diverse European origins—and perhaps even, some journalists suggested, by Algerian Muslims, whose common experience of suffering and codes of aggressive manliness made them natural allies in the fight against the Jews.

Just two years after publishing his account of the anti-Jewish riots, however, Castéran was writing with equal urgency against a new threat—that of the young "Algerian" to the political dominance of a racially and culturally homogenous French nation. "The Jewish question is no more than a myth," he pronounced. "It is the French question to which we must attend."[8] In encouraging the formation of a distinct "Algerian" community based on shared sentiments and their physical expression, the *Antijuif* movement had challenged the political and cultural hegemony of the French metropole. The "breeze of independence" that Castéran had welcomed in 1898 had stirred up calls for separatism, spurring a number of journalists and their readers to openly rebel against the metropolitan government. The threat of separatism and the intensity of the riots, which Stephen Wilson describes as "pogroms on a scale unknown in France," shocked French observers on both sides of the

Mediterranean, who were quick to denounce the insidious influence of Muslims and settlers of foreign European origin.[9] Regretting their previous support for "Algerian patriotism," some *Antijuif* militants, including Castéran, retraced the boundaries of the nation.

The nationalist retrenchment of journalists like Castéran and the wider appeals to French patriotism made by militants throughout the 1890s have led some scholars to view the *Antijuif* movement as a crucible for the transformation of foreign settlers into Frenchmen. Explaining the basis of anti-Jewish prejudice in Algeria, Elizabeth Friedman suggests that "the Christian colonists . . . drawn from throughout the Mediterranean world, all sought to be considered French" and that "they deeply resented the Jews as natives who were trying to become French, as they had done."[10] Friedman's analysis overlooks the continued diversity of identification among settlers following the collective naturalization of Europeans in 1889 and, in so doing, ultimately upholds a binary model of colonial power in which Algerian Jews—as an enfranchised indigenous population—constituted troubling abject figures that disrupted the hierarchical opposition of "colonizer" and "colonized."[11]

More than a simple expression of national chauvinism or religious bigotry, however, the *Antijuif* movement functioned to articulate local, national, and transnational forms of identification among settlers in complex ways. Reaching its apogee at the peak of media furor surrounding the Dreyfus Affair, the Algerian movement was sustained by militants who made strategic use of the ideologies and networks popularized by the affair to advance settler colonial concerns.[12] If militants believed Jews had illegitimately infiltrated the nation, their primary concern was for the threat this infiltration posed to the settler colony, where the Jews were perceived to exercise an even more nefarious influence on politics and commerce. In purging Jewish influence from Algeria, they surmised, they might also refashion the French nation in their own image. Hence, in Stephen Wilson's estimation, the movement "allowed naturalized *colons* to assert their Frenchness *or* their Algerian identity through opposition to the Jews."[13] Similarly, for Pierre Hebey, the movement did not simply reinforce settlers' attachment to France but also amplified their claims to represent "a new race."[14] The claims to "Algerian" specificity voiced at the time of the *Antijuif* agitation, Lizabeth Zack notes, formed the basis of a new and distinct "political identity" among settlers, which would continue to disrupt any binary relation of colonial power and retain a powerful influence on the dynamics of colonial rule until independence.[15]

In addition to defining the common prejudice and shared political objectives of settlers, the *Antijuif* movement contributed to the consolidation of a sense of "Algerian" community through defining a set of gendered sensibilities and encouraging their enactment on a massive scale. Using combative journalism to impart what Castéran called "the *frisson* of lived experience," *Antijuif* militants elicited sensations and behaviors that would remain integral to "Algerian" identification long after support for the *Antijuif* movement began to wane.[16] Even before the widespread militancy of the end of the century, settler journalists had embarked on a quest to clarify and consolidate popular understandings of the "Algerian" character. *Antijuif* militants strove to embody the wider journalistic ideals of manly suffering, youthfulness, and indiscipline, and such journalists encouraged their readers to do the same. The explosion of popular violence in 1897–98 constituted an affirmation of these longer-term ideals.

Far from putting an end to the elaboration of a local community in the press, the French nationalist backlash against the *Antijuif* movement extended the journalistic debate regarding the "Algerian" character and the most suitable administrative context for its development. While many journalists, like Castéran, rallied to the defense of French ideals, they renounced neither their anti-Jewish sentiments nor their support for "Algerian" interests. Rather than simply transform settlers into Frenchmen, therefore, the *Antijuif* movement helped clarify popular understandings of an "Algerian" people and its ambivalent relationship to the metropole. In so doing, moreover, it confirmed the definitive exclusion of Muslims from the "Algerian" community imagined by settler journalists. Having initially sought to mobilize Muslim support for the movement, settler journalists retreated from this position when the scale and potential consequences of the uncontrolled violence they had unleashed became fully apparent. In the early years of the twentieth century, *Antijuif* journalists muted their praise for Muslim aggression and reasserted the Latin character of the "Algerian" community. If militants did not permanently abandon their attempts to mobilize Muslims against the Jews—reaching out once more amid the political extremism of the interwar years—subsequent solicitations, as Dónal Hassett notes, would be made not in the name of the "Algerian" settler colony, but in the name of the imperial nation state.[17]

The Local and National Dimensions of the Movement

Announcing the imminent arrival in Algeria of the marquis de Morès, a notorious French anti-Semite, in 1893, a journalist using the provocative pseudonym Aryen (Aryan) urged the readers of *Le Combat* to give their guest an enthusiastic welcome: "a reception apt to prove that the hearts of the French of Algeria beat in unison with those of their brothers in the metropole."[18] Invoking the familial analogy that had expressed settlers' simultaneous desire for both protection and differentiation from France since the early years of the colony,[19] Aryen implied that after decades of neglect, the French of the metropole—or at least, the most enlightened among them—had finally recognized the true worth of the settler colony. This long-standing desire for acknowledgment from metropolitan politicians and publicists motivated local militants' attempts to forge ties with metropolitan anti-Semites, despite the local specificity of the *Antijuif* movement.

Hostility to the Jewish community increased on both sides of the Mediterranean in the decades following the French defeat in 1870. As fears of physical and moral degeneration gripped anxious observers in the metropole, doctors, journalists, politicians, and artists sought ways to explain perceived French weakness, pointing to the destabilizing decadence of modernity and to the corrupting effects of the cosmopolitan crowds it generated.[20] Xenophobia and antisemitism became increasingly prevalent in public discourse as French nationalism turned in on itself and the political right underwent a populist reconfiguration.[21] Jews were blamed for sapping the manly vigor of Frenchmen through their control of public space, depleting national strength, and provoking a series of humiliating national crises, including the Panama scandal and the Dreyfus Affair.[22]

While the *Antijuif* militants of the settler colony followed these developments with interest and praised the efforts of anti-Semitic publicists in the metropole, they focused primarily on the alleged local effects of perceived Jewish influence, thought to be even more execrable: usury, exploitation, and instigation of unrest among the Muslim population. The long-anticipated "Anti-Jewish Revolution in Paris!" certainly made headlines in the settler colony, but local *Antijuif* journalists devoted a far greater number of column inches to praising local leaders and denouncing the actions of figures in the local Jewish community. After all, claimed Max Régis, editor of *L'Antijuif algérien* and future mayor of Algiers, "while France is just waking up to cries of 'Down with the Jews!' Algerians created this movement."[23]

While Régis's claim overlooked a long history of antisemitism in the metropole, it acknowledged the specific local factors that had contributed to increased anti-Jewish sentiment in Algeria since 1870. In this year the emancipation of the Algerian Jews by the Crémieux Decree had sparked widespread opposition among settlers of French and foreign European origin, who feared the impact on their reputation as colonizers in the eyes of a Muslim population who had assigned Jews the inferior, if protected, status of dhimmis under Ottoman rule.[24] The decree was habitually cited by settler journalists as the cause of the Muslim uprising led by al-Muqrani in 1871 and the reason for acts of theft and banditry carried out by dispossessed Muslims in subsequent decades. While Jewish emancipation in fact had little direct effect on Muslims, it exerted a broader influence on the dynamics of settler colonial power in the first decades of civil rule. First, in providing the basis for persistent rumors, circulated in the settler press, of a conspiracy between Jews and "Jewified" French politicians,[25] the Crémieux Decree exacerbated settler suspicion of metropolitan authority. Second, it established the "consistorial bloc" of Jewish electors, leading to a long period of political dominance by the moderate Opportunists and thwarting the ambitions of Radicals and their supporters, whose plans for more imminent social reform included measures establishing financial autonomy in the settler colony.[26]

Disappointed by the metropolitan government, which they accused of protecting the Jews at the expense of "real" French citizens and other civilized European peoples, settlers began to organize anti-Jewish leagues in 1871, campaigning for the repeal of the Crémieux Decree.[27] Prefiguring the National Anti-Semitic League, established by Édouard Drumont at the time of the Boulanger crisis in 1889, and the Grand Occident of France, founded by Jules Guérin ten years later, these local organizations allied as colonial federations—such as the Anti-Jewish Socialist League and the National Anti-Jewish League—through which contact with metropolitan structures was later coordinated.[28] The manifesto of the Anti-Jewish Socialist League, founded in Algiers in 1892 and subsequently extended to Bougie, included a specific set of "economic and Algerian" claims alongside a more general "political program" addressing issues of national import, such as the abolition of the senate, the separation of church and state, and the improvement of conditions for workers. The demands of the "Algerian" program included the abrogation of the Crémieux Decree, the suppression of the general government, and the abolition of the indigénat, a separate legal regime for Muslims.[29] The league held regular neighborhood meetings, as well as a monthly general assembly to which "all the Antijuifs of Algiers" were invited, "French, European, and indigenous Muslims."[30]

One organization among many, the Anti-Jewish Socialist League nevertheless reflected the left-wing leanings of the Algerian Antijuif movement as a whole, as well as the desire of many militants to include Muslims and settlers of foreign European origin alongside settlers from France. That this alliance would be an unequal partnership was indicated by the manifesto's further objective to ensure "the unity of all Aryans in the struggle against the progressive invasion of the Jews."[31] While Muslims largely avoided participating in anti-Jewish militancy,[32] the same was not true of naturalized and foreign settlers, whose anti-Jewish prejudice was openly expressed in the press in a variety of languages.[33]

The liberalization of the press in 1881 accelerated the growth of the *Antijuif* movement as local leagues found a new forum for the discussion and dissemination of their ideas. Newspapers carried anti-Jewish sentiment beyond the confines of league membership, allowing the uninitiated to nurture preexisting prejudice and discover more formal channels for the expression of their views. Writing to *La Lutte antijuive* in February 1898, Madame Aragonès expressed her support for the paper's campaign to boycott Jewish shops and asked in passing how she might join the anti-Jewish league mentioned in previous issues.[34] Boyed by the press, anti-Judaism became a mass movement in Algeria in the 1890s. By 1898 *L'Antijuif algérien*—organ of the central league, based in Algiers—enjoyed a circulation of thirty thousand.[35] Despite its popularity, this publication alone was not enough to satisfy the colony's anti-Jewish readership, and a great number of other newspapers were dedicated to the denigration of the Algerian Jews and the government officials believed to be in their thrall.[36]

While acknowledging the colonial scale of the Jewish problem, many publications focused on its manifestations in their immediate localities. Thus, while *Le Colon antijuif algérien*, for example, explicitly aligned itself with larger publications such as *L'Antijuif algérien* and *Le Télégraphe* in colony-wide combat, it declared its primary purpose to be the unmasking of Jews and their political protectors in the Mitidja plain and the Atlas.[37] Given the plethora of local titles, anti-Jewish newspapers varied greatly in circulation, ranging from the wild popularity of *L'Antijuif algérien* to the more sectional appeal of publications such as the revolutionary socialist *Combat* and the lithographed newspaper *La Guerre aux Abus*.[38] Alongside the rapid rise of publications that explicitly identified with the *Antijuif* movement, there was a perceptible increase in the casual anti-Jewish sentiment of the press as a whole during the 1880s and 1890s.[39] Indeed, the Jewish population in Algeria had few defenders in the colonial press during these decades. Even those journalists who opposed anti-Jewish violence usually did so out of fear of public disorder rather than on principle. Despite his outspoken critique of the *Antijuif* movement, editor E. Nicaise readily admitted, on behalf of his colleagues and readers, "It is certain that we dislike the Jew, whose character is so different from our own."[40]

The development of the colonial press not only reinforced the local character of the *Antijuif* movement but also created new opportunities for exchange with the anti-Semitic publicists of the metropole. Édouard Drumont's *La Libre parole*, launched in 1892 in the aftermath of the Boulanger crisis and on the back of his best-selling work, *La France Juive*, was admired by the militant journalists of the settler colony for its strident prose and its commercial success.[41] New titles launched by Morès and Guérin were likewise welcomed in the colonial press as allies rather than competitors.[42] Sensing that settlers may have finally found a receptive audience on the other side of the Mediterranean for the expression of their grievances, local militants reached out to metropolitan anti-Semites, inviting their collaboration. Eager for publicity, Drumont, Morès, and Guérin, among others, readily accepted these invitations. Their messages of support were highly valued by settler journalists, so long dismissed and ridiculed by their metropolitan colleagues. "We reserve the *prime* position in this *first* copy of *Le Combat*," announced editor Fernand Grégoire, "for our friend Morès, the valiant champion of antisemitism."[43]

Law student turned journalist and *Antijuif* figurehead Max Régis similarly opened the pages of his newspaper, *L'Antijuif algérien*, to Drumont in February 1898 in preparation for the latter's campaign for election in Algiers.[44] Drumont's candidacy had been instigated by Régis, who recognized the potential benefit to the "Algerian" community of collaboration with a renowned metropolitan publicist. "Which French citizen would have enough courage, competence, and talent to win the whole nation over to our cause?" asked Régis in *L'Antijuif algérien*. "Which French citizen of powerful and authoritative speech could rehabilitate Algeria, which has been so discredited, so slandered, so vilified by detractors in the pay of Israel? . . . We see only one man capable of this almost superhuman effort. That man is Drumont."[45] Régis's decision to collaborate with Drumont followed the failure of his own propaganda mission to Paris in January and February 1898, when his attempts "to defend THE

HONOR OF ALGERIANS" by organizing a "grand anti-Jewish meeting" to explain the causes of the recent rioting were heartily disparaged by the capital's journalists.[46] These journalists, concluded *L'Antijuif algérien*, were evidently all "in the pay of the Jews."[47]

While *Antijuif* militants in Algeria actively sought ties with metropolitan anti-Semites, they did not succumb to the metropolitan agenda but instead hoped to use the public influence of these figures to the colony's advantage. Indeed, it was often the metropolitan figureheads who were obliged to adapt their discourse to the particular circumstances of the settler colony. Campaigning to become parliamentary deputy for Algiers, Drumont, for example, was forced to tone down the clericalism that had characterized *La France Juive* of 1886 and remained in evidence in his own newspaper, *La Libre parole*.[48] "In the Jew we do not hate the man of a particular confession," wrote Drumont for *L'Antijuif algérien*, playing to local Radical sentiment; "we hate the traitor, the exploiter, the despoiler, the hoarder, the antisocial being."[49] Not all militants were convinced by this transformation, however. *La Lutte antijuive* echoed the opinion of Morès, who had reportedly dismissed Drumont as "a hypocrite and a liar who thinks only of making money."[50] Régis's press campaign nevertheless carried the author of *La France Juive* to victory in the elections of May 1898. The illustrated supplement to *L'Antijuif algérien* marked the occasion with an image showing Drumont greeting a crowd of European workers and Régis driving the Jews and their political protectors from the colony, the standard of the republic held aloft.[51]

When invoking the republic, *Antijuifs* frequently specified that they were referring to "the true republic"—which was to say not the one governed by Opportunists, whom they considered to be paid lackeys of the Jews.[52] Similarly, the term *citizen* was applied only to those whom the *Antijuif* journalists believed truly deserved this title: the French and naturalized settlers of foreign European origin. As victims of the Jews, settlers were routinely portrayed as French citizens regardless of their origins. Hence *L'Antijuif algérien*, a paper that openly targeted readers of diverse European backgrounds, condemned the actions of

Jewish butchers on the rue de la Lyre in Algiers, who were reported to have wielded meat hooks during the riots of August 1897 in an effort to "pierce the flesh of French citizens."[53]

The frequent references to the French republic and French citizenship in a sector of the press that also spotlighted the particular interests and experiences of "Algerians" served two primary purposes. For one, journalists sought to remind the French of the metropole of their obligation to protect the inhabitants of the settler colony from the nefarious activities of a Jewish community that they represented as "a society apart, a closed society that considers the French and all the Europeans who don't eat kosher as equally foreign to their race, their interests, their future."[54] In addition, journalists hoped to promote the idea that the successful defense of the settler colony would precipitate the regeneration of the French nation as a whole. Appealing to settlers as uniquely capable of reviving the national community, papers such as La Guerre aux Abus presented themselves as "revolutionary organs," poised to set the revolution back on the path from which it had deviated following the emancipation of the Jews in 1791.[55] This belief in the regenerative, redemptive capacity of settler colonialism in Algeria also inspired the title of Le Sans-culotte, whose editors, "Robespierre, Danton, Marat, Saint-Just, Mirabeau, Etc.," saw the creation of colonial society as a second chance at year one.

In the settler colonial context, however, references to revolution and nationhood carried an implicit ambiguity. When Max Régis declared in La Libre parole, "If the government does not respect the votes of the people . . . the people will rely on force to make sure its demands are respected," it remained unclear whether he was speaking of the "Algerian" people, whom he had traveled to Paris to represent, or the French people, to whom he sought to appeal.[56] Increasingly disillusioned with the latter, Régis used the agitation of 1898 to launch more explicit calls for settler independence.

Whether the coming revolution was to be French, "Algerian," or both, Antijuif militants surmised that it would need heroic leaders, and these would be found among the hardy and long-suffering men of the settler colony. Part of the appeal of Morès and Drumont, from the settler colonial perspective, was their apparent failure to conform to the dominant codes of bourgeois metropolitan masculinity, which urged self-control, refinement, and repression of emotion.[57] These behaviors themselves, Christopher Forth explains, were perceived by anti-Semites to be a result of Jewish influence in French society and were held responsible for the physical and moral degeneration of the French people.[58] Constructing their own masculinity in opposition to these characteristics, men like Drumont and Morès presented themselves as strong-willed individuals who spoke their minds and were ready to die in defense of their words. This aggressive form of manliness appealed to a gendered settler colonial sensibility already in evidence in the press, in which journalists habitually emphasized manly strength, suffering, and sacrifice as the very basis of "Algerian" existence. Cultivating a dynamic and embodied style of reporting, *Antijuif* journalists sought to nurture the ideal traits of the "Algerian" in opposition to the supposed characteristics of both the Jews and their effete metropolitan protectors, preparing them for the revolution to come.

Suffering and Violence in *Antijuif* Reporting

Using sensationalist language, illustrations, and caricatures, *Antijuif* journalists sought to elicit an emotional response in their readers (what Castéran termed "the *frisson* of lived experience"[59]), drawing them into a settler colonial community of sensibilities that privileged manly suffering and promoted the regenerative effects of violent self-expression on the part of settler men. From the early 1880s journalists reported with increasing frequency on "the shouts, the pushing and shoving . . . the burlesque or dramatic incidents" that accompanied altercations between settlers and Jews.[60] In 1884 press attention to a skirmish between "Algerian" and Jewish conscripts transformed the incident into a violent mass protest.[61] The resulting riots lasted over two days, led to the destruction of many Jewish businesses, and were finally dissipated only by the intervention of the army. In Castéran's analysis, the event marked the launch of a coordinated *Antijuif* press across the three colonial departments, led by politically and physically engaged journalists.[62] It also established the recurrent tropes of *Antijuif* reporting, which portrayed settler men as the innocent victims of Jewish tyranny, legitimizing their recourse to violence to defend themselves and the wider settler community.

Such reports typically used the present tense, encouraging readers to experience the same feelings of anger and aggression as the *Antijuif* militants they described. Often focusing on scenes of collective protest or rebellion, journalists invited readers to identify as part of the anti-Jewish crowd. An article in *L'Antijuif algérien* placed the reader at the center of an 1897 demonstration in Algiers, where a crowd had gathered to express their opposition to Mantoue, a Jewish butcher who was involved in a legal dispute with editor Max Régis:

> The crowd swells and swells with malcontents, and they are many. All the victims are present, ready to make yids of every variety pay dearly for their numerous provocations. The crowd knows that the previous evening the Jews killed a hawker because he used to sell anti-Jewish newspapers. A feeling of exasperation over Jewish domination can be sensed. A revolution seems to be readying itself, with shouts of "Make way for the French!" But the crowd of our fellow citizens does not seek to provoke confrontation, contenting itself with calling for the downfall of the Jews. The fight would certainly not have broken out if the Jews—supported by the government that protects them—had not had the insolence to shout, "Down with the French, death to the French!" . . . At that, shouts of "Down with the Jews!" spring forth from every mouth, and the Jews—crowded onto the balconies—throw pots of soil and boiling oil onto the crowd.[63]

In casting Jews as persecutors and settlers as victims, such reports established an opposition between the two groups on the basis of their sensibilities and behaviors. While settlers embodied the wider colony's capacity for resistance and survival, Jews were presented as people who, "by their principles and their traditional atavism," were "obstacles to all progress, to the normal and confident expansion of our society." The Jew, stated *Le Progrès algérien*, was a man who was, "by choice or by fate, excluded from humanity and its onward advance." There could be no place for such a man in the emerging "Algerian" society, composed of a youthful new people intent on colonial progress. "He will therefore be our enemy," announced the editor of *Le Progrès algérien*, "and we—along with the whole of Algeria—will remain opposed to him." As Jews possessed "neither conscience nor self-respect," the paper continued, they could not be vanquished in the same manner as other enemies; "they must be attacked via their material assets and not via their feelings."[64] Devoid of both finer feelings and basic sentiment, Jews were thus written out of the settler colonial community of sensibilities.

Jewish antipathy to progress, such journalists argued, was evident in their political behavior—particularly in their tendency to vote as a community in Algerian elections. The practice of bloc voting, settler journalists suggested, was not only detrimental to colonial representation in the metropole but also indicative of the Jewish people's failure to embrace the beliefs and behaviors that defined the modern citizen.[65] "What is more beautiful, more sublime than the free man?" asked a writer for *Le Sans-culotte* as he rallied against the consistory and its control of the Jewish vote. Appealing directly to young Jewish voters to emancipate themselves from this tyranny, the journalist urged them to turn their backs on the older generations within their community: "Do not associate with these men, these slaves who bow down in submission to one person or one clan," he insisted; "they are the lepers of society, whom we must cast out as their touch is contagious and unhealthy. Raise your heads, citizens, look at the horizon before you; there is the freedom and independence of civilized peoples."[66] Invoking the French revolutionary heritage of 1789, the appeal privileged a direct and transparent bond between the citizen and the state over an opaque and inscrutable communitarianism. If strength of will and independence of character were recognized as French characteristics, it was in the Algerian settler colony, and the fight for "the true republic," that they would be revived.

In addition to the political behavior of the Jews, *Antijuif* journalists looked to their economic activities for further evidence of opposition to colonial progress. As the economy faltered in the 1890s, journalists readily blamed Jewish usurers for burdening settlers with excessive debt. Writing for *Le Pauvre colon*, Battesti suggested that the ubiquitous Jewish moneylender had turned the settler population into "a people of slaves." Worse still, he said, the government was doing nothing to remedy the situation, and he denounced "the sickening spectacle of odious bloodsuckers plying their trade under the benevolent eye of those who ought to reprimand and punish them."[67]

Battesti's animalization of Jewish people was a typical strategy of *Antijuif* journalists, who regularly likened Jews to parasites, vultures, or jackals—creatures that, "having drained the intelligence, drain to complete extinction the physical force of the unhappy souls to whom they cling."[68] A number of papers, including *L'Antijuif algérien* and the *Charivari oranais*, made use of caricatures and illustrations to reinforce the representation of the Jews as exploiters of colonial resources. One such illustration showed a map of Algeria occupied by an enormous flea bearing caricatured Jewish features.[69] A similar image depicted Opportunist politicians Édouard Lafferière, Charles Lutaud, and Paul Gérente as vultures feeding on a prone body labeled "Algeria," while "Jewish" vultures circled in the background (fig. 5). The illustration was accompanied by a short text describing how the beasts "threw themselves upon their victim, each one tearing her apart, each strip of flesh to be shared between the Jews, the English, the thieves. Sad!"[70]

Such representations echoed those of the anti-Semitic press in the metropole, which also relied on animalization and caricature to convey its simplistic message.[71] If journalistic strategies were similar on both sides of the Mediterranean, however, the threat posed to the settler colony, local writers argued, was much more severe. *La France africaine* drew its readers' attention to a recent issue of *La Libre parole*, "which showed a Frenchman in chains and working the land, while a Jew, with a whip in his hand, orders him to keep ploughing relentlessly, from the top of a small tower." This image of Jewish exploitation "was true

5. "Feeding Time," *Le Supplément illustré de l'Antijuif algérien*, August 6, 1899

enough in France," alleged the colonial publication, "but it is all the more so in Algeria, where the men and the land are owned by the Jews, for whom we toil incessantly, in all that constitutes the life of society."[72] Not only was Jewish influence greater in Algeria than elsewhere in France, journalists suggested, but its effects were more harmful and caused greater suffering because of the settler colony's precarious stage of development and the scarcity of material resources. It was for these reasons, *La France africaine* explained, that colonial representatives had consistently opposed the Crémieux Decree and "the Algerian press had waged the most ardent campaign."[73]

This suffering was in fact a defining feature of "Algerian" identity, according to local journalists. Conscious of metropolitan objection to rising anti-Jewish sentiment in the colony, Auguste Prax, editor of *L'Algérie française*, excused the actions of settlers in the following terms: "It has become rather fashionable in Paris for newspapers to shout *Shame on the settler!* But how little you know the settler, a man who is always working and is never rewarded for his efforts. He is not the absinthe drinker of whom you speak with disdain; he is robust and sober, and courageous above all else." "If he is poor, that is not his own fault," Prax continued. He blamed instead "the Jew and his usury, the ever-rebellious Arab . . . the sirocco, the locusts, and of course, the *administration*."[74]

This litany of daily disasters was echoed across the settler press, and a number of papers appeared dedicated to the narration of settlers' personal experiences of suffering. Small local papers, such as *Mon journal* of Tlemcen and *La Guerre Aux Abus* of Djidjeli (Jijel), existed primarily as records of their creators' hardships.[75] "Nobody comes to my aid when I must fight not only against locusts but against hunger," complained Léon Bonnenfant, founder of the latter publication.[76] Bonnenfant lay the blame for his predicament squarely on the Jews and the administration. Having had his press confiscated for reasons he did not specify, Bonnenfant went to the lengths of handwriting and lithographing his newspaper, lending a particularly visceral quality to his lament.

If suffering was the "Algerian" condition, it was those at the top of articulated hierarchies of race and gender—settler men—who suffered most, on behalf of the community they represented. Taking the settler male as the incarnation of an "Algerian" ideal, *Antijuif* journalists often described the Jewish threat to the settler colony as a specific attack on the body of the settler man. A typical illustration from the illustrated supplement to *L'Antijuif algérien* depicts a well-nourished and well-dressed Jewish trader riding his carriage past an emaciated, disheveled settler family (fig. 6). Pausing to remove the cigar from his mouth, the Jewish passerby looks at the family with disdain, while the father, standing bowed and frail, watches his children beg at the roadside.[77] Here the contrast between the bodies of the rotund Jewish usurer and the thin European settler served to express what journalists saw as the comprehensive Jewish threat to articulated social hierarchies of race, gender, and material wealth.

A further contrast can be drawn between the battered but persevering figure of the male settler in figure 6 and the defeated and inert figure of the feminine allegory of Algeria in figure 5. Only settler men, such

6. "What Our Councilors Should Be Thinking Of," *Le Supplément illustré de l'Antijuif algérien*, September 18, 1898

gendered imagery implied, could ultimately endure the Jewish threat and ensure the long-term survival of the colony. While such images attempted to generate the public fear necessary to the success of the movement, they did not allow disillusionment, but instead encouraged an active response to the perceived Jewish threat by arousing feelings of anger and resentment. For "from the depths of suffering," *Le Combat* affirmed, "comes anger!"[78]

Amid the generalized suffering that defined settler masculinity, those who sacrificed most or who turned their suffering into righteous anger were lauded as heroes by anti-Jewish journalists. The mass press of the metropole, Edward Berenson observes, closely followed the daring exploits of the era's "heroes of empire," portraying them as exceptional men whose qualities the male public should aspire to emulate.[79] While the heroes held up as exemplary in the metropole were those who acted as "peaceful conquerors,"[80] those favored by journalists in Algeria embodied more specific settler colonial ideals of masculinity, including physical sacrifice and aggression. Max Régis used his paper, *L'Antijuif algérien*, to cultivate an image as something of a role model in this regard. Repeatedly pursued on charges of defamation and breach of public order, Régis willingly publicized his periods of arrest and imprisonment as evidence of his persistent struggle against the tyranny of a state bowed to Jewish influence.[81] Describing a visit "behind bars," Fernand Lafitte emphasized the hostile prison environment, describing how Régis not only endured these conditions but was physically and morally strengthened by his experience: "Three knocks leave a sinister echo. The sound of keys. A door opens . . . the drab, bare walls and pitch black passageways weigh heavily upon me. The dull sound of a door closing, and the *criminal* is led into the jail by two guards. . . . Max Régis is smiling, very calm. Yesterday's events have left no pallor of despondency upon his face. His energy is the same, perhaps even more intense, with the indignation that inevitably brews in his intrepid heart as he thinks of the infamy of which he is a victim."[82]

Eager to claim their place in the settler colonial pantheon, journalists detailed their own experiences of victimization at the hands of Jewish and governmental persecutors. Castéran proudly printed copies of medical certificates describing the injuries he and his colleagues had sustained during a tussle with their enemies.[83] Morès, for his part, had more than war wounds to prove his commitment to the *Antijuif* cause. Killed while antagonizing Tuareg tribesmen in El-Ouatia in 1896, Morès was remembered in the settler press as the brave victim of an Anglo-Jewish conspiracy. Sympathetic journalists in the colony eulogized Morès as a martyr, formally commemorating the anniversary of his death each year, establishing a committee in his memory, and encouraging municipal councilors to name streets after the defunct adventurer "in honor of his supreme sacrifice."[84]

Linked to the movement's leaders by their shared burden of suffering, ordinary settler men could also be elevated to the status of heroes and martyrs. Félix Cayrol, a French settler, became emblematic of the "Algerian" struggle after being killed in the general disorder of the Algiers riots of 1898. Represented in the *Antijuif* press as the ultimate sacrifice made in defense of the settler colony, Cayrol's death was both lamented and glorified by journalists, who encouraged their readers to join the crowd of mourners and pay their respects to the local martyr. According to Castéran, over ten thousand people attended the funeral of this simple "family man."[85] Reporting on how the grief and anger over his death consolidated the community, *L'Antijuif algérien* proudly displayed the headline "Cayrol Is Avenged!"[86]

Their voices drowned out by the loud laments of male settler journalists, women struggled for recognition as both anti-Jewish militants and "Algerians." While male journalists sometimes acknowledged the suffering of settler women, their difficulties were understood as contingent on those of their spouses and male relatives, who bore the full weight of Jewish exploitation. As the discourse of manly suffering legitimized increased militancy, *Antijuif* journalists reminded their male readers that they were also fighting to protect "our mothers, our fiancées, our daughters, or our sisters."[87]

In insisting on the need to protect settler women, militant journalists confirmed the moral righteousness of the manly *Antijuif* crusade and sought to limit the active political participation of women. Rather than exclude women from the movement entirely, however, *Antijuif* journalists devised ways of mobilizing their support in appropriately gendered ways. Recognizing the role of women in the household economy, for example, most anti-Jewish newspapers promoted the boycott of Jewish shops, appealing directly to female readers and even publishing lists to name and shame local women who continued to frequent proscribed vendors.[88] Addressed to "French women, non-Jewish women, and Arab women" or "European women and Arab women," these appeals reflected the movement's wider attempts to include settlers of various European origins and indigenous Muslims.[89] In making purchases, *Le Colon antijuif algérien* instructed its female readers, think of "the efforts made by your father, your husband, your brother or your son to earn and bring back home the few francs so necessary to keeping your household going." Giving this hard-earned money to a Jewish shopkeeper, the newspaper implied, was tantamount to infidelity, as "your hand will brush against his as you pay an inflated price for your goods." Such a betrayal could only augment the despair of women's male guardians: "What disappointment, what anger they would feel if they learnt of it!"[90]

In addition to spending their husbands' or fathers' money in appropriate ways, settler women could demonstrate their loyalty by providing moral guidance to their menfolk, even in political matters. To ensure that women did not overreach themselves in this domain or attempt to participate in political debate themselves, L'Antijuif algérien helpfully provided its female readers with a script, instructing them how to address such questions to their male relatives: "*Without wishing to influence your political opinions*," a loyal anti-Jewish woman might say, "*I would feel somewhat avenged if I knew that Antijuif candidates had defeated the governmental snitches who have dared to insult me ... by begging for your vote.*"[91]

Attempts to mobilize women sometimes received a more enthusiastic response than *Antijuif* journalists could have wished for. Learning that a group of female supporters had established a Feminine Anti-Jewish League, the leaders of the movement released a statement in the press cautioning against their initiative. While the motives of these good "Algerian French women" were to be applauded, the male *Antijuifs* explained, their all-female organization was superfluous: "Such a league already exists, given that the National Anti-Jewish League, of which Max Régis is president, receives women members." The statement instructed women to join the central league rather than form their own "little groups."[92] Although this instruction was ostensibly given in the interests of ensuring the unity of the wider *Antijuif* movement, it was clear that the women's attempt to define their own terms of political and social engagement had not been appreciated.

The incursions of settler women into the hypermasculine world of anti-Jewish journalism were even less favorably received. *La Jeune France antijuive*, established by a group of French and naturalized women in

March 1900, was ridiculed by male militants.[93] *Le Tirailleur* even published an illustration comparing the all-female staff of the new publication to the famous female Dreyfusards of *La Fronde*, thus framing their efforts as counterproductive to the movement as a whole.[94] Seeking to defend their actions as both anti-Jewish militants and "Algerians," the female contributors to *La Jeune France antijuive* emphasized that they belonged to the same community of settler colonial sensibilities, as their male colleagues. The journalist Anza invoked suffering as an integral aspect of women's physical and social experience.[95]

In claiming suffering as "a land in which all women are sisters," however, Anza's feminist vision not only threatened the gender hierarchies of the movement but also risked reestablishing common ground between groups of settlers and Jews.[96] Playing one prejudice against another proved to be an ineffective strategy, and Anza left the paper in May 1900. Soon after, the publication was bought up by Le Parti français d'union républicaine antijuive—a French nationalist faction within the wider movement—and the content was revised to exclude any articles without an anti-Jewish or xenophobic message. In the first edition of the new publication, the editors made an explicit appeal for contributions by male journalists.[97]

While most *Antijuif* journalists readily agreed that there was no place for women in the settler colonial cult of manly suffering, they disagreed about the place to be allocated to indigenous Muslims. "If we are suffering," observed one journalist of their treatment at the hands of the Jews and the administration, "our *indigènes* are one hundred times more victims than we are."[98] In contrast to the Jews, whom journalists claimed had "replaced *human* solidarity with *Jewish* solidarity," Muslims were seen to suffer alongside the French, Europeans, and "old Algerians" of the colony.[99] Like settlers, journalists reported, Muslims had been exploited by Jewish moneylenders, leading to their expropriation and impoverishment. Like settlers, journalists continued, Muslims had been oppressed and neglected by a corrupt administration. "The real cause of the *indigènes'* misery," argued *Le Combat*, "is the form of administration we have imposed upon them—the indolence, the ignorance, the negligence of administrators and those by whom these latter are controlled."[100] This explanation of Muslim dispossession not only obscured the settlers' own responsibility but also raised the possibility of Muslim integration into the imagined community of "Algerian" sensibilities.

For some *Antijuifs*, the common experience of hardship was enough to legitimize greater social provision for Muslims. *Le Colon antijuif algérien*, for example, supported Muslim notables in their calls for a new court of appeal for the indigenous population.[101] This institution, in the paper's opinion, would help safeguard Muslims from the Jews and their official protectors. The paper also endorsed the limited political participation of Muslims, suggesting that they be able to elect their own representatives to the colony's *Conseil général*.[102] A number of settler journalists went further, suggesting that Muslims be granted full political representation. "It is high time to make them all French citizens," insisted *La France africaine* in 1891, in compensation for all they had suffered since the passing of the Crémieux Decree and in recognition of the participation of Muslim soldiers in the recent campaigns of the French Army.[103] "Had the Arab been able to vote [in 1870]," argued Georges Meynié in *L'Antijuif algérien*, "he would naturally have taken the side of the French, and the Jewish 'grand electors' would have been forced to abandon the designation of candidates." The emancipation of the Muslim population could yet provide the solution to the colony's problems, suggested Meynié, who believed, in 1897, that "the same holds true today."[104]

These overtures toward the Muslim population, Dermenjian-Hannequart notes, were motivated more by political strategy than by a genuine interest in indigenous affairs.[105] Nevertheless, in appealing for a pragmatic alliance between settlers and Muslims in the language of suffering, journalists reinforced the basis of an "Algerian" community while more directly posing the question of its ethnic and religious composition. In contrast to the Jews, whom *Antijuif* journalists considered incapable of sentiment, Muslims were seen to exhibit "Franco-Arab sympathy."[106] While journalists consistently invoked the fundamentally alien nature of the Jews, they acknowledged aspects of similarity between settlers and Muslims, whom they portrayed as "two generous and warlike races" separated only by "the gulf created . . . by the stupid Crémieux Decree."[107]

Regardless of their motives, the principal effect of this differentiation of the essential characteristics of Muslims and Jews was the discursive transformation of the complex history of Muslim-Jewish relations in Algeria into a mythologized past of permanent mutual hostility. *La Bataille*, a Constantinois publication that remained anti-Jewish and anti-Muslim in equal measure, criticized its "arabophile" colleagues for elaborating such a mythology, insisting that "the facts are clear: the Jew has always lived alongside the Arab, without his work or commerce being troubled at all. . . . This alleged hatred exists only in the minds of politicians."[108]

The notion of long-standing Muslim hatred of Jews nevertheless served as a model for certain *Antijuifs* in the settler colony, who expressed admiration for what they saw as the unrestrained aggression of Arab masculinity. Journalists such as Baboucha, a regular contributor to *L'Algérie*, regaled their readers with "Arab tales," which invariably celebrated Muslim violence toward Jews. Claiming to have overheard these stories in local *cafés maures*, Baboucha emphasized the impassioned recounting of the tales as much as the events of the narrative, the vivacity of expression supposedly reflecting the pleasure taken by the Muslim raconteur in reliving acts of anti-Jewish violence. Relaying a story about a pascha who had mistakenly castrated nine Jews after receiving orders from the sultan on a smudged piece of parchment, Baboucha explained the appeal of these stories:

> It's true, I admit, that the *café maure* on the rue Saint-Louis is a long way from the Tantonville. But despite the enormous difference that separates these establishments in terms of the luxury of the decoration and the quality of the service, I prefer to take my coffee at the former. Although the second is more magnificent, the first doesn't want for originality. There, anecdotes are recounted, such as the following, which I place before the eyes of my readers

without cutting or adding a single thing, for fear of spoiling its perfume, its flavor—the original raconteur was a witty man.[109]

What Baboucha ultimately admired in the Arab storyteller's self-expression was the same thing he appreciated about the café: a sense of authenticity, a correspondence between their inner essence and outer appearance. As an honest and unrestrained expression of opposition to Jews, *Antijuif* violence held the same appeal. Henri Garrot, another *Antijuif* writer, harbored a similar penchant for indigenous storytellers in local cafés. He described his own meeting with a Muslim man in a similar locale: "*Aia Sidi* (come here, sir), *chouf hallouf* (look at that pig). And with his threatening glare and his outstretched finger, he pointed out a tall Jew with an awkward demeanor and a shifty gaze, who was just arriving in the square, wearing a jacket, pants and embroidered slippers, with a turban and a silk belt. *I cut his father's head off*, he told me, with a self-satisfied air."[110] Garrot's anecdote created a clear contrast between the two men's postures, gestures, and appearances, favoring the transparently aggressive stance of the Muslim over the inscrutability and artifice of the Jew. Conveying his interlocutor's parting words, Garrot warned his readers of the dangers of failing to emulate the Muslim man's violent hatred of Jews: "*There will come a time when the lions will be eaten by the hyenas, and that will be a great shame! The Frenchman protects the Jew! The Jew will devour him!*"[111]

Beyond offering the reassuring image of complicity between settler men and Muslim subjects, such tales also promoted an ideal of colonial manliness in which violence and pleasure were inextricably linked. Many *Antijuif* journalists aimed to re-create the "endless banter" that they claimed circulated in the *café maures*,[112] these spaces of shared male sociability, filling their newspapers with jokes and amusing anecdotes at the expense of the Jewish population. Journalists also encouraged a festive atmosphere at meetings and protests, printing verses and anthems to be sung in the streets by the *Antijuif* crowd. Such jokes and songs acknowledged the Jewish threat, thus maintaining the public fear necessary to the movement, but offered a reassuring vision of the world in which Jewish miscreants inevitably met their comeuppance. The social dimension of the shared joke or the anthem sung in unison served to further legitimize violence against Jews as both acceptable and enjoyable.

In linking prejudice and pleasure, jokes and songs also upheld gendered and social hierarchies within the movement by emphasizing the different sensations of different anti-Jewish bodies. A journalist from *Le Progrès algérien* described the unifying effect of songs and slogans disseminated in the press, recalling how chants of "Down with the Jews!" had been accompanied by "a strange frisson—an awakening of lifeblood and energy—running through the whole population." This energy manifested itself in different ways in "the child who, from that moment on, danced only to the sound to the *Marseillaise Antijuive*; . . . the worker who beat his hammer to the virile rhythm of this glorious hymn; . . . the bourgeois, whose daughter abandoned her recital of Beethoven in favor of this anthem of social struggle."[113]

The festive atmosphere of *Antijuif* demonstrations was often heightened by the participants' experience of sociability and drunkenness. Militants celebrated and displayed their political views with the consumption of *Antijuif*-branded absinthe and cigarettes, advertised in the press.[114] By smoking "Louis Régis cigarettes," militants publicly affirmed their allegiance to the movement and could imagine themselves inhaling the air of charisma and heroism that surrounded one of their celebrated leaders.[115] Some young men were enticed into militancy in this way. Louis Bes, a seventeen-year-old valet who was arrested following the violent assault of Elie Kanouï during the Journée des Antijuifs in Algiers in May 1901, explained that although he was not a member of the Jeunesse Antisémite Nationaliste, he had joined up with a group of youths on the Place du Gouvernement and had gone with them to a café to drink absinthe before embarking on a series of violent acts.[116] The café in question, the prefect of Algiers noted in his report, was a known meeting place of the Jeunesse Antisémite Nationaliste, whose members readily mixed festivity and militancy. Their previous meeting place had also been a café, until "the noise, the violent discourse emitted every evening by the League members, and their anti-Jewish songs were complained about by the neighboring residents."[117]

The *Antijuifs'* café rendezvous, the prefect suggested, also involved the construction of a celebratory narrative of their violent activities in a ritual that recalled the recounting of the Arab tales by Muslim men in the *café maures*: "League members return [to the café] and tell each other about their various exploits." These exploits included the destruction of Jewish property, aggression against Jewish people, and public protests against the imprisonment of fellow militants. It was in this way that a group of men, composed, according to the prefect, of "the most dangerous pimps and criminals of all nationalities," formed a political community based on shared behaviors and sensibilities.[118]

The *Antijuif* press was central to the organization and perpetration of acts of violence. From the 1880s sympathetic journalists had sought to inflame tensions between settlers and Jews. During the 1890s press advocacy of violence became all the more explicit, as journalists employed illustration and photography, as well as provocative language, to incite their readers to use physical aggression. Papers such as *Le Châtiment* and *L'Antijuif algérien* regularly printed images of the movement's leaders in combat with dehumanized Jewish enemies or scenes of angry crowd rebellions.[119] Illustrations such as one depicting the journalist Louis Lionne raising an ax to a "Jewish" spider conveyed the habitual signifiers of *Antijuif* masculinity: the aggressive gesticulation, defiant posture, and unwavering gaze.[120] In other images, journalists explicitly linked these features to the struggle of settler colonial existence, depicting the leaders of the movement as outlaws on the far western frontier.[121] Their sharp features and fixed gazes were deliberately placed in contrast to the hooked noses and shifty looks of the caricatured Jewish figures in these images.

Max Régis, in particular, was adept at cultivating his image as the harbinger of an aggressive new form of settler colonial manliness. As one of the contributors to Régis's newspaper remarked, "Quill, sword, saltpeter, incandescent lava, heroism, abnegation, an unrepentant hatred of Jews, a generous heart . . . all the qualities of a MAN are brought together in his brave chest."[122] Régis's collaborators and rivals within the movement hastened to follow his example, advocating the development of "combat journalism." [123] Many were actively engaged in militancy, at the forefront of the planning and orchestration of riots. Etienne Baïlac, editor of *Le Turco*, for example, was central to the organization of the Journee des Antijuifs in Algiers on May 1, 1901. Police reports concerning the event describe how Baïlac accompanied leaders of a group known as La Jeunesse Anti-Semite Nationaliste into the streets of Bab-el-Oued "in order to recruit young protestors." On the orders of Lionne—head of the youth movement and, by this time, deputy mayor of Algiers—the recruits were armed with sticks, knives, and revolvers before being plied with alcohol and let loose into the streets.[124] Such events demonstrate the extent to which *Antijuif* leaders based their political identity on the wider press discourse of "Algerian" youth and indiscipline and indicate a level of public support for the same ideals.

Responding to the growth of anti-Jewish sentiment among settlers, Jewish journalists launched their own newspapers to represent and defend their community. The creation of such papers often directly coincided with peaks in anti-Jewish activity, with new publications appearing with the passing of the Crémieux Decree and during the violence of the 1890s.[125] "We will respond with energy to all the attacks and insults to which our coreligionists are—alas!—daily subjected," promised the editors of *La Jeunesse israélite*, launched in Oran in 1890, "and we will refute any accusation against them, be it in regard to their political life or their private life."[126]

Jewish journalists employed strident tones that matched those of the *Antijuifs* in their dynamism yet stopped short of invoking popular violence. Instead, these writers engaged their opposition by launching active investigations into the various crimes of which their coreligionists were accused, exposing the real wrongdoers and their threat to the colony. Acknowledging *L'Echo d'Oran*'s descriptions of the insalubrity of the town's Jewish quarter, *La Jeunesse israélite* observed, "This is exactly what needs to be explained to those who pretend they know nothing about the problem—*the mu-ni-ci-pa-li-ty*! Yes! The very institution responsible for the neglect of such a densely populated neigh-borhood!"[127] In this way the paper displaced the blame for "Algerian" suffering—as a result of urban degradation and disease—from the Jews onto an anti-Jewish public and its political representatives. Like their opponents, Jewish journalists also attempted to mobilize popular opinion by using humor to transform resistance into a pleasurable social experience. Countering the anti-Jewish association of Jews with filth and corruption, *La Jeunesse israélite* offered the following joke: "Two men start arguing on the way out of a noisy meeting: "Dirty Jew!" shouts one. "Clean Aryan!" replies the other."[128]

By highlighting the neglect and prejudice suffered by the local Jewish population and drawing attention to the collusion of civil and military authorities in violence against their coreligionists, Jewish journalists undermined *Antijuif* attempts to exclude Jews from the "Algerian" and French communities on the basis of their alien sensibilities.[129] Indeed, the original community of suffering, they suggested, was the French nation itself, born of the struggle and sacrifice of the revolution of 1789. If anyone was straying from that community, these journalists observed, it was not Jewish people but *Antijuif* militants, who presented themselves as "sons of the revolution" while "renouncing the sacrifices made by their fathers and trampling on the principles that the latter were only able to establish at the expense of their property and their lives!"[130] To mark this contrast and affirm the Jewish population's place within the French nation, these journalists consistently supported a policy of cultural assimilation, encouraging their readers to learn the French language and adopt French dress and customs.

If Jewish journalists led the charge to expose the supposedly un-French nature of the ideas and behaviors of the *Antijuifs*, their concerns were increasingly shared by observers in the metropole, particularly following the violent riots of 1897–98. Such indiscipline, metropolitan politicians and journalists concluded, must surely be the result of the influence of settlers of foreign origin, who sought to rile the Muslim population and usurp French authority. The rising threat of separatism, moreover, caused many French *Antijuifs* to reconsider their actions, if not their prejudice. Fearful of the combined force of a looming "foreign peril" and "Arab peril," settler journalists encouraged their readers to reevaluate the relationship between "Algerian" and French cultural and political communities.

"The Anti-Jewish Movement Is No Longer Anti-Jewish"

Following the dramatic eruption of popular violence in 1897–98, metropolitan politicians and wary French settlers in Algeria feared for the security of French authority in the colony. "The anti-Jewish movement is no longer anti-Jewish," warned socialist deputy Gustave Rouanet. "It is French people—the best of them and the most loyal republicans—who are scorned, insulted, and beaten."[131] The civil unrest, Rouanet and a number of metropolitan journalists suggested, was being led by naturalized settlers of foreign European origin, whose disrespect for French authority was inciting Muslims to rebel against the colonial regime.

Although the efforts of militant *Antijuifs* to mobilize Muslim subjects against the Jews in Algeria had been largely ineffective,[132] French officials nevertheless seized on rare incidents of violence as troubling evidence of mounting indigenous unrest. Jewish journalists had highlighted several disturbances at the beginning of the 1890s, noting that Muslims were targeting Jews and leaving Christians unscathed—an indication that *Antijuif* agitators were behind the attacks.[133] Not until they believed such actions could threaten European security, however, did settler journalists and government officials begin to take notice. "By inciting the Arab to hate the Jew, by giving him a sense of self-worth, by making him believe that he is still capable of taking action, his old tendencies to revolt and struggle are revived," warned *La Bataille*.[134] While the paper was not opposed to the wider aims of the *Antijuif* movement—agreeing that "antisemitism has its good sides!"—it objected to the dubious methods of arabophile colleagues, including the strategy of baiting Muslims into militancy with the promise of full citizenship.[135] If the Crémieux Decree had taught the settlers anything, the paper argued, it was that the collective naturalization of indigenous communities was detrimental to the progress of the colony.[136] Furthermore, the paper insisted, Muslims were fundamentally uncivilized and as a result could not be welcomed into a political community that was based on the affinity of sensibilities. Extending the suffrage to this population was tantamount to "*the assassination of all settlers*," the paper declared.[137]

In the wake of the rioting and widespread disorder at the end of the nineteenth century, government officials took such arguments all the more seriously. In 1901 J. Bigot, police commissioner of the second arrondissement of Algiers, reported with no little anxiety on a knife attack against one Joseph Hadjadj, age thirty-eight, perpetrated by "one known as 'sahari' Brahem Ben Mohamed," who was alleged to have launched his assault with the provocative remark: "I'll stab you, you dirty Jew! I'm going to take you to see Régis in the town hall!" While Bigot noted that such occurrences remained isolated, he nevertheless drew the attention of his superiors to "a certain ferment [among our indigenous subjects] that is surely not unrelated to the recent anti-Semitic agitation."[138] This agitation, in Bigot's opinion, had been fueled by the colonial press.

In a special report to the central commissioner of Algiers in July 1901, Bigot highlighted an article by Régis in *L'Antijuif algérien*: "Having congratulated the Arab for his unflappable sangfroid and his immeasurable patience in the face of the numerous crimes for which the government of the republic and administrative officials daily make him their scapegoat, the article continues by inciting veritable hatred against a group of citizens—in this instance, 'the Israelites'—before moving on to talk of the 'Jewified,' meaning those of French stock who do not share the opinions of M. Max Régis."[139]

Such provocation and disregard for French authority, the prefect of Algiers worried, could not possibly go unnoticed by Muslim subjects in Algeria. "Most *indigènes* now know our language," he explained to the minister of the interior; "they are often involved in our lives; they are assiduous readers of newspapers, including *L'Antijuif*. They comment on all aspects of our political and social life, aspects that in Algeria are apt to increase their wariness and hatred of our race."[140] With fresh and painful memories of the bloody uprising in Margueritte in April 1901, Bigot and other administrators feared that "the fanatical instincts" of Muslims, once excited, would be directed not only against Jews in the colony but also against settlers and the French state.[141] Similarly anxious, many settler journalists renounced their Orientalist fascination with Muslim masculinity, falling back on the alternative Orientalist tropes of hostility and suspicion. The increasing press activity of Muslim men in the early twentieth century did little to allay the fears of settler journalists. References to the coming "Arab peril" signaled their rejection of Arabs in particular, and Muslims more generally, from both the overlapping "Algerian" and French communities they sought to embody and protect.[142]

If the "Arab peril" constituted one kind of physical threat to the settler colony, the "foreign peril" constituted another. Described by journalists and other social commentators as a diffuse menace to French cultural ideals, the "foreign peril" was seen as less of an external attack on French colonizers than their internal corruption through association with settlers of other European origins. Demographer Louis Durieu blamed the existence and particular forms of expression of the *Antijuif* movement in Algeria on "the multitude of foreigners who . . . have imposed a moral and political ideal that corresponds with their own desires, passions, and aspirations."[143] The journalist Augustin Castéran felt likewise, qualifying his former "Algerian patriotism" with an ardent declaration of French identity and noting that "these sentiments have nothing in common with our own."[144] Both Durieu and Castéran blamed the 1889 naturalization legislation for causing a disjunction between the French community of sensibilities and the political community of French electors. Settlers of foreign origin and their "Algerian" descendants, Durieu suggested, had not become fully assimilated into the culture, were not knowledgeable about French political precepts, and were ill prepared for French citizenship. As a result, the influx of naturalized voters had corrupted the "Algerian body politic," leading to "the troubles characteristic of these illnesses involving excessive growth, which can destabilize the most robust constitutions."[145]

The violence and indiscipline of *Antijuif* militancy in the colony was, in the eyes of many French imperialists, symptomatic of these unnatural growing pains and of the alien sensibilities of non-French settlers. For many anxious observers in the metropole, as in the settler colony, the behavior demonstrated during anti-Jewish rallies and riots was not confined to the movement's militants but had become a defining trait of the whole "Algerian" population. "The anti-Jewish movement is an explosion of bad Algerian manners and a moral separatism," proclaimed one journalist.[146] Speaking in parliament on May 19, 1899, socialist deputy Rouanet referred to the disorder in the settler colony as an indication of the "strange mental state" of its inhabitants, who displayed a "hardly French mentality."[147] Since 1870, the politician proclaimed, the "French mentality" of those from the metropole had undergone a gradual metamorphosis, transformed by the influence of Spanish, Maltese, and Italian settlers and contact with Muslims and Jews. Citing an unnamed source from the colonial press, Rouanet explained that, deprived from birth of a French cultural environment, young "Algerians" could not help but grow up with values and behaviors different from those that characterized metropolitan Frenchmen. The influx of foreign influences, his source suggested, invoking the popular analogy of the familial relationship, had broken the bond between the metropolitan parent and its colonial child, interfering in the transmission of sensibilities from one generation to the next: "For her [Algeria], France has not been the mother close to whom one lives during the period of development, from whom one instinctively draws one's manners and ideas. For her, France is a somewhat distant mother . . . whom she loves, of course, but whose theories she doesn't understand and whose voice she cannot really hear."[148]

The transformation of the French mentality in the colony, demographer Louis Durieu suggested, warned of an imminent and profound change in the composition of the French race itself. If the "Algerian" could at that time still be considered French, argued Durieu, the failure of the government to intervene and bolster French cultural and civic education in the colony would mean that "he will soon be no more than a métis."[149] Just as the political and economic activity of the Jews was represented by *Antijuifs* as a form of corruption, so the racial debasement threatened by naturalized settlers was described by patriotic French colonizers in the language of disease. It was not only the French settlers in Algeria who were in danger, warned Rouanet, but also the population of the metropole and the whole body politic: "If we let the anti-Semitic gangrene spread and take hold, it will take over the whole body, cover it in necrotic debris, and cause it to rot and die."[150]

Rejected from the French racial and cultural community, naturalized settlers were described by some journalists in the same terms that *Antijuifs* had applied to the Jewish people. Denying claims of shared suffering among settlers, editor Nicaise branded the naturalized Europeans "a horde of beggars who have gotten rich under the folds of the [French] flag . . . who having sacrificed nothing in the conquest of Algeria now want to become its masters."[151] In contrast to the underpinnings of an "Algerian" community, suffering and sacrifice, Nicaise declared, were uniquely French attributes, conferring superior status on French civilization and thereby justifying French domination. Some writers even called the term "Algerian" into question, suggesting that it was employed by naturalized settlers merely "to hide their intentions and allow them to pretend—if not that they are still Spanish, Italian, or Maltese—at least that they are no more French citizens than they were before."[152] "Against the growing crowd of renegades without a homeland," promised Nicaise, "all that is French will rise up, and we will not be the ones to be chased from this French land."[153]

For journalists who sought to defend French cultural ideals and political structures, the reorganization of settler colonial society according to metropolitan gender codes was imperative. These writers criticized the violence and indiscipline of the *Antijuif* militants and "Algerian" protestors, labeling them as "hysterics" and "cowards."[154] Their failure to exhibit self-restraint contravened the dominant metropolitan ideals of masculinity and undermined the image of the "peaceful conqueror" on which the civilizing mission and its justification of colonial control depended. In the metropole, "the newly energized male of the fin-de-siècle could not be a brute," explains Berenson. "An excessively violent man would resemble savages abroad and appear to confirm the feminist view of men as unworthy of their superior position in society."[155] In actively seeking to emulate imagined aspects of Muslim masculinity, *Antijuifs* had embraced the violent expression of their instincts as the basis of a new, colonial form of manliness. Shocked by the scale and political implications of the violence they had unleashed, however, journalists to whom this new model of manliness had initially appealed now confirmed the need for discipline and self-restraint. From this point on, asserted Max Régis, there were "two approaches: temporization or immediate combat."[156] While Régis, accompanied by a reduced entourage, continued to advocate violence as a legitimate form of manly and political expression, other former militants renounced aggression, calling instead for "calm" and "a policy of reason and discussion" in their continued struggle against the Jews.[157]

Their reversion to French cultural ideals was often accompanied by their support for the metropole to have greater administrative authority over local affairs. For Castéran, the foreign corruption of French senti-ments had fostered a destructive desire for political autonomy, a situa-tion that could result in nothing less than "the negation of our virility, of our rights and of our hopes."[158] These staunch defenders of "all that is French" also called for the purification of the body politic through the repeal or revision of the 1889 naturalization law.[159] Equally attached to French values, other journalists suggested that French authority in the colony would be best served not by the exclusion of settlers of for-eign origin, but by their cultural assimilation. "Is it not preferable and more immediately practical to try to bring together citizens who may be divided by petty questions of race or origin?" asked Léon Djian of *La Jeune France*. Bearing the subtitle "Organ for the Diffusion of French and Republican Ideas," the Oranais publication sought to provide a "connection between the diverse elements of French Algerian society." The newspaper presented the policy of cultural assimilation as the best means of achieving social harmony, arguing, "It is important that French and republican ideas are methodically and gradually diffused in the milieus of Algerian society, and—even more so—among the French who were born in Algeria."[160]

Other journalists echoed such sentiments, calling for reform of the colonial education system or the extension of settlers' military service to two years, a period that should obligatorily be spent in the French metropole.[161] The editor of *L'Education sociale* even proposed that all young "Algerians" receive their secondary schooling in mainland France. He was particularly concerned that they be taught contemporary history in order to "learn what the [Second] Empire was, what the reactionary forces were, what clericalism was. They don't know any of this and that is why they are duped by the first agitator or self-interested party to come along."[162] These proposals relied on reinforcing the subordination of the colony's administration to the metropole, eliminating "Algerian" exceptionalism in structural as well as cultural terms.

Rather than making "Algerians" into unidimensional Frenchmen, however, a third group of settler journalists advocated celebrating "Algerian" exceptionalism as a strength within the French national community. This perspective emphasized the existence of a Latin race, regrouping French, Spanish, and Italian settlers within the same broad racial community, while allowing for a certain level of diversity of cultural expression among these European groups. Many journalists thus invoked "Latin blood" as the basis of a united political community that recognized "Algerians" as Frenchmen.[163] These ideas drew on the longer-term expression of "Algerian" identity in the settler colonial press but were more explicitly framed in scientific terminology, as journalists looked to demographic and medical studies to promote an understanding of the settler community as composed of distinct people whose biological inheritance was nevertheless compatible with that of the French.

Research into such questions had begun in the colony in the 1870s, as demographers such as Dr. René Ricoux wondered how they and other Algerian-born Europeans, as "children of this land," would fare in their quest to found a prosperous new society in Africa.[164] By 1911 eminent local doctor Edmond Vidal was describing the heredity and characteristics of "the Algerian child" with precision. Addressing those "systematic detractors of Algerian mentality," Vidal emphasized the relative youth of the "Algerians" as a people: "It must be remembered that in France, it took eighteen centuries of evolution for the revolution of 1789 put an end to the immorality of the *Ancien Régime*. One must give credit to a young people, still in development, and not demand a set of moral characteristics that cannot all be identified in any other people, at any point in history." Indeed, Vidal suggested, the particular moral characteristics of the "Algerian" should be viewed as qualities rather than deficiencies. Their apparent lack of self-restraint, the doctor argued, was in fact a manifestation of youthful exuberance and "a love of pleasure." In this respect, the "Algerians" were akin to "the young Africans of the Roman era, who were also sons of settlers, soldiers, and administrators, of pure or mixed blood"; as such, they were surely destined to form a valuable artistic and intellectual elite.[165]

As this confidence in the properties of Latin blood seeped from the sciences into other disciplines, the language of biological race increasingly made its way into the press, where expert opinions on the "Algerian" people and the Latin race were quoted at length. Trilingual publication *L'Union latine* printed a series of opinions on the matter, favoring the findings of economist Paul Leroy-Beaulieu, who observed, "If, in mixing with Spaniards, Italians, and Maltese, the French race loses its purity, it nevertheless gains a greater resistance to the climate." "The Algerian population of the future," Leroy-Beaulieu predicted, "will be neither Spanish nor Italian, nor will it be entirely French; rather, it will be a neo-Latin people."[166] If this discourse was to be expected in multilingual publications that explicitly sought to create unity among settlers of diverse origins, it was not limited to these publications. Outside of the nationalist press, the celebration of the "Algerian" people and the Latin race was common among settler journalists. Taking pride in the opinions of local "experts," and flattered by the attention of metropolitan observers, colonial publications regularly featured articles on the topic of race in Algeria. Had French history not proved, asked a local philosophy teacher named Beaudroit in *Le Progrès*, "that far from clashing, the most divergent traits can complement one another, when a superior ideal exists to carry along hearts and wills?" The superior ideal evident in Algeria, Beaudroit suggested, was that of civilization itself—an ideal for which French settlers and their "Latin brothers" had all made sacrifices. "In a colony as in a beehive," Beaudroit observed, "the real foreigner is idleness."[167]

Idleness, these journalists concurred, was anathema to true "Algerians," regardless of their country of origin, but remained an essential trait of indigenous Muslims. "What is needed here," announced Oranais publication *L'Africa*, "is harmony and understanding between the diverse nationalities which the republic has brought together to create an Eden of activity and productivity in a place that, under Arab domination, was nothing but a bleak desert."[168] Reviving a long-standing Orientalist stereotype, journalists once again emphasized the perceived indolence of Muslim subjects, dropping the calls for indigenous emancipation that had accompanied the *Antijuif* reporting of previous years. Their retreat from such propositions was further hastened by the campaigns for political rights organized by Muslim journalists in the early years of the twentieth century.[169] In invoking the common efforts of the Latin races, therefore, settler journalists at once acknowledged diversity within local and national communities and limited the extent of this diversity based on a notion of civilization grounded in biological race. Although some writers saw the fusion of Latin peoples in Algeria as "a sort of step toward the cosmopolitanism of diverse races," they remained few in number and invariably qualified their prophecy by noting the remoteness of its realization.[170] For most settler journalists, Muslims simply did not possess the requisite Latin sensibilities to become "Algerian"; nor, as a result, could they be considered truly French.

Despite the settlers' submission to French sovereignty, these journalists insisted that their cultural particularity should be reflected in the political and administrative relationship between the colony and the metropole. Although the settlers' acquisition of a certain amount of fiscal autonomy following the establishment, between 1898 and 1900, of the Délégations financières removed much of the bitterness from journalistic arguments over the political and administrative future of the colony, the debates did not end.[171] As W. Marial of *Le Petit oranais* observed of his peers in 1903, "One is allowed to be an assimilationist or an autonomist, but not to be indifferent."[172] Bearing out the predictions of Leroy-Beaulieu in *L'Union latine*, those journalists who saw "Algerian" and French identities as compatible expressions of a wider neo-Latin community favored the autonomist camp.[173] Algeria could not simply be considered "an extension of France," *Le Trait d'union* agreed, publishing the contribution of deputy Jules Legrand to the ongoing parliamentary discussion over how best to reform the colonial administration in the wake of the *Antijuif* agitation. Despite the proximity of the Algerian departments, Legrand argued, the settler colony required, "in the financial, economic, and administrative domains, its own structures, clearly distinct from those of the metropole."[174]

Decentralization, Legrand argued, was the best means of not only maintaining but actively strengthening the French Empire. Other commentators agreed. Writing in *L'Union latine*, Bazillac, who had worked as a journalist in Algeria before returning to the metropole, presented administrative decentralization as imperative to the representation of the "new nationality" that was developing in the settler colony, as well as to the security of the empire as a whole. Envisaging the federation of separate nations within the empire, he called for repeal of the 1889 legislation leading to the French naturalization of the descendants of settlers of foreign European origin and proposed its replacement with "Algerian naturalization." "I say Algerian and not French," Bazillac explained, "because, while it is genuinely disconcerting to create French citizens who know nothing about France, it is, on the other hand, natural to legally recognize as Algerians those whose interests are based in the colony, who make every effort in its service, and who are essential to its prosperity."[175]

Such debates, continuing throughout the first decade of the twentieth century, long outlived the political success of the early *Antijuif* movement. In reaction to the widespread unrest in the last years of the nineteenth century, the French government took steps to restore stability. In addition to establishing the Délégations financières and thereby allowing settlers to elect their own representatives to oversee the colonial budget, Governor General Édouard Lafferière (1898–

1900) and his successor, Charles Jonnart (1901–3), acted to constrain unrest and militancy, focusing on social reform and the development of the colonial infrastructure. These actions helped reduce popular antipathy toward the French government and subdue support for the *Antijuifs*. Facing waning public enthusiasm and effective opposition from the state, the movement was increasingly beset by factionalism, as its leaders turned on one another with recriminations. By 1902 the colonial *Antijuifs* had lost all four of the seats they had gained in the French parliament four years earlier, without having achieved their principal objective of suppression of the Crémieux Decree. Although *Antijuif* officials continued to dominate municipal councils in Oran and Algiers until 1905, their influence steadily declined in the new administrative context.

Settler prejudice against Jews, however, did not die out with the first wave of the *Antijuif* movement. Latent throughout the first decades of the twentieth century, it once again exploded in the interwar period, nurtured by homegrown and metropolitan far-right organizations. These were, as Dónal Hassett points out, the first far-right groups to take hold in Algeria, where settler colonial ideology had long consolidated racial and ethnoreligious discrimination.[176] Their attempts to balance claims to settler primacy against a desire for intervention and protection from the metropolitan government had a much longer history, stemming from the attempts to reconcile "Algerian" and French communities in the wake of the *Antijuif* violence at the turn of the century. In this context, an "Algerian" community of sensibilities, which definitively excluded indigenous Muslims, had been loosely grafted to the French metropole through an infusion of Latin blood. Once again courting Muslim support, the anti-Semitic militants of the 1930s did so not in the name of "Algerian" sensibilities, but in the name of a French imperial nation state within which an "Algerian" community had claimed its place.

Despite the electoral defeat of the *Antijuifs*, the debate on the nature of the "Algerian" character lived on in the press and in the research of doctors and demographers in the setter colony. If the backlash against the *Antijuif* movement did indeed contribute to the reconfiguration of relations between the settler colony and the metropole, it did not simply transform foreigners into Frenchmen. Instead, the movement served to consolidate popular understandings of the "Algerian" character, crystallizing elements from long-standing journalistic debates about the settler community's racial composition, cultural sensibilities, and political representation. Seeking to cultivate an "Algerian" community on which to build their political agenda, anti-Jewish journalists imagined a patriarchal society structured by a form of colonial manliness that privileged physical suffering, strength, and violent self-expression. If such an imagined community entirely excluded Jews and left women's political participation severely circumscribed, it offered possibilities for the cultural and political integration of settlers of foreign European origin and, to a more limited extent, indigenous Muslims.

The violent disorder of 1897–98, however, was viewed by many journalists in Algeria and France as evidence of a malady that jeopardized the future development of the colony and the stability of the empire. Within Algeria, journalists began to reconsider the form of cultural and political community that they sought to create and the nature of its relationship to the French nation. In the press debates that followed, Muslims were rejected from both the "Algerian" and French communities and were depicted as uncivilized religious fanatics who threatened both settler security and imperial authority.

For many settler journalists and social commentators, the "Algerian" of the early twentieth century was not simply French, but the local product of a transnational community of Latin peoples. If, in 1874, Ricoux had cautiously looked forward to the day when French settlers would mix not only with other Europeans but also with Jews and Muslims to produce a strong and acclimatized colonial population, this prospect was explicitly rejected in most formulations of the Latin race described at the turn of the century.[177] As well as clarifying the racial boundaries of the "Algerian" people, the journalistic debates provoked by the *Antijuif* movement popularized understandings of this people as unique. Whether journalists embraced or abhorred the "Algerian" character following the riots of 1897–98, the diffusion of their opinions discursively defined its composition: impulsive and undisciplined, youthful, and uncertainly French.

4

...

Pages without Borders

Local Publications in Global Networks

Looking back over his long career as a journalist in Algeria, Ernest Mallebay—contributor to numerous publications and founder, in the 1880s and 1890s, of *La Revue algérienne, Le Turco,* and *Annales africaines*—remembered with particular fondness the decades that preceded the First World War.[1] "At that time," he reminisced, "Algerian settlers—those from the interior as well as those in the towns—read the newspapers from Algiers with an impassioned fervor. They read them not for their snippets of information transmitted by telegraph at a cost of three centimes per word, which barely took up half a column, but for the articles of [local journalists] Allan, Marchal, Arthur de Fonveille, Narcisse Faucon, Tillier, Vaille Marial, Marteau—anagram of Aumerat, director of *Solidarité.*"[2] These writers, as proud contributors to "an ardent and combative press," produced the kind of "sweeping judgements," "vehement ripostes," and "grillings" of public figures that, Mallebay lamented, had become impossible to publish in the interwar era—at least for those who lacked the funds and elite backing required to set up their own newspapers.[3]

Already caught up in the ever-expanding global telegraph network,[4] settler journalists in Algeria in the 1880s and 1890s were not yet subsumed by the standardized information order that some scholars argue emerged in the colony in the first decades of the twentieth century.[5] At this time of transition between artisanal and commercial mass production and oscillation between local and global points of reference, settler journalists enjoyed considerable liberty of expression, and their readers were free to let their imagination wander. "As our newspapers talked a lot about Algeria, and very little of the metropole," mused Mallebay, "we had the impression that France was far, very far away."[6]

The distance perceived by Mallebay runs counter to scholarly interpretations of the contemporaneous effects of new technologies within continental Europe, where, in Roland Wenzlheumer's estimation, the "telegraphic network fulfilled its central purpose and brought most places in Europe closer together." Although certain cities—notably Paris, London, and Berlin—became the most active and well-connected nodes in the network, the density of the network meant that by the early twentieth century, "most places were—telegraphically speaking— equally close or far from each other."[7] Yet if settler colonies were more securely attached to this network than were other colonial territories, their connections were significantly fewer than those enjoyed by the European countries that had ruled, or continued to rule, them.[8] Often bound within the "circuits of empire" identified by Alan Lester, the principal telegraphic links available to settlers remained intrinsic to the imperial formation of which they had been, or still constituted, a part.[9]

Despite the existence of trans-Mediterranean submarine cables since the 1850s and the subsequent installation of overland cables between the Moroccan border and Tunis, the inhabitants of Algeria remained dependent on steamships for communication with the metropole until 1870. Once established, however, the direct telegraphic connection between the settler colony and the metropole was rapidly reinforced, and by the end of the 1890s multiple cables linked Bône, Algiers, and Oran to Marseille, which in turn enjoyed a direct connection to Paris.[10] The integration of Algeria into the expanding global telecommunications network had the effect, according to Arthur Asseraf, of bringing "European Algerians closer to France at the same time as it brought Algerian Muslims closer to other Muslims around the world."[11] A technology perceived by contemporaries as a force for connection and civilization thus came to act as a force for creating difference and enforcing division in the colonial context.

While the capacity of such technology to reinforce inequalities between colonizing and indigenous populations cannot be underestimated, the internal divisions within each population must also be examined. For example, one must question the extent to which "for Europeans in Algeria, events in Paris were domestic news"[12] during these crucial prewar decades of press development, both in light of Mallebay's emphasis on distance and in recognition of the various notions of "home" that existed among the mixed European settler population. If settlers in Algeria had limited direct telegraphic connections with countries other than France, the wider telecommunications network—by its very nature—brought them closer to their diverse countries of origin and to other places of interest around the globe. This proliferation of external points of reference also encouraged journalists and readers to more completely situate the settler colony, and their immediate localities, within their conceptions of home.

These multifaceted understandings of domestic and foreign news among settlers have often been overlooked in histories of the press in Algeria, in part because of the well-observed historical association between publishing and the social elite within Europe.[13] This association has carried over into the scholarship on the colonial press, albeit sparse, where newspapers have been perceived primarily as instruments of the French political and commercial elite.[14] Certainly, it was not uncommon for landowners and businessmen to associate in providing capital for colonial newspapers in the nineteenth century, in pursuit of their own interests. Louis Pierre Montoy cites, by way of example, the long-running *L'Indépendant* of Constantine, whose primary shareholder, Marcel Lucet, was elected deputy, then senator after 1870.[15] Newspaper ownership by groups of investors became increasingly common in the twentieth century, much to the chagrin of old hands like Mallebay, who lamented interwar journalists' loss of independence, as they found themselves obliged "to accommodate so many things and so many people, starting with the members of the newspaper's board!"[16]

Despite the existence of such powerful groups of investors in the last decades of the nineteenth century, the range of newspaper formats and production processes remained vast. Mallebay's experience provides a case in point: having worked alone on the lighthearted *Alger-Saison*, which was owned and financed by a local businessman named L. Chappuis and for which Mallebay wrote every article under a different pseudonym, he went on to enlist a team of collaborators for his subsequent venture, *La Revue algérienne*, which he financed independently until the enterprise became self-sustaining.[17] Produced without support from the general government, Algeria's first literary review went on to attract between four thousand and five thousand subscribers.[18] While most local titles could not boast such figures and lacked the aesthetic appeal of well-funded publications like *L'Indépendant*, their number and the tenacity of their creators—who often persisted in the face of prior failures—testify to the pervasive appeal of journalism beyond the narrow dictates of market forces. These papers existed as cris de coeur but also as forms of social action; even the hastily lithographed pages of short-lived productions such as Leon Bonnenfant's *La Guerre aux Abus* have more to reveal to the historian than the views of their solitary and disgruntled authors.

Newspapers, argues Tony Ballantyne in reference to settler colonial New Zealand, "fashioned social connections and routinely linked individuals into public conversations."[19] In Algeria, too, newspapers functioned as more than ideological instruments or barometers of public opinion. Even the smallest-scale operations, from the conception of the editorial program through their production to their eventual diffusion and consumption, were necessarily interwoven in the social interactions of the settler colony, and as a result, they bore the traces of the conversations, negotiations, and reinventions that constituted settler colonial existence. As assemblages, settler colonial newspapers—even the small ones—were necessarily bigger than their investors or owners.

The process of press assemblage in Algeria at the end of the nineteenth century grew ever more multidimensional as the expanding global telecommunications network brought news from all over the world. Viewing this development alongside the activities of news agencies and interested groups of investors, historians have argued that the transition to an information-based press effaced the previously dominant polemical expression of local concerns and affiliations. [20] Yet, as Ballantyne observes for New Zealand, "telegraphic services did produce a repertoire of news stories that were widely reproduced, but these were always mixed with original reportage on local developments, accounts of meetings, speeches and community occasions, and stories on the politics of the district to produce distinctive news mixes in the newspapers that served various localities."[21] In Algeria, too, preexisting practices persisted, and existing informal journalistic circuits of information endured. Most significantly, integration into a global network of information did not subdue expression of a distinct settler perspective; rather, it provided new points of reference and comparison for settlers' processes of identification. Heightened awareness of events elsewhere, posits Terhi Rantanen, actually strengthened nineteenth-century readers' "sense of place" by making it possible for them "to be both here-and-there at the same time."[22]

Although the stream of electric news reached Algeria through Paris, much of it had originated somewhere else to begin with. Thus, while the telegraph was capable of binding settlers in Algeria to France, it could also encourage links with other nodes on the global communications network. Then as now, local editors and journalists played an active role in selecting and "domesticating" foreign news, through rewriting or translation, for its new audience.[23] Events in Spain and Italy featured regularly in the overseas coverage presented to settler readers. Both countries were experiencing newsworthy political and economic upheaval at the end of the nineteenth century, and many readers in Algeria had affective ties to these countries, from which they or their ancestors had emigrated. Spanish and Italian interests in other areas of North Africa were consequently also addressed, especially where journalists identified potential conflict with the imperialist designs of the French government. While some writers exploited these tensions to promote division between settlers of different origins, others found ways to encourage their peaceful coexistence as fellow members of the "civilizing races."

Developments in the colonies and former colonies of the Spanish Empire were similarly assumed to be of particular interest to readers, as were events across the French and British colonial domains. Journalists frequently directed their readers' attention to other settler colonies around the world, attempting to measure the relative progress of each and to evaluate the pros and cons of their respective political structures—often with a view to pursuing administrative reform in Algeria. Beyond providing possible models of development, other settler colonies were also of interest in this era as settings for the kind of sensational and dramatic events apt to capture readers' attention: if the economic ascendency and scientific advances of the United States furnished readers with an appealing success story, news of horrors in the Transvaal and Cuba cautioned journalists and their readers in Algeria against too hasty a leap toward independence.

In considering these events on the other side of the Atlantic and at the other end of the African continent, settler journalists in Algeria encouraged their readers to reexamine their relationships to each other—as Europeans of different national origins—and to the French state. Although the examples of settler nationalism set by their counterparts elsewhere in the world proved attractive to a mixed settler population keen to resist the assimilative drive of the "one and indivisible" French Republic, journalists ultimately privileged a transnational Latin community capable of uniting Europeans of French, Spanish, and Italian origin, while accommodating real differences of cultural practice and patriotic sentiment, as well as perceived differences of race.

In this way, the global connections of the press in Algeria seem to have operated differently from those examined by Simon Potter, John Lambert, and Alan Lester in the settler colonies of the British Empire, where, they argue, telecommunications networks structured processes of identification in such a way as to promote a sense of imperial community, or an imagined "British world."[24] As the Algerian example demonstrates, however, connections between empires could challenge the neat correlation of national and imperial communities, extending and transforming the dynamics of identification for all sectors of colonial society. Further research into interimperial connections, argues Antoinette Burton, is essential if historians of empire are to "think beyond the nation."[25]

The Latin identification sustained by the global outlook of the settler press in Algeria provided just such a means of thinking for contemporaries, encouraging them to see beyond the nation—French or otherwise. More than part of a commercial strategy to attract readership in a diverse market, representations of a Latin settler community in Algeria constituted an evolving cultural response to a geopolitical climate that privileged national unity and national identity. Not only did the mobilization of Latin unity in diversity constitute a form of cultural resistance against the assimilative projects of the French state, but it also reflected a profound ambivalence toward sovereignty. By using Latin identity to underscore, at once, settlers' similarity to and difference from the French of the metropole, settler journalists sought to defend the colony's cultural and administrative autonomy without ultimately renouncing French political authority and the protection it afforded the European demographic minority.

Expanding Networks and Broadening Horizons

The interaction of journalists of different origins in the settler press in Algeria created a situation markedly different from that found in many British settler colonies, where, as Simon Potter explains, "migrating journalists carried with them their experiences of newspaper work in Britain, and imposed metropolitan models on the colonial press."[26] The contacts cultivated by those settlers in Algeria who had previous journalistic experience were dispersed in "diasporic homes" rather than concentrated in a single metropole.[27] The imposition of any one coherent journalistic model in Algeria was further complicated by the relative lack of professional infrastructure. Until the early years of the twentieth century the settler press was characterized by local production and distribution.[28] Although a small number of major titles—such as *L'Echo d'Oran*, established in 1844, and *La Dépêche algérienne*, established in 1884—benefited from close ties with large news agencies and commercial organizations, many settler publications were launched with limited means and untrained, if enthusiastic, personnel.[29] Contributors to these papers often had no experience in newspaper work before settling in North Africa.

Many, like Ernest Mallebay, were drawn into journalism by the experience of settlement and a desire to defend the particular interests of their local community.[30] Mallebay, a history teacher who settled in Blida in 1880, felt compelled to give up the relative security of a job in state education to take up journalism—a profession that, as one contemporary biographer explained, he "always viewed as a kind of apostolate."[31] Like many other journalists in the settler colony, Mallebay denounced the complexities of the administrative apparatus and called attention to the precariousness of settlers' existence. He supplemented this political mission with a cultural quest for "a literature that was truly Algerian, and not simply a reflection of that of the metropole."[32] Mallebay's memoirs—a nostalgic ode to a form of journalism transformed by the technological and commercial developments of the early twentieth century—reveal a world of informal social connections and improvised production practices.[33] Mallebay recalled having used, as a young journalist, "a small rectangular zinc basin into which I poured a copying-paste that I had melted in a *bain-marie*" to produce 350 copies of an "Algerian Chronicle" designed to attract the interest of metropolitan publications.[34]

The widespread desire to use journalism in the defense of settler interests generated mixed feelings among settler journalists toward the principal French news agency, the Agence Havas. Originally established as a translation agency in 1832, Havas quickly developed into one of the leading structures of news transmission in Europe, alongside the British company Reuters and the German Wolff Telegraphic Bureau. Havas opened an office in Algiers in 1880. Its first director, Émile Muston, went on to establish a successful rival operation, the Agence Africaine. In many ways, the overseas expansion of these agencies complemented the international perspectives of local journalists and facilitated their task; it was no coincidence that Muston was viewed by journalists at the end of the century as "one of the most influential people in the colony . . . the most renowned perhaps, after the governor general and Senator Mauguin."[35]

These agencies' ties to both the French state and a metropolitan journalistic field regarded as either indifferent or hostile to the interests of settlers, however, led journalists to view their activities with suspicion. The "loyalty of the information" provided by such agencies, *Le Petit fanal* suggested, was "rarely perfect" and could mislead settler journalists into destructive quarrels instigated by the metropolitan press.[36] It was surely because the Agence Havas was "in vassalage to" former governor general Jules Cambon, the paper insisted, that it had failed to disseminate the results of the 1897 elections—"an Algerian plebiscite" revealing a lack of public confidence in the allies of Cambon and a rejection of the former governor's close ties with the metropole.[37] Although these suspicions did not prevent settler journalists from making increased use of the telegraphic services provided by the Agence Havas or Agence Africaine, they remained circumspect in their interpretation of news originating from outside the settler colony and maintained alternative circuits of information among contacts overseas.

In addition to these local factors, the failure of the French government in this era to create an independent network of submarine cables worked against the creation of a French "imperial press system" equivalent to the one that connected the colonies of the British Empire.[38] While the circuits of information available to settler journalists in Algeria were transformed by the increasing availability of telegraphic technology, they were neither precisely aligned with French imperial space nor tied to the interests of a single national group within the settler population. The information they carried was instead selected and reworked by editors and journalists in accordance with their perception of their readers' demands.

Consequently, most of the externally sourced news came from the French metropole, Spain, or Italy, replicating the migratory trajectories of the settlers themselves. The prevalence of news from these countries reflected both the interests of settler readers and the relative ease of obtaining information from destinations with direct telegraphic connections or transport links to Algeria. Nevertheless, settler publications could be more or less selective in their treatment of French, Spanish, and Italian national news, depending on their target readership. If some papers, such as the aptly titled *Le Trait d'union* (Hyphen), keenly awaited the arrival of postal steamers from France in order to focus on the dissemination of extracts from the major French dailies, others, such as the appropriately named *L'Union latine* (Latin Union), might, within a single edition, inform their readers of the latest decisions of the French parliament, the earthquakes in Calabria, Italy, and the expansion of the railways in Spain.[39] By the late 1890s, *La Dépêche algérienne*—the best-selling francophone title in the territory at that time[40]—regularly included sections devoted to Italian and Spanish news in addition to more general coverage of international affairs.[41] While the emergence of a press focused primarily on the dissemination of information did not eliminate publications that favored selective national treatment of news from France, Spain, or Italy, it multiplied the trans-Mediterranean connections of journalists and exposed the reading community to a range of perspectives—all the more so at a time when, as Ballantyne observes, readers rarely limited themselves to a single source of news.[42]

This range of perspectives was further broadened by the frequent reproduction or summary of news from the neighboring territories of Tunisia and Morocco. Following the establishment of the French protectorate in Tunisia in 1881, a number of editors of francophone and italophone newspapers in Algeria set preferential rates for French and Italian subscribers residing on the other side of the eastern border. Some papers, including *La Revue algérienne et tunisienne* and *La Lega franco-italiana*, hired correspondents from the Tunisian settler population.[43] News also flowed into Algeria from French and Spanish settlements in Morocco, both before and after military intervention led to the creation of protectorate governments in the territory.[44] These connections across the Maghreb simultaneously reinforced separate French, Spanish, and Italian national communities across North Africa and created the conditions for the mutual recognition of these distinct communities at the local level. Hence, although newspapers in Algeria echoed French national anxieties surrounding the numbers of Italians in Tunisia or Spanish national anxieties concerning French influence in Morocco, they also sought to avoid conflict between groups of settlers by referring to their shared Latin interests.[45] "The common enterprise of civilization in North Africa," Franco-Spanish publication *L'Africa* asserted, "will become the most glorious achievement of France and her Latin sisters, Spain and Italy."[46] Spanish-language newspapers in particular extended the Latin connections of the local press by diffusing news from the former and remaining colonies of the Spanish Empire in Central and South America and in the Caribbean. These regular connections were supplemented in settler publications in Algeria by more irregular news of scientific discoveries, diplomatic crises, and military conflicts elsewhere in the world.

Although some newspapers' horizons were broader than others, they found common ground in the systematic publication of Algerian colonial news alongside information from other territories. The rubric "Algerian Questions" was common to many francophone, hispanophone, italophone, and multilingual publications, reflecting the widespread recognition in the press of a local "Algerian" community comprising the disparate national groups of the settler population. In many newspapers, external news was selected to correspond to the particular interests of "Algerian" readers. Even *Le Trait d'union*, for all its dedication to the much-anticipated missives from the French metropole, reproduced extracts from metropolitan titles only "when the subject under discussion is of particular or general interest to Algeria."[47] Indeed, although the relative weighting of external and regional or provincial news could vary from title to title and from issue to issue, the treatment of "Algerian" affairs remained a constant. The juxtaposition of different combinations of local and external news with "Algerian" questions ultimately gave definition to each category and encouraged an image of an "Algerian" settler community able to accommodate a range of national and regional perspectives.

Whether this community was based solely on the diverse migrant groups' mutual recognition of a common Muslim enemy or also reflected their shared tastes and sensibilities remained a matter of debate among journalists. Although few papers were as explicit as *L'Union latine* in insisting on compatible tastes and mentalities as the basis of a distinctive "neo-Latin race" in the colony, many acknowledged the existence of an "Algerian" community with shared experiences, fears, and aspirations.[48] Frequent journalistic references to a common struggle to render the land productive and to overcome the dangers of the North African environment and its indigenous inhabitants helped create an enduring pioneer myth. Such experiences, journalists habitually claimed, had shaped settler sensibilities, meaning that there was a difference between "understanding Algeria" and "*feeling* Algeria." Metropolitan claims that Algeria was simply "'an extension of French territory'" were thus routinely dismissed by settler journalists, who recognized "Algerian" cultural specificity even when they supported French cultural influence.[49]

The expansion of the circuits of information in which the settler press was integrated therefore was accompanied by a renewed focus on local specificity. Indeed, according to Mallebay, it was the continued attention to "Algerian" issues that later allowed a press based on the dissemination of international news to flourish.[50] As the space afforded to external and foreign news grew, local news and opinions did not disappear; rather, the simultaneous appearance of these perspectives in the press provided coordinates for the imagination of a settler community whose internal diversity was marked and not masked.

News from the Old Republics of France and the United States

The unity in diversity of this community, however, was not easy to maintain in the contemporary political context. If unity among settlers was often threatened by tensions in Franco-Spanish and Franco-Italian relations, diversity of settlers' cultural practice was under pressure from the assimilative apparatus of the French state. Assimilation was not only an ideological principle of a republican regime that declared itself to be "one and indivisible" but also a policy specifically directed toward settlers in Algeria by this regime, whose representatives feared that the settler "mentality" was "strange" and "not very French."[51] Such fears, which had persisted following the collective naturalization of Europeans in 1889, were heightened in the last years of the century, when the growth of anti-Jewish sentiment among settlers precipitated levels of popular violence that far surpassed those seen in the metropole, even at the height of the Dreyfus Affair, and provoked a small but militant separatist movement.[52] As French political commentators discussed how best to transform settlers into Frenchmen, settler journalists drew on their global perspectives to reflect on the colony's relationship with the French Republic. At once attracted by the protection offered by French authority and frustrated by restrictive administrative ties with the metropole, journalists expressed ambivalence toward French sovereignty.

The advent of the French Third Republic in 1870 had precipitated a transfer of authority in Algeria from military to civil structures. Many settlers welcomed this transition, believing that it would herald a period of stability and sustained economic development in the colonial territory.[53] As journalists at *La France algérienne* explained in 1871, in the wake of the revolutionary Algiers Commune, "the colony can only be saved and regenerated by a totally different form of organization—or, rather, disorganization—than the one that has prevented growth up to this point." "The republic, and only the republic," they insisted, could safeguard the future of the settler colony.[54]

Enthusiasm for the new regime was not confined to settlers with French citizenship, who acquired greater political representation and access to land requisitioned from the Muslim population, but was also expressed by many settlers of Spanish origin, who hoped that the victory of the republic in France would precipitate a similar victory in the peninsula. In a front-page illustration titled "The Sublime before the Ridiculous," Spanish-language publication *El Mosquito español* compared the verdant "tree of liberty," next to which stood a gleaming bust of the Marianne, with the decaying "tree of absolutism," flanked by vultures and a pompous masked scarecrow (fig. 7). Noting with approval the progress of the revolutionary movement in Spain, the paper assured its readers, "Soon . . . we will be able to kick out the foreign king and

7. "The Sublime before the Ridiculous," *El Mosquito español*,
November 16, 1884

shout along with the rest of you, on the other side of the Pyrenees, 'Long live the republic!'"[55]

The republic itself, another Spanish title reminded its readers in an article celebrating the French revolutionary date of July 14, was an eminently Latin invention; if the revolution was "a lesson given by France to its kings," it was now the duty of the French to "make the most of it, in order to return the lesson to the countries that had taught France in the first place."[56] A shared belief in the regenerative power of republicanism thus helped bring settlers of French, Spanish, and Italian origin together within an imagined Latin community that superseded national boundaries. "Long live the French Republic and long live the Latin Republic!" proclaimed editor Francisco Zavala in *El Patuet*, intimating that the former was but one iteration of the latter.[57]

Settlers' particular appreciation of the French Republic, however, was increasingly tempered in the 1880s and 1890s by their frustration with the inefficiency of the colonial administration and their sense of neglect at the hands of a privileged and distant metropolitan authority.[58] Under these conditions, a more general enthusiasm for republicanism—and revolution—threatened to outweigh any commitment to the particular republican regime in place. References to the French Revolution, as Jan Jansen demonstrates in his examination of celebrations of Bastille Day in Algeria, could be used by different groups of settlers in strategic ways to express different relationships with the French nation.[59] In the settler press of the 1880s and 1890s references to the revolution of 1789 no longer served as straightforward affirmations of French sovereignty, but rather were calls to arms for settlers eager to seize control of their own fate.

"The administration is a new Bastille against which an assault must be launched," announced E. Nicaise, writing amid the political disorder of the late 1890s.[60] The excessively centralized system, a journalist at *L'Algérie* pointed out, meant that "today, under a republic, France has the same administrative machinery as at the time of the monarchy."[61] This system, already deleterious in the metropole, was even more harmful in the settler colony, where, journalists argued, it was fundamentally unsuited to the interests and character of the "Algerian" people. "It is even worse in Algeria," explained E. Nicaise, "as our old legislation . . . is ill suited to the needs of a new land and the needs of a people who came to this colony seeking a form of liberty that is incompatible with our outdated procedures."[62] As a politically mature people, journalists insisted, settlers should be entrusted with their own decisions. "Arrived at adulthood," another journalist asserted, "Algeria would like to be freed from her reins, which—instead of helping her walk—today hold her back and force her to march on the spot."[63]

For all their references to rebellion, settler journalists rarely advocated revolution and the establishment of an independent settler republic. Indeed, even the most radical publications—such as the Jacobin news-papers *Le Sans-culotte* and *Le Bonnet phrygien*—explicitly sought to reinforce French authority by regenerating the nation from the colonial periphery.[64] The question remained, however, of how to organize the relationship between colony and metropole in a way that accounted for settlers' sense of specificity. To answer such questions about the social composition and political development of their community, journalists reflected on the news brought to them from other settler colonies around the world.

The United States, which was widely considered to have set the stan-dard for what could be achieved by a settler society of mixed origin, especially captured the imagination of journalists. Reports gave regular updates on the United States' economic, technological, and scientific progress, which journalists attributed to the "particular qualities of the American citizen, who raises himself up through his energy, his virtues, and his labor, becoming *somebody* and *something* after enduring many years of struggle without faltering or becoming discouraged."[65] These qualities, *La France africaine* suggested, were to be emulated by those who sought to lead settlers in Algeria to a brighter future.[66] Although politicians in Europe might try to explain American progress with ref-erence to the many resources of the "virgin lands" of North America, *Fraternidad obrera* noted, this was only because "their pride would not allow them to admit that this young people owes so much to the insti-tutions that they themselves had never imagined and are incapable of understanding."[67] Acutely aware, and proud, of their status as a "young people," settler journalists and readers in Algeria pondered the applicability of such institutions to their own society.

The American experience was of especial interest to journalists in the colony, as it provided one possible model for managing the interaction of settlers of diverse national origins. In the debates surrounding the naturalization of Europeans in Algeria, both preceding and following the naturalization legislation of 1889, journalists regularly took the American model as a point of reference. A number of writers pointed to the positive effects that the legal equality of diverse migrant groups had produced in the United States.[68] In emulating this policy and creating new French citizens in Algeria, some journalists suggested, the French nation would similarly gain in strength and prosperity.[69]

For others, however, an accurate application of the American model required first creating an independent Algerian nation, and then welcoming migrants as "Algerian" citizens.[70] Most journalists rejected this course of action in the present, but the common belief that the "Algerian" people were progressing toward cultural specificity and political maturity allowed some to envisage this as a possibility in the future. Although journalists at *L'Algérie* denied wanting to break with the French mother country in the same way that "the United States once treated their mother, England," they could not help but pose the question, "But *if* we wanted to renounce you as our mother—which would never happen—wouldn't we have the right? Is not a state, according to modern ideas, formed of the voluntary union of citizens?"[71]

Other journalists were less guarded in their warnings to the French state. One dissatisfied writer at *La France africaine* simply declared, "If there is a general feeling of hostility to the metropolitan government, then the Algerian provinces will rebel and a new, robust, and young republic will be born under the name of the United States of Africa."[72] This course of action would certainly simplify the policy toward Muslims, mused one reader in a letter to the newspaper; while Americans were "imperiled" by land-grabbing "negroes" and settlers in Algeria were threatened by acquisitive Muslims, the former at least had the means to defend themselves: "Over there they are fortunate to have revolvers that go off of their own accord, whereas here it is the French who are forced to make way for the insolent demands of the *indigènes!*"[73] These threats of violence, toward both the French authorities and the Muslim population, presaged the actions of settlers almost sixty years later, on the eve of a very different form of Algerian independence, as they finally resorted to open rebellion in a seemingly paradoxical effort to maintain French presence.[74]

Reactions to Settler Rebellion in Cuba and the Transvaal

If the United States provided a historic model of settler rebellion, the expanding communications networks of the late nineteenth century brought news of more contemporary examples. Journalists and readers in Algeria avidly followed the anticolonial struggles in Cuba and the Transvaal in the 1880s and 1890s. In both territories, fledgling republics were engaged in epic struggles against imperialist powers. In their desire for domination of these territories, the governments of Spain and Great Britain, respectively, demonstrated the readiness of imperialists to turn the violent tactics of the colonial regime—expropriation, starvation, population displacement, and concentration—against people of European and mixed colonial origin. The impact of these conflicts on debates about social and political development in Algeria was noted by former governor general Cambon in his memoirs of his period in office.[75] Whereas Cambon, as a representative of French authority, sought to learn from these events in order to strengthen French rule, journalists of the colonial press reflected on the inherent lessons in settler uprising and political independence. Their widespread support for Boer insurgents in the Transvaal, however, was not echoed in their coverage of rebellion in Cuba. The comparison of press reactions to these two examples of settler uprisings reveals the imagination of a transnational Latin community by local journalists and their attempts to situate "Algerians" within such a community.

The South African War of 1899–1902 attracted unprecedented levels of international media interest and transformed journalistic practice in the twentieth century.[76] Integrated by 1899 into both a global telecommunications network and a web of press contacts, settler journalists in Algeria contributed fully to the media furor surrounding the conflict. *La Dépêche algérienne*—the first newspaper in the colony to have subscribed to the reports from the Agence Havas—featured news about the war every day between January and June 1900, often on the front page.[77] Coverage continued following the British capture of Pretoria and the reversal of Boer fortunes, albeit on a less regular basis. Most reports summarized information offered by papers in Paris and London or elsewhere in the United Kingdom. Updates from publications in Berlin, Frankfurt, Rome, Amsterdam, Dublin, and Washington were also frequently included. Additional telegrams relayed from London, Paris, and Cape Town through the Agence Africaine supplemented these reports. Smaller local newspapers benefited from the connections of papers such as *La Dépêche algérienne*, providing further analysis and commentary on the information they printed.

The great public demand for news of the war enhanced the status of journalists, whose access to information transformed them into experts and public advisors. Following the alliance of the governments of the Transvaal and the Orange Free State in February 1900, a public lecture on the war given by Viator of *La Dépêche algérienne* was attended, the paper claimed, by more than a thousand listeners, two hundred of whom were obliged to stand at the back of the Algiers Velodrome for want of seating. The audience, boasted the paper, was "the most select, including several well-known personalities of Algiers, many ladies, and a great number of officers." The opinion expressed by Viator at this lecture aligned with that regularly expounded by the metropolitan journalists whose views on the war were reproduced in *La Dépêche algérienne*: support for the Boers and opposition to the "greedy Englishman."[78]

Anti-British sentiment had been a standard refrain of French journalists since the Anglo-French standoff at Fashoda in 1898. This sentiment was reinforced by news of British atrocities in the Transvaal, which journalists in France exploited in an effort to defend their own ideal of beneficent imperialism in opposition to the violence and egotism of their imperial rivals. While the Parisian publication *Le Petit journal* dedicated the front-page illustration of the issue of January 28, 1900, to a celebration of the French occupation of In Salah—depicting Muslim soldiers rallying to the French flag—the back-page illustration showed the death and destruction caused by the British imperial conflict in the Transvaal. The Boers, the newspaper's editorial confirmed, were "the object of the heartfelt admiration of all humanity, while the indignation of the civilized universe against odious and extravagant British jingoism increases ever more each day."[79] The idea that the mighty British Empire could be shaken by a small and poorly equipped colonial population appealed to French journalists in the metropole, as it did to the more privileged sectors of settler society in Algeria, who often identified with metropolitan opinion. Writing in January 1900, Viator could barely conceal his excitement at the successive defeats suffered by the British that month: "A humble people, too few in number to populate a city, has broken the legs of the colossus, and the colossus is left staggering. England has no longer has an army; England no longer has any gold."[80]

Like a number of right-wing militants from the French metropole, some settlers in Algeria saw the conflict in the Transvaal as an opportunity to capitalize on British failures and regenerate a French nation rendered weak by ineffectual republicanism. The settler press reprinted and commented on the missives of Action française founder and volunteer in the Boer army, Col. Georges de Villebois-Mareuil, inciting young men to engage in combat alongside the hardy Boers.[81] The presentation of these letters foregrounded the strength and resolution of frontier masculinity: "The Boers are soldiers of an extraordinary temperament," insisted one extract of correspondence in *La Dépêche algérienne*, "men from one hundred years in the past, fighting with modern weaponry."[82]

The struggle of the Boers also garnered the support of republicans in both the metropole and the settler colony, who portrayed the Boers as defenders of republican liberty against the tyrannical forces of the British monarchy. As the *Bulletin municipal officiel de la ville d'Alger* reported in December 1899, "The municipal council of Algiers expresses its greatest sympathy for the republicans in the Transvaal and the Orange Free State, who, in this time of cowardice and platitude, are fighting so heroically for their independence and their freedom."[83] *Le Petit mascaréen*, whose title banner declared it a "Patriotic and Republican" publication, printed a series of illustrations depicting the European tour of President Paul Kruger, leader of the South African Republic, echoing those of popular illustrated titles in Paris.[84]

While many Europeans in Algeria shared the various motivations of the metropolitan French to support the Boers, they also had reasons of their own, based on their identification with a fellow settler community. Hence even Viator, who ultimately sought to use the example of the conflict in the Transvaal to bind settlers in Algeria closer to the French nation, could not complete his public lecture without evoking for his listeners "the tribulations that the first Dutch and French settlers were forced to endure."[85] According to many settler journalists, these tribulations—which commonly included the experiences of migration, working the land, and fighting against disease and indigenous enemies—had helped develop the qualities of honesty, perseverance, and simplicity that formed the basis of the "Algerian" character. These distinctive qualities, E. Cat of *L'Algérie* explained, were also the result of "living in a new country where everything is yet to be created, everything yet to be imagined, and being in contact with diverse races."[86]

Settler journalists in Algeria recognized themselves in the Boer people and empathized with their plight. President Kruger was particularly admired for being "precisely the type of hero—of the land and of independence—that seems to have disappeared from the [European] race." "In this age of corruption and spinelessness," continued *La Croix de l'Algérie et de la Tunisie*, "he shows us what can be achieved with simple values and an energetic character. Never is a man better able to defend his home than when he is not encumbered by the mollifying luxury of excessive civilization."[87] The difference in character between Europeans living on either side of the Mediterranean, many journalists in Algeria argued, was exemplified by the failure of any European government to take decisive action in support of the Boers.[88] The "Algerian" people, by contrast, would prove more hospitable: the *Petit fanal* gladly circulated rumors that the new general governor, Jonnart, had requested that land be made available "to encourage the immigration of the Boers, should they be defeated by the English."[89]

Support for the Boers, as settlers engaged in a struggle against an oppressive imperial power, inspired some Europeans in Algeria to promote the independence of their own settler community. For anti-Jewish militants in Algeria, who felt that colonial growth had been stunted by the actions of a weak French government corrupted by Jewish influence, the Boers were seen as an example to be followed. Having been accused by a fellow journalist of espousing the same politics as the Boers, the anti-Jewish writers of autonomist publication *Le Républicain* reveled in the comparison: "The likeness is striking," they boasted, and as for their "Jewified" French political opponents, "they would quite deserve the title of Englishmen."[90] Max Régis, foremost anti-Jewish publicist and proponent of "Algerian" settler independence, expressed his intent to join the Boer struggle, hoping, perhaps, to gain insight on how to achieve his political objectives in Algeria.[91] The tendency of the separatists to use the experience of the Boers as a template was later denounced by some of their former followers, such as Augustin Castéran, who came to believe that the "foreign danger" posed by settlers of non-French origin was greater than the "Jewish danger"—or even the "Arab danger"—in Algeria and rallied to support French authority.[92]

Other journalists, however, drew different conclusions from the South African War and the public interest it had elicited among settlers in Algeria. The horrors of the conflict, Jules Aime of *L'Union latine* suggested, served not as an incitement to embrace nationalism, but as a clear warning against it. While he readily joined his colleagues in condemning the inaction of "civilized and civilizing nations that have impassively allowed the massacre of these unhappy settlers," he could not agree that emulating such egotism served his readers' best interests. Instead, Aime exhorted, settlers should become "men who know how to reach out across borders, because fraternity cannot be contained by mountains and rivers."[93] It was the fraternity of Latin peoples, in particular, Aime suggested, that would not only ensure prosperity at a local level but also safeguard against "Germano-Saxon" aggression in Europe and lay a strong foundation for "universal peace."[94] Rather than pursue a violent struggle for independence from France, settlers were encouraged to see themselves as part of a wider Latin community of which the French nation was already a part.

This emphasis on Latin fraternity had been similarly reinforced by local press reactions to the ongoing struggle between the Spanish government and independence fighters in Cuba in the 1880s and 1890s. The conflict was covered in detail in a number of francophone, hispanophone, and bilingual newspapers. Coverage was based on the retransmission of news featured in overseas publications and the additional commentary or analysis of local settler journalists. As the conflict assumed international dimensions in the 1890s, with the diplomatic and then military involvement of the United States, the circuits of information that sustained local reporting similarly expanded. Whereas during the early 1880s small bilingual newspapers such as *El Patuet* and *Fraternidad obrera* had relied primarily on information from colleagues in Spain and Cuba,[95] by the late 1890s more widely circulating papers such as *El Correo español* and *La Dépêche algérienne* were also referring to the publications and opinions of fellow journalists in France, Italy, Austria, and the United States.[96]

Despite the extensive coverage of the events in Cuba, the insurgence of the racially diverse Cuban population failed to garner the same level of popular support in Algeria as had the struggle of the Boers. Although some journalists of Spanish origin expressed admiration for the Cuban rebels, based on their shared republicanism, most opposed the rebellion as a threat to Spanish national strength. Hence, while journalists at *El Mosquito español* declared their support for "the aspirations of the Cuban leader and ardent republican, Don José Maceo," their colleagues at another republican newspaper, *El Patuet*, denounced the conflict as a "political cancer" that depleted Spanish resources.[97] This latter interpretation was shared by journalists at the more conservative hispanophone paper *El Correo español* and at the francophone Oranais publication *L'Ami du peuple*, both of which encouraged Spanish nationals to enlist through the Spanish consulate in Algeria to support the national campaign.[98] The widespread opposition to the Cuban rebellion expressed by journalists of Spanish origin in Algeria echoed that of their colleagues in the peninsula, where, as Christopher Schmidt-Nowara explains, the common defense of the empire encouraged Spaniards to overcome the fractures and tensions of domestic politics.[99]

The Cuban rebellion, as some francophone journalists in Algeria pointed out, also ran counter to the interests of the French nation. Not only did French authority over its possessions in the Caribbean depend on stability in the region, insisted French journalist A. Bloeme in the Franco-Spanish newspaper *Fraternidad obrera*, but also French security in Europe depended on promoting good relations with their Spanish neighbors.[100] This opinion was reiterated in extracts from the French metropolitan papers that were widely disseminated in *El Correo español* and *La Dépêche algérienne*.[101] *El Correo español* was particularly pleased to relay an article titled "Viva España!" from the Parisian daily *Le Gaulois*, which attempted to dissuade French journalists from showing support for the Cuban insurgents: "What would these supporters say, writes the journalist, if Spaniards made the same arguments in relation to Tunisia, Algeria, or Madagascar!"[102] Local reporting on the events in Cuba thus encouraged settlers of French and Spanish origin in Algeria to recognize the distinct interests of their separate national communities, while acknowledging the mutual benefit of supporting each other's claims to sovereignty across their respective empires.

This mutual recognition of sovereignty, some journalists suggested, was the natural result of the wider Latin community of which each national community was a part. As well as encouraging readers to identify as Spaniards or Frenchmen, reactions to the events in Cuba encouraged them to see themselves as Latin. In addition to the particular threats posed to Spain and France, warned journalist A. Bloeme, the uprising in Cuba would be "*the curse . . . of the entire Latin race.*" Instability in the Caribbean, Bloeme explained, would enable the intervention of "the Yankees," who would not only extend their political influence but also exert cultural domination, imposing the English language on a Latin population.[103] Hostility toward "Yankee jingoism" increased in the 1890s, particularly in the Spanish-language press, as reports of American political and media hyperbole reached settler journalists in Algeria.[104] Antipathy toward American actions strengthened settler journalists' suspicion of Germano-Saxon aggression, which had been similarly identified in British and German foreign policies.[105]

The coincidence of the war in Cuba with nationalist uprisings in the Spanish Philippines, Italian setbacks in Eritrea, and bloody riots in Milan in 1898 served only to reinforce local journalists' calls for stability through Latin solidarity. *L'Ami du peuple*, whose revolutionary-inspired title masked its clerical perspective, saw in these events collectively not only proof of an international conspiracy of freemasons but also evidence of a malevolent "Teutonic" or "Anglo-Saxon" hand.[106] "If the lesson could at least serve to prove, once and for all, to our Latin brothers," pleaded the paper, "that there is nothing to be gained but cynical exploitation and irremediable decadence in letting ourselves be absorbed by countries of the Anglo-Saxon race."[107] As journalists reacted to these shifts in geopolitics and demographic developments within Algeria, a Latin community increasingly imagined in terms of race, rather than republicanism, came to unite the disparate political tendencies of the settler press.

Although the racial dimension of Latin identity was not absent from contemporaneous calls for solidarity from sectors of the French metropolitan press in the tense decades preceding the First World War, it held particular salience in Algeria, where demographers, scientists, and journalists believed that a "new white race" was already in the making.[108] "It is certain that in Algeria," explained *L'Union latine*, referring to the opinion of Gaston Laforêt of the *Bulletin des Renseignements Coloniaux*, "the various peoples of Latin civilization have found the crucible in which to effect their intimate fusion."[109] The local "fusion of races," the paper asserted in another article on the topic, would produce "the neo-Latin race, composed of diverse elements each attenuated by their union." This new racial community would not efface the specificity of each national group of settlers, but would ensure their harmonious interaction for the benefit of the colony, their nations of origin, and indeed, the whole world. "In maintaining our own originality let us each use our particular qualities for the benefit of all," the paper exhorted its mixed readership.[110]

The format of the paper echoed this advice, designating separate French, Spanish, and Italian sections, but featuring local news in each. Yet if the multilingual *Union latine* was the most determined of settler publications to pursue the creation of the Latin race, it was not alone in recognizing its development in Algeria. Even *La Dépêche algérienne*, which remained unambiguously loyal to French authority, could not deny the evidence put forward by local demographers: "A slow but sure fusion of races is taking place in Algeria," reported journalist Eugene Lagadec, "which, over a period of time as yet unknown, will lead to the formation of a distinct new race." It was only to be hoped, he added from the French perspective, that the French racial contribution would continue to predominate.[111]

In portraying the "Algerian" settler colony as the crucible of a neo-Latin race, journalists helped shift the focus from the question of independence to the goal of greater autonomy within the French Empire. If settlers could ensure that France remained connected to a global community in which degrees of Latin difference were recognized, then they had no urgent need to break from the French nation. Instead, they could use their status as gatekeepers to a wider Latin world to renegotiate their relationship with the metropole. Press campaigns for greater autonomy gained momentum in the 1890s, as some journalists began to suggest that the example to follow was not, after all, that of the United States, but that of the British self-governing colonies in Canada or Australia.[112] In these territories, a journalist from *Le Progrès algérien* explained to his readers, settlers had their own parliaments and armed forces and could decide for themselves when cooperation with the metropolitan government was advisable. Though settlers in Algeria may not choose to seek such extensive liberties, the journalist added, "it is the desire and expectation of each of us that, financially and politically, we will be endowed with bodies that allow us to develop our wealth and make use of the resources of this land while taking account of its needs."[113]

These expectations were only partially met by the creation in 1901 of the Délégations financières, an elected colonial assembly with a measure of responsibility for the distribution of the colonial budget.[114] For many journalists and their readers, the autonomy provided by this institution was both illusory and costly. As one angry reader of Le Tell fumed in a letter to the editors, "It is said that they [the Délégations financières] are left to foot the bill, without having a say in how to spend the money!"[115] To reinforce the political authority of settlers, some journalists suggested a process of devolution that would end settler representation in the French parliament and replace it with the settler government of "French Africa"—a space including both Algeria and Tunisia and opening onto the rest of the continent. "With the adoption of financial autonomy and North African colonial unity, there is no more need for [settler] parliamentary representation," explained a journalist from Le Petit oranais. "It is not in Paris but in Algiers—the capital and heart of French Africa—that the representatives of Algeria must be based: it's a matter of logic."[116]

The results of devolution, warned Félix Dessoliers in L'Algérie, could not be predicted. Although it was possible, he supposed, that the process might ultimately lead to settler independence, it was certain that in the interim a productive relationship between metropole and colony could be achieved—such was the lesson he took from observing the development of the British self-governing colonies.[117] In creating a system in which separate states were united within the same community, however, the British Empire had also provided a model for those journalists who sought to place the settler community in Algeria at the center of an alliance of Latin peoples. In strengthening the bonds of Latin fraternity among France, Spain, and Italy, a journalist at Oran journal explained, settlers in Algeria provided "the basis of a Latin confederation intended to protect humanity, maintain peace, and illuminate and beautify the world."[118]

Absent from settler journalists' discussions of the new Latin racial formation were the Algerian Jews and Muslim *indigènes* of the colonial territory. Their exclusion from both the local "Algerian" community and the global Latin community imagined by settler journalists was justified in terms that increasingly combined the language of race with that of cultural or religious difference. This imagination depended in part on a process of identification supported by the multiple new points of reference provided by an expanded global telecommunications network. Although this network privileged connections between the settler colony and the French metropole, it also brought Europeans in Algeria into ever closer contact with their diverse countries of origin, the empires and former empires of these countries, and other settler colonies around the world. As the horizons of journalists and their readers broadened, their sense of place became more sharply defined. As Latins and "Algerians," their rejection of indigenous peoples was even more clearly articulated.

Increasingly drawn into the global telecommunications network in the 1880s and 1890s, settler journalists nevertheless maintained a diversity of production practices, enabling them to assemble the news from multiple sources rather than submit to a stream of information from the metropole. Although the process of press assemblage reflected the triangular dynamics of the settler colonial situation, journalists called on a wider set of referents provided by the expanding network of telegraphic connections across the globe. While this network tied the settler colony to the French metropole, it also reinforced journalists' and readers' preexisting connections with their diverse countries of origin and provided them with points of comparison in other settler colonies around the world. As news flowed into the settler colony from these various locations, journalists promoted an understanding of "Algerian" community that allowed settlers to move freely among local, national, and transnational senses of affiliation.

In framing processes of identification among journalists and readers, the global telecommunications network also shaped local press debates on autonomy, assimilation, and administrative reform. Profoundly attached to the revolutionary heritage of the French Republic, many journalists wondered whether settlers should launch their own revolution to establish a new source of national strength to replace that long since exhausted in the metropole. Tempted by the economic and political success of the United States since its independence from Great Britain, journalists in Algeria looked to other settler colonies to discern their path to progress. While the hardy Boers' stand captured their imagination, the violence of the South African War served as a precaution against too hasty a move to rebellion. News of the bloody conflict in Cuba, moreover, deterred journalists from this path, especially when the consequences for the balance of power within Europe and the fate of their own readers' countries of origin were taken into account.

Rather than pursue an independent "Algerian" nation, therefore, settler journalists emphasized the transnational Latin dimension of the local settler community. If references to a Latin republic served for a time to forge ties between settlers of French and Spanish origin and encourage their Italian counterparts to renounce tyranny and militate against the Triple Alliance, these references were increasingly supplanted by the language of racial belonging. As Latins, bound by blood, journalists and their readers were able to invoke the protection of the French state without sacrificing their cultural and linguistic differences.

The positive affirmation of such differences among journalists, however, did not extend to the Jewish and Muslim populations of Algeria. If the telegraph and the news it brought had the power to bring differently situated groups together, they also had the potential to divide. These divisions were less the result of a dichotomy between those who were encouraged to regard events in France as domestic news and those who were not than the consequence of unequal access to the global points of identification that allowed journalists and readers to combine local, national, and transnational senses of belonging. Latin by neither blood nor culture, Muslims and Jews were violently rejected by settler journalists from both the local community of "Algerians" and the wider community of the French nation.

The dynamics of inclusion and exclusion inherent in the imagination of a Latin people in Algeria were further exposed by the contemporaneous development of bilingual and multilingual publications. These publications provided another means of forging connections across frontiers, yet they remained freighted by the inequalities of the settler colonial context.

5

...

Algerians of Any Nationality

Articulating Communities in Multilingual Publications

"One for all and all for one," exclaimed the editors of the new publication *L'Union latine* in April 1903.[1] It was, they felt, an apt slogan for a multilingual publication that aimed to ensure the unity of settlers of diverse national origin. "All for one and one for all," reprised the editors of bilingual Franco-Arabic publication *El Hack* several years later, encouraging solidarity among Muslims in their quest for greater religious diversity within the French nation.[2] Slogans of this kind became the rallying call of the significant number of multilingual publications that appeared in Algeria between 1870 and 1914.[3] The era marked the heyday of the multilingual press in the colonial territory, as such newspapers attained greater numbers and a wider diversity of formats than in preceding and subsequent periods. Alongside trilingual newspapers in French, Spanish, and Italian, readers encountered bilingual publications that combined French with Spanish, Italian, Arabic, or Hebrew. Each title combined different languages in specific ways in pursuit of particular political objectives. Despite their differences, these newspapers were founded on the common belief that in promoting the interaction of languages and cultures, the press could help construct a new society. In providing a forum for this interaction, multilingual newspapers became physical manifestations of what postcolonial theorist Homi Bhabha refers to as a "third space," a space from which new forms and codes might emerge.[4]

Multilingual publications reflected the social reality of Algeria as a zone of "language contact," in which multiple European and indigenous languages were spoken and high levels of bi- or multilingualism were present among certain migrant and indigenous communities.[5] Linguistic diversity persisted in this era despite official attempts to impose the use of the French language through education, military service, and the forced naturalization of some sectors of the population. Indeed, as Juan Bautista Vilar observes in his study of language use among Spanish settlers, multilingualism was as much a result of the success of the French assimilation policy in Algeria as it was of its failure, giving those with access to French schooling and citizenship a new language in which to ask questions about their preexisting cultural heritage.[6] Such was the experience of the Algerian Jews, collectively enfranchised in 1870, and the descendants of European settlers born in Algeria, who became French citizens in 1889. For Muslims, however, this access remained restricted. While around 90 percent of Algerian-born Europeans were attending French schools by the early years of the twentieth century,[7] only a small number of Muslim children were enrolled in colonial schools. According to Charles-Robert Ageron, only 2 percent of the Muslim school-age population received a primary education in 1890, and 5 percent in 1914; of these students, only 100 to 150 progressed to secondary school each year.[8] Consequently, few naturalized and French-educated Muslim elites ever expressed themselves in French in the press.

In a context in which language marked social status and political authority, journalists' primary motivation in founding multilingual publications was a desire to effect social or political change. This objective certainly overrode any commercial consideration: although particularly vibrant in this era, bi- and multilingual publications remained but a small niche in the wider field of the press in Algeria. Franco-Arabic papers, estimates Zahir Ihaddaden, attained circulation rates of three hundred to three thousand,[9] and even given the greater access to French education for foreign European settlers beginning in the late 1880s, papers targeting this readership were unlikely to have exceeded the upper figure by any considerable amount. Like the multitude of other local weeklies produced in this era, these publications were sustained by hardworking individuals or small teams of contributors driven by their desire to reimagine the boundaries and hierarchies of colonial society. They hoped to achieve this through promoting and managing interaction among different ethnolinguistic groups. If evidence of language contact could also be found in monolingual French newspapers—in short stories in the local dialect of *pataouète*, letters from readers written in *sabir*, or articles composed in phonetic spelling[10]—it was in multilingual papers that contemporary journalistic debates about the relationship between language and society were made explicit.

Imbued, like their contemporaries in Europe, with the romantic belief that language revealed the unique character of a people, journalists in Algeria attempted to use language as a tool to refashion the internal and external frontiers of the society in which they lived.[11] Yet language mixing, Jocelyne Dakhlia observes, "is not in itself . . . a positive value; it may denote oppression, power struggle, and hatred as much as, or more often than, it denotes harmonious coexistence."[12] While the inclusion of different languages within the pages of a single publication encouraged differently situated readers to recognize one another as part of the same public, interactions within this public were framed by editorial choices concerning the column inches given over to each language, their spatial arrangement on the page, the degree of linguistic interference and exchange, and the direction and frequency of translation. These decisions revealed the highly political nature of language use in the settler colony and could mean the difference between a journalistic declaration of equality among ethnolinguistic communities and the assumption of cultural supremacy by one party intent on transforming or assimilating another.

The political nature of language use in colonial and postcolonial settings has been widely recognized by scholars, who have pointed to "linguicism," or the elaboration of linguistic hierarchies by politically dominant groups.[13] In Algeria, writes Mohamed Benrabah, "the colonizer's monolingualism and accent were allocated much higher prestige than the colonized's linguistic forms."[14] The devaluation of indigenous languages sustained the representation of indigenous peoples as uncivilized and served to justify their exclusion from public debate and political participation. Within this broad division between the languages of the colonizer and the colonized, the French attributed different cultural values to different indigenous languages, distinguishing, for example, between Arabic and Berber languages within the ideological framework of the "Kabyle myth."[15] This differential treatment left its mark in postindependence Algeria, where Tamazight speakers have struggled to overcome the effects of the official policy of arabization, instigated by the government in an effort to reverse the effects of linguistic imperialism.[16]

The impact of the specific dynamics of the settler colonial situation on language politics, however, has attracted significantly less attention from scholars. Although most settler colonies were populated by migrants from diverse European countries, the question of their linguistic differences has often been overlooked amid the scholarly focus on the "register of sameness" underpinning settlers' quest for cultural and political sovereignty.[17] Even those studies that recognize the transnational character of settler colonial formations emphasize the prior elaboration of cultural or political unity among migrants of disparate origins. Hence the question of linguistic difference has been posed neither of the "British world," which linked Great Britain and the self-governing dominions, nor of the wider "Anglo world," which incorporated the United States, where anglophone arrivals, according to James Belich, simply "swallowed" other European migrant populations.[18]

That the linguistic hierarchies elaborated by politically dominant groups in settler colonies also attributed inferior status to the languages of other European migrant populations is beyond doubt. In Algeria, Andrea Smith observes, Orientalist perceptions of the Maltese language, derived from a form of Arabic, contributed to the social marginalization of settlers from Malta by the French and other Europeans.[19] Linguistic prejudice supplemented class prejudice as socially elite French settlers disparaged the expression and accents of their Spanish and Italian counterparts.[20] Yet these linguistic hierarchies—while framing the extent and nature of language contact among settlers of different origins—did not prevent contact altogether.[21] The existence of this contact, and the forms of community it engendered, cautions against assumption of the monolingualism of the colonizer in a settler colonial setting.

Language contact in the press in Algeria has been further obscured by the historiographical focus on the role of the press in France in the consolidation of the "one and indivisible" national community that had defended its freedom since the revolution of 1789.[22] The national frame of reference, Diana Cooper-Richet points out, has limited historical inquiry into publications in foreign languages, despite their potential to illuminate the "vast network of international cultural transfer and journalistic practice" that developed in the nineteenth century.[23] Such studies as do exist, moreover, emphasize the role of foreign-language publications in the preservation of national forms of identification among discrete ethnolinguistic communities.[24] In their strategic combination of languages, however, bi- and multilingual newspapers destabilized the widely accepted contemporary belief in the triangular correspondence of language, nation, and identity. This powerful triumvirate was especially potent in the French political imaginary,[25] and in combining French with indigenous and foreign European languages, journalists in Algeria offered new ways of imagining the French nation.

The proposed nature of this reimagining depended on the relationship to the French national community of each journalist and the group of readers that journalist claimed to write for. As French citizens and targets of settler prejudice, Jewish journalists proved to be the most ardent champions of assimilation. In Franco-Hebraic and Franco-Judeo-Arabic publications, therefore, bilingualism was framed as a temporary measure—a practical necessity that would bring about the full francization of the local Jewish population. While some Muslim journalists took a similar approach, presenting Franco-Arabic publications as an extension of the pedagogical mission of the republican government, most others in this era used bilingualism as an expression of equality between two peoples with different beliefs and customs. This approach, which journalists referred to as "rapprochement,"[26] reflected a wider shift in French colonial policy from "assimilation" to "association" in the context of the establishment of protectorate governments in Tunisia in 1881 and Morocco in 1912.[27] Both strategies represented responses to the social and political vulnerability of Muslims and Jews in Algeria and aimed ultimately to improve the material conditions and status of these groups by demonstrating the ability of Judaism and Islam to reside within the French nation. The efforts of journalists to navigate between national unity and religious diversity in these years were rendered all the more perilous by the growth of anticlerical sentiment under the Third Republic and the political suspicion toward religious communities, which would lead to the separation of church and state in 1905.[28]

While Jewish and Muslim journalists were obliged to prioritize the construction of a more diverse French national community, often subordinating local and transnational forms of identification to this end, foreign European settler journalists sought to evade French nationality until it was imposed on them by the collective naturalization of 1889. Bilingual settler publications of the early 1880s thus emphasized the separate national identities of settlers of different origins. Faced with imperialist rivalry and diplomatic rifts between European governments, however, editors also found it necessary to emphasize the shared local experience and common Latin heritage of migrant groups in an effort to calm tensions in the mixed settler colony and protect migrants of foreign European origin. Journalists increasingly defined Latin heritage in terms of a compatibility of racial origins and sensibilities, allowing them to circumvent the language of religious community.

The emphasis on local experience and transnational Latin civilization proved especially useful to settler journalists in the wake of the 1889 law, as bi- and multilingual newspapers sought to offer readers a way of reconciling their cultural heritage with their newfound political status as French citizens. As did the use of the regional dialect of *pataouète* spoken by settlers of lower social classes, therefore, multilingual settler publications actively contributed to the definition of a local "Algerian" settler community conscious of its cultural particularity.[29] Unlike this dynamic, primarily oral form of communication, however, multilingual newspapers attempted to codify the interaction of different European languages and safeguard their distinctive traits. In so doing, they sought to extend the privileges of the colonizer beyond the framework of a linguistically homogenous French nation to a Latin racial community that included native speakers of Spanish and Italian and excluded Muslims and Jews.

For calling into question the correspondence of language, identity, and nation, multilingual papers earned the suspicion of the French authorities and some settler journalists of French origin, who worried about "the deformation of the French language in Algeria" as a result of contact with other idioms. In an article that appeared in both *Le Tell* and *Le Petit oranais*, W. Marial expressed concern that local particularities of expression reflected the deformity of a local "mentality" that appeared "somewhat different from that of the metropole."[30] Similarly perceived as incompletely French in form and spirit, bi- and multilingual newspapers were sometimes simply categorized as foreign newspapers by the colonial government, rendering them subject to suspension by administrative decree in accordance with article 14 of the 1881 law regulating the press. The vulnerable status of these papers—which could find themselves accused of antigovernmental discourse by zealous administrators, members of opposing interest groups, or professional rivals—contributed to the ephemeral nature of many titles and frequent revisions of format, as journalists rearranged the order and ratio of articles in different languages in an effort to demonstrate their benign intent. This vulnerability was amplified for Franco-Arabic publications, which were regarded as a particular threat by the administration and settler journalists alike.[31]

Regarded with suspicion by the French authorities and ill equipped to compete with the information-based commercial productions that consolidated their hold on the colonial market in the interwar period, bi- and multilingual publications all but disappeared after the First World War. The forms of community they advocated, however, lived on in the imagination of journalists and their readers. If Jews in Algeria were obliged to continue defending their place in the French national community and Muslims were pushed to imagine an alternative national community, this was due in part to settlers' increasing identification with a transnational Latin community of race and sensibility that had found its most direct expression in the local context.

National Unity and Religious Diversity

Bilingual papers combining French with Arabic, Hebrew, or Judeo-Arabic provided the first experience of engagement with the press for many writers and readers from Muslim and Jewish communities in Algeria. Working alone or in collaboration with French colleagues from the metropole, Muslim and Jewish journalists in Algeria produced papers that defended the place of their coreligionists within the French nation. Differently situated in relation to French authority, however, journalists from these two religious communities moved between languages in different ways. While most Muslim journalists in this era adopted bilingualism as a potent symbol of contact between two peoples who respected each other's cultural and religious differences while working toward an equality of status, others emulated their Jewish colleagues in using the bilingual format to promote the assimilation of their coreligionists into French cultural ideals. Despite their different approaches to language use, the journalists at these publications privileged the reimagining of the French national community, often subordinating the local and transnational dimensions of their readers' identification to the process of developing their sense of national belonging.

From Information to Rapprochement
in Franco-Arabic Publications

The first example of a bilingual publication in Algeria, *Le Moniteur algérien*, launched by the colonial administration in 1832, was but the second newspaper to be printed in the colonial territory. Divided into two distinct sections, French and Arabic, the official newspaper publicized laws and decrees, royal proclamations, and scientific studies related to colonial development.[32] The paper, later criticized by settler journalists for its selection of "laudatory articles" concerning the colonial administration,[33] was designed to serve the needs of the colonial government by disseminating selected information and openly promoting French authority. A second official newspaper, Le Mobacher, followed in 1848 and maintained the bilingual, Franco-Arabic format.[34] Founded by French administrator Ismaÿl Urbain, a convert to Islam and a defender of the Muslim community in Algeria, the paper was envisaged as a means to educate Arabic readers about the nature of the French polity.[35] Rapidly reduced to little more than a rough summary of the news presented in the French version, however, Le Mobacher disappointed Urbain and, notes Christiane Souriau-Hoebrechts, "enjoyed a monopoly on the Arabic-language press in Algeria *almost until the end of the century!*"[36] Subsequent bilingual publications established by the administration and distributed in Algeria—Le Sada in 1876 and L'Astre de l'Orient in 1882—were printed in Paris, reinforcing by their proximity to the seat of government what Zahir Ihaddaden identifies as "the French authorities' preoccupation with limiting the [Arabic] press to its simplest expression as a means of communication."[37]

Although official attempts to control the use of Arabic in the press continued in the decades around the turn of the century, the administration increasingly moved away from the bilingual format. While Le Mobacher continued to appear in both French and Arabic, from the 1880s all new governmental publications were to be monolingual, produced in one language or the other. This change of approach signaled the transition to the policy of association, under Governor General Jonnart, who favored the parallel development of Muslim civilization under French guidance over the imposition of French customs and values on the Arabo-Berber population. The absence of intercommunal dialogue in these official publications, however, left considerable room for doubt as to how the French hoped to achieve the moral and material uplift they had promised. For the European and Muslim journalists who supported the new objectives of the administration, explains Ihaddaden, "the best way to serve this policy was to encourage the development of a bilingual press."[38] As well as being a symbol of the effective association of two peoples, bilingual publications also provided a strategic means of holding the government to account.

These origins and objectives framed the development of an independent bilingual press for Muslim readers, encouraging the use of a Franco-Arabic format. Linguistic and ethnic differences among Muslims themselves were thereby subsumed to their community of faith as journalists sought primarily to defend the place of Islam within the French nation. Supportive of French rule and focused on establishing a dialogue of equals between Muslims and the French colonizers, independent Franco-Arabic publications defended the principles on which the French nation had been founded and used these principles as the basis of their arguments for a reimagining of the national community.[39] The earliest such publication, *El Montakheb*, announced, quoting from the revolutionary *Declaration of the Rights of Man and Citizen*, "The first article of freedom is this: 'all citizens are equal before the law.' Well, we want indigenous Muslims to also be equal before the law."[40] This guiding principle underpinned a program of demands, including the suppression of the separate legal regime applied to Muslim subjects, an end to land expropriation and administrative corruption, and the political representation of the Muslim population. In establishing this program, *El Montakheb* set the tone for many of the Franco-Arabic publications that appeared in the following decades.

This, indeed, was the second objective of *El Montakheb*, which aimed to instruct the Muslim subjects of Algeria in the political uses of the press. "You don't yet know what the press is, you don't know its power, you don't know its value!" exclaimed the paper, addressing its "coreligionists" in French and Arabic. "It is a lever that can lift up a world and take it out of the orbit it has followed for centuries."[41] Although the publication presented itself, upon its launch in April 1882, as the creation of a group of Muslim notables from Constantine, the sustained hostility of settler journalists forced the editor, Paul Etienne, to reveal that "those behind the creation of *El Montakheb* are of French race."[42] The publication had close links with the Society for the Protection of Indigènes, established in Paris in 1881 by Paul Leroy-Beaulieu, and it is likely that this organization facilitated the publication of the newspaper. Created by indigenophile Frenchmen rather than by Muslims themselves, the paper nevertheless explicitly solicited contributions from Muslim readers, reminding them that "*El Montakheb* is their newspaper, that it is entirely at their disposition, that it is their organ, their tribune."[43] By entering the public sphere through participation in the press, Etienne urged, Muslims would also guarantee their place in the national community. "All races, all sects, all religions, all strands of opinion have a banner, and civilization has made this banner the newspaper," proclaimed the opening article of the first edition of the paper. In creating this paper, Etienne announced, he and his collaborators had given Muslims in Algeria "the means to defend themselves through the great voice of the press."[44] In so doing, he continued, *El Montakheb* had led Muslims "into a new phase," a phase in which demands would be conveyed by the peaceful yet powerful means of the press, rather than through revolts and uprisings.[45]

Paternalistic in their approach, the founders of *El Montakheb* overlooked the extent to which Muslims in Algeria were exposed—despite the best efforts of the colonial administration—to other models of press production, originating in the Eastern Mediterranean.[46] The paper nevertheless influenced Muslim writers in Algeria in the final decades of the nineteenth century, contributing to the development of a new sector of the colonial press. Writing in the first issue of *El Hack* of Bône in 1893, Baba-Osman acknowledged the support of "indigenophile" French journalists before declaring, "Today, we speak for ourselves." The paper's editor, Omar Samar, writing as Zeïd ben Dieb, hoped that their voices would be "heard and taken into consideration by the government."[47] Subsequent publications sought to consolidate the place of Muslims within the French public sphere. In 1912 the editors of another newspaper, also called *El Hack*, took this endeavor quite literally, organizing a two-week tour of France for readers in the hope that it would deepen their love for their adoptive mother country and expose the French public to Muslims' views on a variety of topics.[48] The mutually enriching dialogue envisioned by the editors was an extension of the bilingual format they also came to espouse.[49]

In addition to contributing to the growth of press activity among Muslims in Algeria, *El Montakheb* helped establish a precedent for bilingual expression. This format remained prevalent even after the administrative injunction to provide the French translation of Arabic text was lifted in 1886. The injunction had little troubled *El Montakheb*, in which French constituted the principal language and selected articles were translated into Arabic. The newspaper experimented with a number of formats, first printing French and Arabic articles on each page, then printing a first page in French, a second page in both languages, and a third page in Arabic, and finally settling into a pattern of providing a French section of two to three pages followed by an Arabic section of one to two pages. This model was taken up by the majority of Franco-Arabic publications established in subsequent years by both Muslim and indigenophile French journalists and expressed their desire to change the experience of Muslims under French rule without challenging this rule itself. These newspapers typically presented themselves as Muslim publications, addressing both the indigenous elite, among whom they urged solidarity, and the wider French public, whom they hoped to disabuse of Orientalist stereotypes of Islamic fanaticism.

Among the changes required for Muslims to be truly accepted into the French national community, journalists at these publications agreed, was the abolition of the *indigénat*, the separate legal regime applied to Muslim subjects in Algeria as a result of the perceived incompatibility of their faith with French civil law. The differential legal treatment of colonial populations began during the first years of the conquest, when Muslims and Jews were defined as French subjects without full national status.[50] Access to this status was finally afforded by the *sénatus-consulte* of 1865, which reiterated the distinction between citizens and subjects and authorized the naturalization of the latter on the condition that they renounce the particular civil status defined by their faith.[51] Although the Jews of Algeria were collectively emancipated in 1870, the Muslims were not, and the legal distinction between citizens and subjects legitimized a range of restrictions on the latter, denying or severely limiting their freedom of movement, reunion, and expression and authorizing particular forms of punishment, including the nefarious principle of collective responsibility.[52]

These restrictions were codified in 1881, giving added impetus to the development of a bilingual press that aimed to show how both linguistic and religious differences could be accommodated within the national community. Disparaged as "arbitrary" by *El Montakheb* in 1882, the *indigénat* became the principal target of critique for Franco-Arabic publications, including some that favored assimilation over association. For the journalists at these publications, the separate legal status of Muslims was incompatible with both the French mission in Algeria and the wider values of the French nation.[53] It served, noted *Le Croissant*, as "a code of *servile*, not *civil*, education," preventing the exercise of true liberty.[54] "Let us list . . . the abuses of the gentle name of *Liberty*, which is one of the principal symbols of the republic," proposed A. Risa at *El Hack*, citing a range of activities that were forbidden to Muslim subjects. Alongside activities formally proscribed by the law, such as traveling without prior authorization, Risa noted with irony the inability of the Muslim subject to "express his grievances without being accused of stirring up trouble" or "read an independent newspaper without being imprisoned or threatened."[55]

The campaign against the *indigénat* was accompanied by fierce opposition to land requisition, which Muslim subjects found themselves legally prevented from effectively resisting, and to administrative corruption, which thrived as those subjects who were able to do so attempted to buy their way out of the restrictions imposed on them. Both practices, noted journalists, were detrimental to French authority in Algeria: not only did the vulnerability of dispossession render Muslim subjects "inactive and unproductive" but also the obligation to deal with corrupt intermediaries weakened their trust in the administration.[56] While specific instances of expropriation or corruption were localized, journalists suggested, their consequences were felt across the territory. "Injustice," noted *Le Croissant*, was "unanimous," with bribery the only guarantee of leniency toward Muslim subjects "from Oranie to Numidia, from the Mediterranean to the Sahara."[57] Hence, while journalists readily called on localized examples to illustrate their points, they presented these examples as evidence of a national problem that France needed to solve, in its own interests. In so doing, they further reinforced the claims of Muslims as devoted members of a French national community.

If local examples could be employed in service of a larger national cause, transnational forms of identification among Muslims were more explicitly denied in order to reassure the authorities and the volatile settler population that Islam posed no threat to French rule. Journalists at Franco-Arabic publications were thus at pains to fend off repeated accusations of Pan-Islamism. Settler journalists, *Le Croissant* and *El Hack* lamented, were liable to see a Pan-Islamic conspiracy behind every complaint or request made by a Muslim journalist or any other representative of the Muslim community.[58] European suspicion of Pan-Islamism mounted as diplomatic fractures on the continent made the prospect of war ever more likely and raised the dual questions of whether and how the Ottoman Empire would be accommodated in the system of alliances among European powers.

In France, this looming prospect also generated debate about the loyalty and reliability of the nation's Muslim subjects and framed discussions over conscription in Algeria between 1908 and 1912. Anxieties among French journalists—in both the metropole and the settler colony— became increasingly apparent in the context of the Italo-Turkish conflict from 1911 to 1912, giving renewed vigor to stereotypes of Muslim cruelty and barbarity in some sectors of the press. These attacks prompted a series of articles in *El Hack* of Oran, in which journalists emphasized the peaceful and reasonable nature of Islam. "It is said that Muslims are fanatics," wrote a Muslim woman from Constantinople whose complaint to *Le Temps* was reproduced in *El Hack*. "My God, what a mistake! The fanatics are those who rally against Islam and invent a thousand untruths about it, each one more ridiculous than the last." Islam, assured El-Faradj of *El Hack*, was no obstacle to French patriotism: "We are Muslims, it's true—but in contrast to what the arabophobes claim, this in no way prevents us from having France as our homeland and Humanity as our dogma."[59]

This sentiment was consistently put to the test over the course of the era, as French influence spread into the neighboring territories of Tunisia and Morocco. Faced with the reality of French domination in North Africa, journalists at Franco-Arabic publications affirmed their support for French influence and pointed out the positive effects they believed it would have on Muslims across the region. Launched in the same year as the protectorate in Tunisia, *El Montakheb* closely followed the debates surrounding the administrative organization of the territory, promoting French intervention in both its French and Arabic language sections.[60] As French intentions in Morocco were clarified in the early twentieth century, journalists frequently held up the Tunisian protectorate as an example of association policy at work, pointing out the relative vitality of the indigenous press and learned societies. Islam in Tunisia, observed *El Hack*—as in other Muslims countries with a lively press and contact with Europeans—was a more progressive force than Islam in the sultanate.[61]

Such observations constituted attempts both to advise the French government in its Moroccan policy and to reconcile Muslims across North Africa to French rule. This latter objective contributed to the decision of the editors of *El Hack* to adopt a bilingual format in 1912, noting that "the Cherifian people are waiting with great impatience for our Arabic edition to appear."[62]

Support for French expansion in Morocco, moreover, was motivated by the hope that Muslims in Algeria would benefit from the consolidation of French authority and the administrative reforms that this might engender. For many journalists at Franco-Arabic publications, the relative freedom of the protectorate context seemed preferable to the situation endured by Muslims in Algeria. In addition to regularly comparing administrative arrangements across North Africa, journalists at Franco-Arabic publications pointed to reforms in colonial territories elsewhere in the world as evidence of how an empire might be differently managed. Comparisons with France's greatest imperial rival, Great Britain, were of particular strategic value. Noting a measure in India that would allow for greater indigenous representation at municipal and provincial levels, *El Montakheb* asked, "Why not, in Algeria, be inspired by these useful and humanitarian reforms that England—the nation that is said to possess colonizing genius par excellence—offers as an example?"[63] Characteristically, *Le Croissant* was more forthright in making the comparison: "Will it be said that the great, humanitarian France, defender of the rights of man, follows a more heinous policy than Albion?"[64]

Le Croissant indeed was the only Franco-Arabic newspaper to openly oppose French expansion in North Africa. In a series of articles, journalists at the paper denounced the ways in which their metropolitan colleagues, "supported by financial syndicates whose only aim is . . . to spoil everything, use their columns to spread dissent between peoples, disseminate outrageously exaggerated news, and inflate the smallest incidents to ridiculous proportions" in an effort to provide a "plausible pretext" for French intervention.[65] In rejecting France's Moroccan policy, the newspaper developed the basis of a wider anticolonial discourse: the invasion of the sultanate, one journalist noted, would be but the latest in a series of morally questionable French military operations, "after Annam and Tonkin, after Madagascar and the Chinese war, after the horrible sacking of Dahomey." "By what right do we impose our faults on them?" demanded the writer, seemingly of French origin. "By what right do we seek to become masters in their lands? Europe never asked itself these questions. It just saw a new field of exploitation, and the delegates of the great powers came together in the Bay of Algeciras to discuss how to divide up the most beautiful country in North Africa."[66] This line of argumentation earned *Le Croissant* the disapprobation of its Parisian allies and local rivals, and the paper was forced to close in 1907. Its fate suggests that the support for French imperial expansion shown by other Franco-Arabic newspapers was a matter of expediency, as well as an opportunity to insist on the primacy of a sense of national community among Muslims in Algeria.

The most obvious way journalists at Franco-Arabic publications sought to create a place for Muslims within the French nation was by campaigning for their political representation. Newspapers were all well and good, noted *El Montakheb*, but elected representatives would undoubtedly provide a more direct means of "enlightening the government as to our rights, our situation, and our needs."[67] *Le Croissant* and both versions of *El Hack* likewise argued for the emancipation of Muslims on the grounds of democratic principle and in recognition of the tax burden under which they labored.[68] In the years immediately preceding the First World War, moreover, journalists were able to use an additional argument in favor of the political rights of Muslims. In 1907 a proposal for the conscription of Muslim subjects had been submitted by Adolphe Messimy, deputy of the Seine and wary observer of German military strength. After years of discussion, the government finally announced its plans for indigenous conscription in February 1912, prompting a number of Muslim journalists to renew their demands for political rights. "For us," explained the journalists of *El Hack*, "it seems logical that the 'blood tax' should correspond to all the prerogatives of citizenship."[69]

Not all Muslim journalists, however, shared this opinion, and some even openly called for resistance to conscription.[70] Divergent perspectives on the question cut across policy lines to some extent, with support for conscription coming from *El Hack* as well as the new assimilationist organs of the Jeunes-Algériens movement. Differences of opinion were commonly expressed as differences of language, with supporters of the initiative writing in French and opponents expressing themselves in Arabic. This division appears to have contributed to the collapse of the bilingual *El Hack*, whose two sections found themselves supporting opposing positions. Having adopted the bilingual format in May 1912 in an effort to acknowledge the diversity of reactions to conscription, the newspaper could not bridge the gap that had emerged in Muslim public opinion.[71] Omar Racim, editor of the Arabic section of *El Hack* and strong opponent of conscription, went on to found the Arabic-language *Dou-el-fakar* in 1913.[72] His opinions, as Ihaddaden points out, also earned him a number of years in jail on suspicion of espionage.[73]

Language and Assimilation in Franco-Arabic, Franco-Hebraic, and Franco-Judeo-Arabic Publications

While indicative of the fragility of bilingualism as a political strategy in the context of colonial domination, the breakdown of the pro-associationist Franco-Arabic press amid the debates on Muslim conscription did not signal the collapse of the Muslim public sphere. Another strand of bilingual Franco-Arabic publication, which instead favored the assimilation of Muslims into French cultural mores, had begun to emerge amid the political discussions leading to the 1905 separation of church and state. Representative of the interests of the French-educated Muslim elite, papers such as *L'Algérie franco-arabe* and *El Misbah* were more cautious in their representation of Muslims as a necessarily separate community, emphasizing instead their capacity to adapt to French customs and values and reserving questions of faith for a newly acknowledged private sphere. While such papers remained rare in the period preceding the First World War, their perspective would come to dominate the French-language indigenous press of the mid-1920s.[74] For the journalists who espoused this perspective, bilingualism effectively represented a necessary but temporary phase in the integration of the Muslim and national publics.

As with other publications involving Muslim journalists, the assimilationist strand of the Franco-Arabic press originated with indigenophile Frenchmen. A settler of French origin, J. Manhalt d'Anhalt of Constantine, created *L'Algérie franco-arabe* in 1898 to "bind ever closer . . . the already powerful ties of friendship and interest that unite Arabs to the French nation." While he employed an indigenous translator and secretary and hoped that the newspaper would become "a tribune open to all legitimate demands," Manhalt d'Anhalt remained the central voice of *L'Algérie franco-arabe*, focusing less on dialogue with Muslims than on their instruction. In particular, the director announced, the paper would "attempt to spread among the Muslim population some of our notions of scientific progress useful for agriculture and commerce." This eminently colonial concern was in fact motivated by a suspicion of foreign European migrants, whom the director feared were taking jobs from French settlers in Algeria and destabilizing French rule. The French would do better to learn from their Germanic rivals, he suggested, and promote "national colonization." As French nationals and subordinates, Muslim subjects were, according to Manhalt d'Anhalt, preferable to foreign settlers, who retained their own nationality and concomitant legal rights.[75]

By 1904, however, a small number of French-educated Muslims were attempting to take the civilizing mission into their own hands and thereby raise their status within the French national community. Larbi Fekar, a naturalized Muslim and former teacher at the Franco-Arabic school in Tlemcen, founded *El Misbah* in the hope of ensuring "the ever closer rapprochement of the French and the Arabs, for their common well-being, their common security, and for the greatness of France." This was to be achieved by "spreading French influence to the indigenous masses" via official initiatives and the Muslim administrative intermediaries who helped carry them out. *El Misbah* existed, Fekar explained, to "lend a loyal and disinterested hand to French and indigenous administrators and elected officials in the intellectual emancipation of Muslim society."[76]

The bilingual format served the pedagogical mission of *El Misbah*. "In a family," explained Fekar, "once one brother has followed lessons from the schoolmaster, he passes them on to his younger siblings or to those of other children who are unable to go to school because of work or some other reason."[77] Having received instruction in the French school system, Fekar saw his paper as a means of extending an education in French language and values to other Muslims. According to Fekar and his colleagues, mastery of the French language allowed for the full expression of civilization. Muslims who were known to express themselves in French with fluency and erudition—such as the Tunisian journalist and reformist Béchir Sfar, who gave an address to the Congress of Geography in Tunis in 1904—were held up to readers as examples of all that they might achieve with the right guidance from the French state and its Muslim intermediaries. The paper's editors agreed with their colleagues at Parisian newspaper *Le Temps* that in hearing such men as Sfar talk, one might be forgiven the impression that "there is no fundamental difference between the two races."[78] Acutely aware that most Muslim subjects had no such relationship with the French language, however, Fekar and his team provided Arabic translations of a number of articles on the third page of their four-page publication. Other articles appeared in Arabic alone, particularly those—like the summary of the meeting of the Tlemcen municipal council—that were intended to help less-educated Muslim readers understand "the efforts our councilors are making to bring them as many advantages as possible."[79]

This differential use of language was designed to promote the development of an indigenous elite whose assimilation into French culture would ensure their own privileged status, promote more efficient government, and improve the conditions of the wider Muslim community in Algeria. Despite its explicitly nonpolitical stance, the paper led a discrete campaign for the expansion of French education in Algeria to promote the creation of an assimilated elite like that in neighboring Tunisia.[80] Carefully detailing the legal framework of French education in North Africa, one article called for the decree of November 8, 1887—which had made the provisions of the 1882 law on obligatory primary schooling applicable to Algeria—to be extended to cover the Muslim population.[81] As in other publications, local examples were used to illustrate this wider national issue, such as an open letter to the mayor of Tlemcen requesting the creation of a new class for Muslim children—both boys and girls—at the local primary school, reminding municipal councilors of the "sentiments of justice and benevolence" that were supposed to motivate their actions as Frenchmen.[82] The inclusive nature of the request, in terms of the gender of those it would benefit, served to further underscore the publication's commitment to supposedly progressive French ideals. This commitment was reinforced in another article, titled "The Advance of Feminism," which welcomed the increased number of female candidates for medical qualifications.[83] These articles, along with other pieces marking the republican festival of secular education and celebrating the inauguration in Algiers of a new *medersa*, or juridico-religious school, by the minister of public education, served to educate Muslim readers in aspects of French history and society and solicit official support for the greater integration of Muslims into the national community.[84]

The nation not only overshadowed the discussion of local affairs but also loomed large in Fekar's evaluation of French expansion across North Africa. Like most other Franco-Arabic papers, *El Misbah* strongly supported French intervention in Morocco, drawing attention to the work already being carried out in the sultanate by French pedagogues and envisioning future benefits for its Muslim population.[85] Here, too, Fekar and his collaborators saw opportunity for French-educated Muslims who offered their services in the pursuit of a pacific conquest. "France has access to an inestimable resource with which to definitively and firmly establish its influence," noted Benali Fekar, brother of the director. "It can penetrate Morocco with its elite Muslim subjects in Algeria, whose common religion will ensure them at least a cordial reception, if not a warm welcome."[86] In offering these services, Benali Fekar transformed the transnational dimension of Islam into a potential source of French national strength.

At the same time, the journalists of *El Misbah* insisted, the guidance of the French nation would produce a widespread "Islamic renaissance." "Under the aegis of France," predicted Alladin, "whose role in this world is ever that of the educator of peoples, the Arab race will be reborn."[87] Although publications promoting assimilation in this era were not as explicitly politically engaged as their associationist counterparts, they ultimately sought the same objective: the creation of a French community united in its religious diversity. Muslims, noted the editors of *El Misbah*, in agreement with their colleagues at Parisian newspaper *Le Temps*, "realize that the political role of Islam is finished, and they accept this disappearance as inevitable—though they certainly don't renounce their right to their own beliefs."[88]

In pursuing this objective, Franco-Arabic publications employed many of the same strategies as the bilingual Franco-Hebraic and Franco-Judeo-Arabic publications that existed in this era. Such publications, which emerged in the context of debates within the provisional government regarding the collective naturalization of the Jews of Algeria, consistently supported assimilation and worked to disseminate French ideals to a local Jewish readership. Nessim Benisti, a jurist from Algiers, set the tone in July 1870 when he launched *L'Israélite algérien* to "defend the interests" and "communicate the aspirations" of the local Jewish community. These aspirations, confirmed Benisti, were easily summarized by the motto "REFORM, EMANCIPATION, PROGRESS." "At a time when the government is considering bestowing upon us the glorious status of French citizenship," the editor explained, "we all hope that the Israelite population of Algeria—which by its devotion, intelligence and capability has earned this sign of favor—will soon find itself, in accordance with its liberal aspirations, on the same footing as its brothers in the metropole." At such a time, Benisti stressed, it was important for Jews in Algeria "to show that we are worthy of this benefit." The paper was presented as proof of this readiness, evidence that Algerian Jews cherished the same values of progress and civilization as all French citizens. "Would . . . retrograde men," Benisti asked, "have created or supported a newspaper?"[89]

For any Jewish readers who did not feel quite as ready as Benisti, the editor adopted a bilingual format with the explicit intention of accelerating their advance toward French civilization. "For those of our coreligionists who are unable to easily understand modern ideas of progress expressed in the French language," reassured the editor, "we will explain these ideas to them via a translation elaborated in their mother tongue." The newspaper thus provided two sections, one in French and one in Judeo-Arabic. While the use of translation would improve readers' familiarity with the French language, the bilingual format would "activate their natural predisposition toward progress, making them understand that it is time to unite with us through shared liberal aspirations and divest themselves of certain prejudices that conflict with our holy religion, and bring them to these aspirations by reason, example, and instruction."[90] The paper intended, in short, to provide an education in the values of French citizenship.

As settler prejudice against Algerian Jews grew steadily following their collective naturalization by the Crémieux Decree of October 24, 1870, other publications appeared that used the bilingual format with the same objectives of defending the local Jewish population and encouraging their rapid assimilation into French culture. *La Jeunesse israélite*, a Franco-Hebraic newspaper established in 1890 by Elie Karsenty, declared its intention to "spread an appetite for education among the Israelite youth, enhance their emancipation, and prepare good citizens who are aware of their status and grateful to the country that has granted it to them."[91] Karsenty renewed these efforts in 1902 with *Le Nouvelliste oranais*, established in the wake of a period of intense violence against the Jewish community. The paper promoted "the diffusion of French ideas" as a bulwark against such violence, working to "propagate the wholesome ideas of civilization, progress, and emancipation among the most disadvantaged of our coreligionists," particularly those who, "alas, have not had the fortune to attend French schools."[92] As model French citizens, Karsenty's Jewish readers would remember what French settlers—"sons of the French Revolution"—seemed to have forgotten in "renouncing the sacrifices of their fathers and trampling on the principles that the latter won at the cost of their property and their lives!"[93] The French language, these papers agreed, was the language of citizenship, and the bilingual format was a necessary tool of assimilation: "In trying, by way of simple yet substantial translations, to popularize notions of common science, history, philosophy, or morality; in seeking to constantly guide [our readers] in the practice of their rights and their duties as citizens; in trying, in short, to emancipate them and make them French, we believe we are carrying out a useful, patriotic task."[94]

By insisting on integration into the national community, these papers sought not only to unite the Jews of Algeria with other French citizens but also to reaffirm the national character of French Judaism as a whole. This had been the work of the Central Israelite Consistory of France since its creation by Napoleon Bonaparte in 1808.[95] The consistory emphasized its national affiliation throughout the political turbulence of the nineteenth century in an effort to protect French Jews from religious prejudice and conducted its own civilizing mission among the Jews of Algeria, whose local customs were perceived as a threat to the security of the wider Jewish community.[96] Its efforts were publicized by Franco-Hebraic and Franco-Judeo-Arabic newspapers in Algeria.

Welcoming Zadoc Kahn to the post of chief rabbi of France in 1890, *La Jeunesse israélite* reiterated his appeal "that Jewish Algeria continue on the path of social progress on which it has so resolutely embarked, becoming each day more permeated by the duties incumbent on the honorable status of French citizenship."[97]

The drive to subordinate local particularism to national community was also evident in the treatment of these different categories of news, in which the rubric "Local News" most often examined stories of national import, such as the unofficial creation of a corps of Tirailleurs Israélites Algériens in August 1870 by a group of young Jewish men eager to serve their country.[98] Similarly, although *Le Nouvelliste oranais* declared its intention to give simple translations of French texts concerning the history of Algeria, the paper did so as a means of reinforcing its readers' sense of national belonging: "On learning of the eminently civilizing role of our beloved France in this once barbarous land," the paper explained, "their patriotism will become yet more ardent."[99]

In their haste to dispel any trace of local particularism, however, journalists at Franco-Hebraic and Franco-Judeo-Arabic publications were sometimes moved to make comparisons between the Jewish and Muslim populations of Algeria, emphasizing the greater integration of the former. "French writers who know little or nothing about Algeria," warned *L'Israélite algérien*, "sometimes emit erroneous opinions about the Israelites of this land, whom, under the vague title of *indigènes*, they confuse with Arabs and Kabyles in regard to their degree of civilization."[100] In an effort to correct this error, the paper pointed out the cultural differences that separated Jews from these other groups, including their more rapid and complete adaptation to the gender codes of the French colonizers. "In the religion that forms the civil code of the Muslim people," explained Benisti, "the woman is, from a social perspective, a nonentity and most often unaware of the interests of the household. . . . This example that our forebears observed over many centuries may have influenced a number of Jewish families who— lacking education—strayed from the path of our sacred traditions. . . . Since France has planted on this land its glorious flag, which has for us become a symbol of deliverance and civilization, our fathers have understood the advantages of the education that was unavailable to them in previous times." Like other French women, concluded Benisti, a Jewish woman in Algeria could now look forward to being "at the center of the household," where she would "become the mother of children destined to provide the pride and joy of her old age."[101]

The discrepancy between this image of French gender relations and that presented by the Muslim paper *El Misbah*, which supported the entry of women into the liberal professions, reveals much about the conflicting expectations placed on women of all backgrounds by the male-dominated journalistic profession in this era. The comparison invoked by Benisti also indicates that although these journalists were able to imagine a form of national unity that recognized religious diversity, the extent of this diversity was threatened by the rivalries and competition engendered by the differential treatment of religious communities in the colonial context. Without a forum for dialogue among the differently situated elements of the colonial population and the elaboration of local or intercommunal ties, the unity of the proposed French nation remained precarious. It was, paradoxically, the development of just such ties in the multilingual settler press that bound foreign European settlers to the French nation, even against their will.

Diverse National Communities in the Franco-Spanish Press before 1889

In contrast to the journalists of bilingual publications that sought to represent the interests of Muslims and Jews in Algeria, those established to defend European settlers of non-French origin tried assiduously—at least until 1889—to prevent their readers from being drawn into a French national community. The first such papers appeared in the early 1880s, combining French with Castilian Spanish. Like the monolingual Castilian and Catalan newspapers that began to appear at the same time,[102] these publications were dedicated to the defense of Spanish nationals in Algeria, denouncing the hardships and discrimination to which they were exposed in a territory under French control. They also served to maintain a sense of patriotism among migrants from the peninsula, uniting them around the discussion of Spanish news and celebrations. Given these shared objectives, the bilingual character of a number of these publications has been overlooked by historians, who have simply categorized these newspapers as Spanish and focused on their role in the construction of expatriate national identity.[103] Although the editors of these papers may have set out with the intention of bolstering national sentiment among Spanish settlers, they found themselves unable to do so without simultaneously acknowledging the transnational Latin and local "Algerian" communities which also afforded displaced Spanish nationals protection and a sense of belonging.

Arriving in Algeria in 1879, editor Francisco Zavala was among the first Spanish migrants to establish newspapers for the large hispanophone populations of Algiers and Oran. His first title, *El Patuet*, appeared in Algiers on a semiweekly basis from July to October 1883, followed by a second publication, *La Fraternidad obrera*, from October 1883 to November 1884.[104] The latter was relaunched in 1887, following Zavala's relocation to Oran. In both papers, Zavala rallied against what he saw as the dangerous dissipation of national sentiment among Spaniards in Algeria. Outraged by the growing tendency of his compatriots to refer to themselves as "Algerians," Zavala used his publications to revive patriotism and create solidarity among readers of Spanish origin. In one acerbic response to *La Lanterne des Issers*, which had published an article defending "Algerians of any nationality," Zavala insisted, in Spanish, that settlers identify as "Spaniards or Frenchmen, not Algerians!!"[105]

Zavala's first task, therefore, was to resurrect a sense of national belonging among Spaniards in Algeria. As the journalist writing under the pseudonym of El Tio Paborde acknowledged, there was already, in 1883, a distinction between "the number of *people designated as Spanish*" in Algeria and "the number of Spaniards ... who are conscious of being so." National sentiment among the first generation of settlers, he feared, had been dulled by the passage of time, "so that neither their customs, nor their language, nor their patriotic love retain the purity that they had when they first came to this continent."[106] Of those who still had memories of their lives before emigration, moreover, many might prefer to recall their home village or region rather than a national community into which they had felt incompletely integrated. The majority of Spanish migrants, Vilar indicates, were from "impoverished and over-populated areas with serious deficiencies of infrastructure."[107] These regions—primarily Almeria, Murcia, Alicante, Valencia, and the Balearic Islands—harbored diverse linguistic groups, further complicating journalistic attempts to promote a homogenous Spanish national culture.[108] "Those who arrive here with little education," complained Zavala, "mix with the children of this country, accepting their customs and even their confused language, which is not French, Arabic, or Spanish, but incorporates elements of all three. This produces such a carnivalesque result that after just four years of residence in this country, they neither know nor maintain their nationality."[109] As for the children of these first-generation migrants, one journalist lamented, "What civic love for Spain could we hope to find in the thoughts of those who do not even know the language spoken there?" Those Spaniards born in Algeria, he claimed, "know nothing more of Spain than its geographical location . . . on the other side of the sea."[110]

For Zavala and his colleagues, therefore, the key to restoring a sense of national identity among Spanish settlers was the promotion of unified linguistic expression in the form of Castilian Spanish. "The beautiful language of the one-armed man of Lepanto" thus became the dominant idiom of both *El Patuet* and *La Fraternidad obrera*.[111] Beyond providing a direct means of binding Spanish settlers to each other and to the peninsula, the language was used by journalists to educate Spanish readers about their national history and legends. One journalist explained their objective: "to propagate and inculcate in the minds of our fellow countrymen our Spanish glories, educating those who—having been born in foreign lands—are not aware of them or those who—having been absent from the mother country for many years—have forgotten them."[112] These glories included overseas expansion, and readers were offered regular articles about Spanish colonial possessions, past and present.[113] "The imagined community of *la España ultrama-*

rina," argues Christopher Schmidt-Nowara, was integral to the attempts of nineteenth-century Spanish writers to heal "the conflicts endemic to political life in the metropolis."[114] Avoiding such political disputes was all the more important in Algeria, local journalists reminded their colleagues, imploring them to subordinate political machinations to their larger pedagogical mission.[115]

Despite the dominant nature of the Spanish language in his publications, Zavala nevertheless chose to describe both *El Patuet* and *La Fraternidad obrera* as Franco-Spanish newspapers. Although neither title featured a regular French-language section, expression in French remained an important dimension of each publication's social mission. In these papers, the French language was reserved for discussion of the more practical aspects of colonial existence, such as the implications of new laws and decrees or proposed infrastructural developments.[116] "As our lead article is of purely Algerian interest," noted the Spanish preface to a discussion of public investment in the colonial territory, "we think we must publish it in French."[117] No direct Spanish translation of this article was provided. The distribution of languages thus served to differentiate between a supposedly authentic national community based on tradition and shared values and a more ephemeral colonial situation born of historical contingency. The bilingual format attempted to mediate between these two temporalities, serving the wider aim of protecting Spanish nationals in a territory under French control. "Our wish," Zavala explained, "is to demonstrate that if French people in Spain are grateful to their hosts without ceasing to be French, Spanish people [in Algeria] feel the same faith in their own homeland and the same gratitude toward France."[118]

More than a gesture to appease the French authorities, therefore, the Franco-Spanish format constituted an attempt to cultivate cordial relations between settlers of Spanish and French origin. The vision of a harmonious entente among the various migrant groups of the settler colony, safeguarded by the influence of the press, was further elaborated in an illustration titled "The Dreams of *El Patuet*," which appeared on the front page of the Algiers-based paper in 1883 (fig. 8).

SUEÑOS DEL PATUET

8. "The Dreams of *El Patuet*," *El Patuet*, September 9, 1883

In this somewhat self-aggrandizing dream, the oversize figure of the journalist was given prominence, reflecting the influence that Zavala hoped the press would exert on colonial society. The objects arranged around the figure indicated the supposed nature of this influence, with books representing his pedagogical mission, a guitar symbolizing his efforts at cultural elevation, and a pickax extolling the virtues of hard work. The desired outcome of the journalistic mission could be seen in the series of figures on the right-hand side of the page, which represented, as an accompanying article explained, "the war on fanaticism," "the education of the masses," and "Latin fraternity."[119] This last ideal was depicted by the embrace of three national allegories—France, wearing the *bonnet phrygien*, and Spain and Italy, adorned with their flags and crowns. Brought together under the beneficent sun of Algeria, the three nations remained, in Zavala's dream, mutually supportive but separate entities.

Invocations of Latin fraternity provided a basis for peaceful relations between settlers of French and Spanish origin. The need to encourage peaceful cohabitation was rendered all the more urgent by the ongoing diplomatic tensions surrounding what journalists commonly referred to as "the Moroccan question." Rivalry over Morocco persisted between the French and Spanish governments until the agreements of 1900 and 1904 defined their respective zones of influence in the sultanate, in anticipation of the formal establishment of protectorates in 1912. During the last decades of the nineteenth century this rivalry was heightened by the overtures made by the Spanish government toward Germany, object of French revanchist sentiment and member of the Triple Alliance.[120] The political debate was closely followed by journalists in Algeria, who recognized that the occupation of the neighboring territory by one or another of the vying European powers risked destabilizing relations in the mixed settler colony. Journalists of Spanish origin found themselves torn between a desire for Spanish influence in North Africa and a need to ensure the security of their compatriots in Algeria. Hence, while *La Fraternidad obrera* readily reprinted a provocative article from the Tangiers-based paper *El Eco de Ceuta*, supporting Spanish intervention in Morocco, journalists felt bound to point out that they did not approve of the tone of the original piece. "We are faced with two conditions to which our colleagues [in the peninsula] are less sensitive," *Fraternidad obrera* explained: "the pride of the nation that hosts us and also the general lack of education that characterizes the class of migrants to this colony."[121]

If the need to avoid conflict among settlers over the Moroccan question encouraged journalistic references to a shared Latin identity, the reaction against cooperation between the Spanish monarchy and the German Empire grounded this Latin identity in republicanism. Although Zavala and his collaborators often eschewed overt expressions of political allegiance, the threat of the Triple Alliance becoming a Quadruple Alliance pushed them to appeal for a united effort from settlers to protect Europe and its people from the "yoke of monarchs and emperors, fortresses that launch their poisoned arrows against free nations." Making use of simultaneous articles in French and Spanish, Zavala urged his readers to "unite against the crowned heads and respond to their threats with a clenched fist and a gaze that shows the force of our conviction."[122] An accompanying illustration reinforced the editor's message, depicting the readers propping up a feminine allegory of peace while a German soldier and an Italian cleric attempt to topple her, to be torn apart by the political vultures circling overhead.[123]

The multilingual press of the colony, Zavala indicated, had both the responsibility and opportunity to bring French and Spanish nationals together to prevail in this struggle. "Here in the humble columns of *El Patuet*," he announced, "we raise the first cry: long live the French Republic and long live the Latin Republic!"[124] In their defense of a Spanish national community, therefore, neither *El Patuet* nor *La Fraternidad obrera* could avoid its articulation with a wider transnational community of Latin peoples and states. But what of the local "Algerian" settler community that Zavala had so hoped to deter?

In a second line of defense for settlers of Spanish origin, journalists frequently pointed out their substantial contribution to colonial development as agricultural laborers. In focusing on the figure of the lowly peasant—a figure celebrated in the title of *El Patuet*—journalists hoped to create a sense of unity among the rural migrants from Valencia, Alicante, and Catalan-speaking areas, who had come together in Algeria as "*patuets* of the pickax" to ensure that "precious fruits and produce sprang from the arid African mountains."[125] As agents of colonial prosperity, these journalists argued, Spanish settlers had clearly distinguished themselves from indolent Muslims and parasitic Jews and should therefore be recognized by the French as their equals in civilization. As equals, the journalists emphasized, Spanish settlers should not be subjected to the same indignity as indigenous peoples—the indignity of imposed French nationality or, worse still, French citizenship.

A front-page illustration in *El Patuet* reinforced this point in 1883, in the context of renewed proposals for the collective naturalization of settlers of non-French origin. The illustration, which depicted a Jewish character diverting the product of settlers' labor into a secret "bottomless pit," asked readers to compare these two elements of colonial society and decide, "Who most deserves French protection?"[126] For Elizabeth Friedman, such expressions of antisemitism among European settlers stemmed from the desire of "the Christian colonists . . . to be considered French" and their concomitant resentment of Algerian Jews "as natives who were trying to become French."[127] Yet the Spanish article accompanying the illustration in *El Patuet* explicitly rejected plans for the collective naturalization of Europeans, presenting them as an insult to the national pride of civilized peoples. Spaniards, these journalists suggested, did not want to be considered French, but rather wished to be seen as a "virtuous people who have worked tirelessly to render fertile the land that has offered them hospitality."[128] The imposition of French citizenship onto a group of people who had contributed so much to colonial development, journalists at *Fraternidad obrera* suggested in 1887, not only would be against the French values of equality and fraternity but also would show "a lack of gratitude that nothing could justify to the eyes of the civilized world."[129] The few articles that appeared in French on the topic took a different position, however, supporting naturalization on the grounds that it would ensure all settlers enjoyed equality before the law of the land. In the opinion of francophone journalist Emilio Alberti, moreover, the naturalization of European settlers of non-French origin would serve less to create French citizens than "French Algerians."[130]

In emphasizing the extent of their contribution to colonial development, journalists inscribed Spanish nationals into a local "Algerian" community defined by a common mythology of settler self-sacrifice and struggle on the land. These experiences were presented as the "shared legacy of glory and defeat," which contemporary thinkers such as Ernest Renan considered to be fundamental to the "soul" of a nation itself.[131] Together, journalists emphasized, French and Spanish settlers had toiled to make the land productive. "Without the honorable children of Spain," insisted one journalist, "France would find in Algeria nothing but the tomb of her own precious offspring."[132] Their mutual struggle, journalists explained, had been carried out in the face of opposition from the French of the metropole, who had been "misled by politicians who find it easier to colonize from parliament than to come out here and see for themselves the supposedly *gentle* character of the natives."[133] In distinguishing settlers of French and Spanish origin from both metropolitan authority and indigenous populations, journalists revealed the dynamics of the settler colonial situation and elaborated a framework for the imagination of a distinct settler community.

As local, national, and transnational communities became increasingly articulated in *El Patuet* and *La Fraternidad obrera*, Zavala found it difficult to maintain the differential use of language with which he had hoped to distinguish Spaniards from Frenchmen. Journalists writing in Spanish occasionally strayed from the staple themes of national legends and Spanish overseas influence to consider local questions of administrative reform and colonial development.[134] Some writers even engaged in creative forms of bilingual expression, underscoring both the unity and the distinctiveness of the French and Spanish languages by using code-switching in their articles.[135] By mixing the two languages within the confines of a single article, or even a single sentence, journalists communicated the specificity of a local situation in which settlers of diverse origins came together in recognition of their differences to function as a meaningful whole. This unity in diversity, the writer of regular column "The Weekly Review" suggested, could be seen in the way Spanish nationals had used their relocation to French Algeria to overcome differences in regional background or social class. In ending the following sentence in French, the role of the French territory and the French language in creating Spanish unity was emphasized: "España nos enviara un beso de amor maternal por la conducta magnifica, digna de todos los elogios, que sus hijos de Argel tienen *les uns envers les autres*."[136] (Spain will send us a kiss of motherly love to reward us for the good behavior, worthy of high praise, which her children in Algiers show *toward each other*.)

Through the prism of local transformations in a French context, the journalist suggested, the Spanish nation itself had been strengthened. Switching to French as the matrix language, the journalists reinforced this point: "Instead of being divided, let us be united!" he exclaimed. "Instead of being *enemigos*, let us be *amigos*! . . . Are we not sons of the same country, for heaven's sake!"[137]

In other editions of the column, the journalist used the same strategy to mark the unity in diversity of European settlers of different national origins. Rejecting reports of violence between French and Spanish settlers in Oran, for example, one article repeatedly alternated between French and Spanish to enact the fraternal relations it sought to promote; sections in Spanish in the original text are italicized here, while those in French are not: "Some of our readers believed that our compatriots were *massacring* the French, *our brothers, in the town of Oran*, just as the vicious Moors had massacred the Spanish in Saïda. *We are pleased to prove them wrong. Absolute harmony reigns—ad majorem gloriam!— between the two populations of our beautiful Algeria, our beloved adopted homeland*. Goodbye my friends, *and may the heavens bring you joy* until next Sunday."[138]

Throughout the article, neither French nor Spanish served consistently as the matrix language, producing a hybrid form of bilingual expression. Taken together, these experiments in bilingual composition sought to preserve a distinct sense of Spanish national identity, while integrating Spaniards into a local community that recognized limited diversity. In marking this diversity, they differed from the local oral dialect of *pataouète*, in which, as Christian Flores explains, "Spanish and French seemed to have fused into a single system" based on the linguistic interference of Spanish in the French matrix language.[139] If *pataouète*, therefore, creatively expressed the emergence of an "Algerian" community of mixed European origins, multilingual publications exposed the dynamic instability within this community and its maintenance of multiple forms of identification.

Despite his initial intention to defend the Spanish national community, Zavala ultimately found that he could not achieve this without acknowledging and fostering forms of local and transnational unity. His invocations of Latin and republican fraternity were reappropriated by other journalists and readers in Algeria to express identities that were simultaneously national and local. As settlers themselves, Zavala's own journalists could not always support their editor's injunction to recognize an "Algerian" community. Instead, many sought to promote "the union and the entente of all Algerians, without distinction of nationality."[140] In 1889, however, this distinction was all but erased by the French Republic's collective naturalization of the descendants of European migrants. Far from disappearing, multilingual publications expanded, finding renewed purpose in their mission to defend the eclectic cultural heritage of French citizens of diverse Latin origins.

Building a Latin Union in Multilingual Settler Newspapers after 1889

The law of July 26, 1889, imposed French nationality on the descendants— born on French territory—of foreign nationals who had been born on French soil. In Algeria, where several generations of European migrants found their home, this led to the immediate creation of 21,696 new French nationals and 50,798 cases of "suspended naturalization" concerning young people who had not yet attained the age of majority.[141] Far from spelling the end for multilingual publications, the legal transformation of foreigners into Frenchmen led to the creation of a number of new Franco-Spanish and Franco-Italian titles, as journalists sought to guide settlers in reconciling their official political status with their personal affiliations and foreign cultural traditions.[142]

The balance of allegiances was sometimes difficult to achieve, as reflected in the frequent experimentation with form that characterized the bilingual settler publications of the early 1890s. In the space of two weeks in January 1892, for example, the Franco-Spanish newspaper *Le Tonnere* underwent a series of transformations: a version with the first page in French and the second in Spanish; a longer publication featuring the first two pages in French, a page of advertisements, and the back page in Spanish; and another version with the first page printed in French, the second in Spanish, and the third presenting a mix of articles in either language.[143] These persistent modifications not only reflected a degree of caution in adapting to the new legal framework of settler identification but also exemplified the ever-fluctuating nature of the multidimensional process of identification itself. As journalists sought to guide their readers through this moment of transition, they developed the themes of colonial productivity and Latin fraternity that had emerged in the Franco-Spanish press of the 1880s and explicitly used these themes to legitimize the imagination of a local "Algerian" settler community. In promoting the cultural specificity of this local community within the French nation, they hoped to shield the distinct cultural heritage of settlers of Spanish and Italian origin.

The first Franco-Italian newspapers appeared in the years following the legislation of 1889. Less numerous than their Spanish counterparts in Algeria, and less imbued with the republican ideology that formed a basis for affinity with their French neighbors, settlers of Italian origin took longer to become involved in bilingual publications. Relations between the French and Italian governments, moreover, had soured considerably since the establishment of the French protectorate in Tunisia in 1881, contributing to some cultural distance between settlers of these two nationalities—albeit on a much smaller scale than in the protectorate itself.[144] The new administrative context, however, encouraged the emergence of Franco-Italian publications, as journalists induced these two migrant groups to recognize a mutual interest in promoting better relations between their nations of origin. In the opening editorial of the *Trait d'union* in 1891, journalists lamented the rupture in trade between the two countries and declared their intention to use the newspaper "to reestablish and strengthen the bonds that formerly existed between the two peoples." "We thought that Algeria, as a neutral territory, or as a territory in which a large number of Italians live a French life and have the same interests as us," explained the editors in both French and Italian, "was a marvelous place to launch a publication that aims, calmly and without emotion, to discuss and identify the many causes that have led to the actual state of affairs."[145] In describing Algeria as "a neutral territory," the editors of *Le Trait d'union* sought less to question French sovereignty than to affirm the complex national identification of settlers, which allowed them to feel at once French and Italian. It was precisely this duality, the writers suggested, that allowed them to be balanced and objective in their discussion of international affairs.

The Franco-Italian convention of 1896, which helped subdue the long-standing rivalry over Tunisia, gave further impetus to the Franco-Italian press. A new publication, *Lega franco-italiana*, marked the restoration of "union and harmony" between the two governments and worked to preserve this fragile new entente. This objective, the opening editorial observed, served the multiple affiliations of Europeans in North Africa: "Our journalistic program is the result of who we are. Italians by birth, willingly naturalized as French, we will strive to show our friends, our compatriots in Algeria and Tunisia, that to be strong we must come together under the double flag of our two Latin sisters, France and Italy."[146] This tripartite sense of attachment—to France, to Italy, and to the settler community—was reflected in the structure of both *Le Trait d'union* and *Lega franco-italiana*. The spatial arrangement of the text in both cases differentiated between national languages through the use of separate sections, but the papers drew both linguistic groups into the same community of readers through the direct translation of leading articles.

Many of these leading articles, moreover, dealt explicitly with the triangular relationship among France, Italy, and North Africa, as journalists endeavored to situate national and local communities in relation to each other.[147] The settler colony was thus presented not simply as a site of contact among national cultures, but as a productive space of cultural transfer. This representation was enhanced by the increased willingness of journalists to disrupt the strict correlation between national news and national language. It became possible, for example, to read articles in French about the king of Italy's birthday celebrations or the organization of Spanish festivals.[148] Articles in Italian or Spanish about the domestic affairs of the French metropole, however, remained much rarer. This imbalance suggests that the primary function of the multilingual publications of the 1890s was to help recently naturalized settlers reconcile their particular cultural heritage with their new political status and immediate cultural context.

This context, journalists affirmed, was resolutely local and "Algerian." If it was rare to read news about the French metropole in Italian or Spanish, it was increasingly common to read local news in all languages. Regular columns such as "Notizie Cittadine" (Municipal News) in *Lega franco-italiana* or "Crónica Local" (Local News) in the Franco-Spanish publication *Le Tonnerre* constructed a multilingual local space that transcended national divisions.[149] Discrete national communities, journalists suggested, were an invention of the French of the metropole and did not reflect the settlers' allegiances. *Le Trait d'union* criticized metropolitan observers for referring to settlers of non-French origin as "foreigners." If these observers "would take the trouble to study the history of colonization in Algeria," the journalist suggested, they would see that all Europeans "had fought together to make the land fertile" and that "the Spanish, Maltese, Italians, and French form but one group for whom the word 'foreigner' means tourist." Visitors from their own country of origin, by these standards, would be considered more "foreign" by settlers than their counterparts of a different national origin. Indeed, national origins were of secondary importance to the settlers, the same journalist argued:

"Ask any child his nationality; he will tell you that he is Algerian and not of this or that origin."[150]

Bilingual publications in Italian and French further contributed to the consolidation of an imagined community of "Algerian" settlers by expanding the definition of Latin identity suggested by Franco-Spanish publications of the 1880s. While the latter had referred to a shared "Latin Republic," the Franco-Italian press invoked a "Latin Union" based less on political ideology than on the perceived compatibility of language, cultural practice, and racial group. This extended version of a Latin community was expedient given the formal alliances in place between the Italian, German, and Austro-Hungarian governments and served to encourage unity among settlers of different origins when international political developments threatened to tear them apart. "Everybody knows," declared Giovanni Gasparri in the first edition of *Lega franco-italiana*, "that between France and Italy—two peoples of Latin race who have held out their hands to each other at various moments in history—there exists an obvious community of aspirations, interests, and values." These shared traits, Gasparri suggested, outweighed any political differences: "*Lega franco-italiana* will always maintain the utmost respect for the form of government in each country," he affirmed, attempting to render differences of regime and ideology irrelevant.[151] Despite the republican leanings of many journalists of Spanish origin in Algeria, they often found it expedient to follow suit, subordinating national differences of political regime to the common aspirations and sensibilities that they insisted united all Latin peoples. Thus the Franco-Spanish newspaper *L'Africa* could "profess as much respect for the Spanish monarchy as sympathy for the French Republic," when what counted most was that "in this African land, so long closed, inhospitable and hostile to Europeans, Latin races have come together to carry out the great task of pacific conquest, civilization, and assimilation."[152]

When journalists could not ignore the reality of political circumstances and the tension it risked generating among settlers of different origins, they encouraged their readers to recognize the discrepancy that existed between the divisive actions of distant political officials and the sentiment of entente that united the masses. "Many Italians recognize that the alliance of their country with Austria and Germany is not natural," insisted an article in *Lega franco-italiana*.[153] In promoting a Latin community based on such supposedly "natural" factors as race or culture, journalists encouraged settlers to set right the mistakes of European governments and forge new local alliances capable of reforming international relations. In so doing, they suggested that local, national, and transnational forms of identification were mutually constitutive rather than fundamentally opposed.

To articulate these multiple communities, journalists not only relied on the familiar tropes of shared sacrifice and common enemies but also fostered new forms of local and transnational commemoration. *Le Trait d'union*, for example, gathered together a "group of patriots in Algiers, without regard for nationality," to commemorate the birth of Giuseppe Garibaldi.[154] Garibaldi, who had seen his hometown of Nice pass from France to Piedmont-Sardinia and back again before his death in 1882, was evidently an apposite choice. A patriot, a republican, and—in the end—a pragmatic supporter of the monarchy, Garibaldi had traveled around the Mediterranean and lived among settler populations in Latin America. The nature and diversity of Garibaldi's experience meant that he held broad appeal for settlers in Algeria, and journalists sought to capitalize on this in a series of articles and slogans in French and Italian.[155]

The broader definition of the Latin community elaborated by the Franco-Italian press in the 1890s paved the way for the emergence of trilingual publications at the turn of the century. These papers served to ensure that the dialogue about settler identification was multidirectional and endeavored to minimize potential conflict between Spaniards and Italians as rival migrant groups in a French territory. Newspapers such as *L'Union latine* and *Pro-patria* actively promoted the notion of a transnational "Latin Union" or "Latin family" and held up the local "Algerian" settler community as a model of interaction to be emulated by Latin peoples across Europe and around the world.[156] This model, journalists explained, was one of unity in diversity: "We take it as axiomatic that variety within unity strengthens the common will," declared *Pro-patria*.[157] The principle, *L'Union latine* elaborated, was that "each of us use our strengths for the benefit of all, while maintaining our own particularities." "This is not internationalism," the paper clarified. "Each of us has a homeland and must hold to it." Nevertheless, the passage of time would herald the inevitable creation of "a neo-Latin race composed of complex elements each attenuated by their interaction."[158]

Nation and race, according to this proposition, were not synonymous. National communities were instead to be considered as variations within a given racial type. The Algerian settler colony, journalists claimed, was the ideal "testing ground" for such a theory, combining as it did the principal national variations of the Latin race.[159] In bringing these variations together in one society, moreover, the settler colony would allow the Latin type to evolve. The conditions of settlement, one journalist affirmed, citing the opinion of a French colleague at the *La Revue bleue*, meant that Latin society in Algeria "differs fundamentally from that on the other side of the Mediterranean." The coming together of migrant groups, "each with their own particular preoccupations and even their own particular ideas brought over from their countries of origin," these journalists argued, offered "the exciting spectacle a bubbling mixture in which the future is being prepared."[160]

Beginning in 1903 the trilingual weekly *L'Union latine* directly addressed the question of "Algerian" cultural and racial specificity, devoting numerous articles to the consideration of the special "mentality" or "individuality" of settlers.[161] These articles were inspired by contemporary scientific research produced on both sides of the Mediterranean, though the editors clearly favored the opinions of experts who had lived and worked in North Africa. The ideas of geographer Onésime Reclus, who had served as a Zouave in Algeria before developing the politically useful concept of francophone unity in the 1880s, were particularly pertinent to journalists of this multilingual publication.[162] While Reclus was hopeful that French authority in Algeria would contribute to maintaining a significant role for the French language on the world stage, he explicitly renounced any pretensions to linguistic hegemony and instead promoted multilingualism.[163] Reclus's belief that community resulted primarily from affinities of language and milieu rather than biological inheritance lent weight to the idea that "Algeria produces Algerians" as a variation of a Latin type: "[In Algeria the milieu] is not shaping an anti-French race, but varieties of our own race: Spaniards, Italians, 'Mediterraneans' are our brothers, with almost the same mixed inheritance as us; they speak dialects of the same language, they bear the imprint of the same language, they bear the imprint of the same civilization, they believe, to all appearances, in the same religion."[164]

The notion that Algeria produces Algerians, however, held serious implications for the political relationship between the settler colony and the mother country. If the "Algerian" was another variation of the Latin type, journalists wondered, was the settler colony—like France, Spain, and Italy—destined to become an independent nation? Discussions of "Algerian" cultural specificity and its potential political consequences spread far beyond the pages of multilingual publications in this era, as journalists in all sectors of the settler press deliberated the relative merits of administrative assimilation, autonomy, and independence. By the early twentieth century all but the most radical journalists had resigned themselves to a greater or lesser degree of colonial autonomy. It was in the midst of this newfound consensus—brought about by the Algerian provinces obtaining fiscal autonomy in 1900 and the public reaction against the instability generated by anti-Jewish separatism— that the multilingual *Union latine* emerged. Its appearance signaled another reason for renewed support for local autonomy: the existence of a sense of a settler community that functioned to make multiple and simultaneous cultural and political identifications possible in a way that most national communities, particularly that of the "one and indivisible" French nation, did not. Indeed, identification with an "Algerian" settler community in which Italian or Spanish specificity was recognized acted as a precondition for naturalized settlers' acceptance of their status as French. It was in multilingual publications—given their explicit mise-en-scène of an internally differentiated local community—that the

Pro-Patria

Semanario español de unión franco-española y alianza latina || *Hebdomadaire espagnol d'union franco-hispano et d'alliance latine* || *Ebdomadario spagnolo dell'unione franco-spagnolo è d'alleanza latina*

9. *Pro-patria,* July 14, 1910

cultural causes of the preference for autonomy, over French assimilation or national independence, were expressed with the most acuity.

In defending a transnational Latin community, newspapers such as
L'Union latine and *Pro-patria* were able to cultivate French, Spanish,
and Italian patriotism without limiting the horizons of their readers to

national identification. This drive for balance was evident in the cover image of the July 14, 1910, issue of *Pro-patria* (fig. 9).[165] Although the title of the publication was an obvious reference to national sentiment, and the editors even solicited funding for their newspaper from the representatives of the Spanish government in Algeria,[166] the front page depicted an allegory of the Spanish nation cut adrift from the peninsula, hovering somewhere between the coasts of the Mediterranean—at once Spanish, "Algerian," and Latin.

Making similar use of imagery to cultivate multiple identifications among its readers, the *Union latine* followed its presentation of an illustration of President Émile Loubet—printed at the time of his voyage to Algeria in 1903—with illustrations of the Italian and Spanish sovereigns, French and Italian cabinet ministers, and metropolitan and local politicians.[167]

These publications further affirmed their commitment to Latin unity in diversity through the spatial organization of texts in different languages. Eschewing the formatting conventions of bilingual publications, which had favored defined sections in each language, both *L'Union latine* and *Pro-patria* featured three languages on each page. A single page from the July 14, 1910, edition of *Pro-patria*, for example, featured an article in Italian marking the French national holiday, an article in Spanish discussing Spanish military activities in the Sahara, and an article in French about the dangers of sunstroke.[168] In this way, each page represented a local community of readers in which linguistic, cultural, and political differences were acknowledged without challenging the unity of the whole.

Such direct expressions of unity in diversity, however, were not always appreciated by French nationalists in Algeria or by the French authorities, who feared the consequences for settlers' attachment to France and for French domination in North Africa. Catholic newspapers in Algeria, including *La Croix de l'Algérie et de la Tunisie* and *La Semaine Religieuse d'Oran*, were especially quick to point out the dangers of letting settlers of foreign origin maintain their native languages.[169] Their critiques were leveled in the context of debates surrounding the separation of church and state and the impact of such a separation in Algeria. Conscious of their vulnerability as representatives of church authority in a territory designated as a principal target of the republican civilizing mission, clergymen in Algeria had long presented themselves as valuable instruments of colonization, rallying to the republic even before Pope Leo XIII issued his encyclical of February 16, 1892, on the church and state in France. Without the continued support of the state, Catholic journalists warned, the number of French clergymen in Algeria would surely diminish, while "the influx of foreign priests, encouraged by the Italian and Spanish governments, will grow and grow." Although Spanish, Italian, and Maltese migrants "all have Catholicism in their bones," noted *La Croix*, it was certain that without the guiding hand of the French clergy, they would "choose priests of their own nationality and language." Referring to the demographic studies of Victor Demontès, *La Croix* warned of the creation of "a new people" though the fusion of European migrants in Algeria, asking whether the law of separation, "in subordinating the conquering race, will threaten its hegemony."[170] In a context in which the public expression of Catholicism in the press was necessarily voiced as a patriotic declaration, the evocation of a Latin community based primarily on race and sensibility provided a means of reestablishing a transnational connection among French, Spanish, and Italian settlers. Multilingual publications for settlers thus assiduously avoided all reference to religious community—unless it was in Orientalist rejection of Islam or Judaism.

Sensitive to accusations of foreign conspiracy or separatism, the editors of multilingual publications were sometimes obliged to revert to the use of separate sections for each language. Responding to charges of "internationalism and antipatriotic sentiment" in 1907, the editor of *Union latine* announced, "We have decided that each section of the newspaper will be entirely autonomous, and that the French section— which is the most important—will be the reflection and expression of Latin thought."[171] *Pro-patria* managed to maintain a less structured organization of linguistic elements until at least 1911, even devoting an increasing number of column inches to articles in Spanish and photos of Spanish dignitaries. By this time, however, the notion of an "Algerian" identity forged by the local interaction of Latin races had become commonplace in the settler press of all languages. Indeed, journalists were already engaged in the quest for "an original Algerian literary genre" as an expression of a distinctive "Algerian consciousness."[172] It was this local "Algerian" consciousness, as developed in the settler press and exemplified in multilingual publications, that had transformed settlers into Frenchmen—and had done so without divesting them of the cultural heritage of other nations.

The independent bi- and multilingual publications that appeared in Algeria between 1870 and 1914 expressed a common hope on the part of the Muslim, Jewish, and European journalists who launched them: the hope that in the context of the manifold ruptures brought about by the imposition of French authority in Algeria, a new society could be imagined and brought into being by carefully managed forms of interaction among ethnolinguistic groups. The ideal societies imagined by these differently situated journalists varied considerably, from a newly expanded French national community strengthened by its recognition of religious diversity to a transnational Latin racial configuration inspired by the local experience of settlers of French, Spanish, and Italian origin.

In each case, journalists proposed competing configurations of local, national, and transnational community as scaffolding for the ideal society of their imagination. If political exclusion or vulnerability led Muslim and Jewish journalists to either deny their local or transnational sense of community or find creative ways of turning these connections to the advantage of the French nation, settler journalists enjoyed greater liberty to differentiate within, and move beyond, national borders. This privilege was based on the security of their rights as foreign European nationals on French territory or, after 1889, their rights as French citizens. Both before and after the collective naturalization of 1889, journalists of foreign European origin protected these rights with reference to their racial and cultural compatibility with the French colonizers and their local contribution to imperial stability. This claim ultimately proved more appealing to settlers of French origin than the calls for unity in religious diversity advanced by Muslims and Jewish journalists, despite their use of the republican language of liberty, equality, and fraternity.

The "third space" opened up by multilingual publications was closed by the advent of the First World War. In the wake of that conflict, the efforts of Muslim and Jewish journalists to defend their place within the French nation continued to be hampered by settler journalists' references to a Latin community that allowed Frenchmen to be Spanish, Italian, or "Algerian," but not Jewish or Muslim. Unlike their Jewish colleagues, Muslim journalists could not rely on their status as French citizens or the support of institutions in the metropole to help combat the exclusionary practices of the settler community. Faced with the state's continued rejection of their appeals for inclusion, Muslim journalists added another form of community to those imagined in the prewar era—an Algerian national community recognizing the Arabic language and the Islamic faith.

Conclusion

Newspapers in Algeria in the nineteenth and early twentieth centuries served as much more than vehicles for the dissemination of information useful to the French Empire. Although the degree of liberty afforded journalists in the colonial territory varied significantly according to their legal status in colonial hierarchies, their language of expression, and the regime under which they operated, their publications continued to express the diverse hopes and fears of Algeria's inhabitants and contribute to the reimagination of the French national community, alongside the elaboration of communities of local and transnational dimensions.

As elsewhere on French soil, the press in Algeria expanded rapidly following the fall of the Second Empire in 1870, producing ever greater numbers of titles and reaching ever greater numbers of readers following the republican legislation of 1881. Much like their counterparts in the metropole in the decades surrounding the turn of the century, journalists and readers in Algeria also witnessed the growing influence of commercial interests and the effects of new technologies. To a greater extent than in the metropole, however, small-scale operations persisted, serving as outlets for individual self-expression and the defense of distinct communities of readers. Such was the nature of press production in a settler colonial context, in which neither professional structures nor social codes nor political destinies appeared fully fashioned, and in which journalists of diverse backgrounds seized on the opportunity to shape the new world they inhabited. Far from contributing to the "homogenization of the national body," at work in other French provinces in the same era,[1] journalists in Algeria consciously gave recognition to the diversity of religions, cultures, nationalities, and languages evident within French borders, in the hope of changing the shape of the national body.

For many settler journalists, indeed, the contours of the nation were reconsidered from the perspective of an "Algerian" body understood to be racially distinct. This "new white race" was born not only out of the interaction of Latin migrants but also out of the transmission of unique sensibilities forged by acclimatization to the North African environment. As in other settler colonial contexts, the claim to a unique biological connection between the body of the white settler and the conquered land served to legitimize settler presence.[2] In presenting settler presence as legitimate, the journalists of the colony sought to shape the French authorities' approach to the management of local resources and indigenous populations. Framed as the cultural value of Latinism, the racialized designation of "Algerian" provided a basis for a transnational form of identification that sustained settlers when they found themselves at odds with their French governors.

Disillusionment with the state grew steadily throughout the nineteenth century, as settlers' aspiration to achieve legitimacy was left unfulfilled by Napoleon III, with his vision of an Arab kingdom, and by the Third Republic, which emancipated the Algerian Jews and promoted a seemingly arabophile civilizing mission. Settler opposition to French authority was expressed as a form of aggressive frontier masculinity, which encouraged violence toward indigenous peoples and rejection of their perceived protectors. The gendered dynamics of settler colonialism, more widely studied in relation to the British Empire,[3] were thus equally important in French Algeria, where they similarly framed the quest for sovereignty. Unlike their counterparts in the United States, Australia, and South Africa, however, "Algerian" settlers stopped short of claiming their independence following the partial rehabilitation of dominant codes of masculinity in the wake of President Loubet's visit in 1903. This key difference in the French Algerian settler colonial experience was as much a result of the mitigating effects of Latin identification, which allowed settlers to cultivate multiple senses of attachment beyond and alongside that to France, as it was of the demographic realities made evident by the Margueritte Affair.

The articulated discourses of race and gender that underpinned "Algerian" identification were echoed in the professional milieu of colonial journalism. However, despite their efforts to exclude settler women, as well as Algerian Muslims and Jews, male settler journalists provided a rhetorical framework for the claims of those they sought to marginalize by insisting on the possibility of equality in difference. Appropriating this same principle, settler women and Algerian Muslim and Jewish journalists seized on the ambivalence of the settler colonial situation as an opportunity to fashion the world anew. For some of these writers, the dynamic possibilities of a nascent "Algerian" people allowed for the reimagination—and regeneration—of the national community as a space of equality. While some saw acceptance of dominant metropolitan codes of civilization as the best means of protecting their own interests, alongside those of a reinvigorated French Empire, others argued for multiple and equivalent forms of Frenchness, in which particularities of linguistic expression, faith, and gender existed within the political community.

For those journalists frustrated by the precarious balancing act of equality in difference, the press offered alternative imaginaries on a transnational scale. Existing or anticipated ties of language, cultural heritage, and faith inspired settlers and indigenous writers alike as they forged paths for the Algeria of the future. Although many of the paths imagined by journalists were cut short by the First World War and its impact on the relationships among settlers, Muslims, Jews, and the French state, the hopes and fears raised by journalists in the prewar era resonated long into the twentieth century, shaping the actions of future generations of writers and their readers.

For many of the Muslim journalists and elites who had pledged their support to the French state at the outbreak of the war, and who had seen 25,000 of their coreligionists fall on European battlefields while another 119,000 upheld the war effort of a beleaguered French nation,[4] the subsequent failure of the government to enfranchise Muslims in national elections or to abolish the *indigénat* constituted both a disappointment and a betrayal. Using more limited, local electoral reform to their advantage, Muslims in both rural and urban areas devised new forms of mass political mobilization in the 1920s and 1930s, forcefully arguing for their political rights as members of the French national community.[5] A newly invigorated press played a key role in sustaining these forms of mobilization as new political groupings, including the federations of elected Muslim officials and the reformist *ulama*, or religious leaders, who sought public support for their competing visions of French citizenship for Algerian Muslims.[6]

Frustrated by the narrow French horizons and elite origins of these reformist groups, however, other Algerian Muslims advocated an alternative source of sovereignty: that of the independent Algerian nation. In the 1920s and 1930s the *Étoile* nord-africaine and Parti du peuple algérien relied on trans-Mediterranean labor, press, and political connections to swell the ranks of their populist revolutionary movements.[7] While these competing sources of national sovereignty came to dominate political debate among Muslims in the interwar years, other forms of community remained imaginable. Pan-Islamism and identification with other "colonized" peoples, Arthur Asseraf suggests, were also sustained by Muslim engagement with news flowing through Algeria.[8] These forms of identification were more widely diffused by the technologies of the interwar era, but the outlines of such imagined communities could already be traced between the points of reference indicated by the first generation of Muslim journalists, including those of *Tout ou Rien*, who had imagined a new religious community across the Muslim world, and those of *Le Croissant*, who, alongside settler contributors, had denounced French intervention in Indochina, Madagascar, and Morocco.

Increased press activity among Muslims in the decades following the First World War met with settler journalists' renewed hostility. The instability engendered by the conflict heightened settlers' ever-present feelings of vulnerability, provoking a conservative outlook that reified racial hierarchies and entrenched dominant gender codes. Tentative government projects to extend the franchise to Algerian Muslims provoked reactionary campaigns in the settler press, as European journalists pointed to the sacrifices of their own community for the French war effort. In subsequent decades, these sacrifices would provide an additional argument for settler journalists and political leaders who sought to protect the European settler community by emphasizing its loyalty to France.[9] At the same time, and much to the chagrin of old journalistic hands like Ernest Mallebay, the changing landscape of professional journalism increasingly favored larger-scale press operations and a more standardized model of news formatting based on metropolitan models.

Despite these strengthened affective ties and structural links with the metropole, settler journalists did not abandon discourses of "Algerian" and Latin identification in the decades following the First World War. Indeed, the conceptualization of the French nation as but one expression of a wider Latin race was reinforced in this era by activities promoted by journalists in both the cultural domain, such as the development of an Algérianiste school of literature, and the political arena, in the support of extreme-right, anti-Semitic movements such as the Unions latines.[10] In many ways, discourses of "Algerian" and Latin belonging constituted increasingly important resources for journalists in this era, as expressions of Frenchness also increased in the press.[11] As settlers' hopes for recognition and appreciation by the French of the metropole mounted, so too did their vulnerability increase; in promoting notions of "Algerian" and Latin belonging, journalists confronted the charged emotional dynamics of the settler colonial situation, creating reassuring narratives of affective and political distance from the metropole, which sustained settlers without jeopardizing their privileged status.

While such narratives could be, and often were, strategically deployed by settler journalists who sought to make demands of the state, from 1860 onward they were more than politically useful negotiating tools. These discourses must be understood as products of the specific emotional dynamics of settler colonialism in Algeria and, as such, recognized as motivating forces capable of shaping settlers' actions. These forces contributed as much to the violent public disorder of the 1890s and 1930s as to the elaborate expressions of gratitude to the French Republic during President Loubet's visit in 1903 and during the celebrations for the centennial of the invasion in 1930.[12] This profound ambivalence toward the French national community would find its most acute and violent expression during the Algerian War, as the most militant settlers resisted and then fought the French government in a vain effort to maintain French sovereignty following De Gaulle's recognition, in 1959, of Algerians' right to self-determination.

Although French withdrawal from Algeria was an immediate shock to settlers and the catalyst for longer-term feelings of trauma and nostalgia, as expressed in the literary and political discourse of some *pieds noirs*,[13] this withdrawal had never been unimaginable. Indeed, it had been a persistent and fearful imagining of settler journalists since the 1860s. If these journalists had often preferred to focus on the promise of progress—the chance to set modernity back on course after the decadent detours it had taken on the European continent—they had never been able to fully dispel the visions of colonial dystopia threatened by the inefficiencies of the colonial administration, the lack of interest of other Europeans in their pioneering efforts, and the size and increasing political activity of the Muslim population. Nor had French withdrawal been unimaginable for Muslim and Jewish journalists in Algeria, who formulated their own emotional responses and shaped their own political strategies accordingly. What had been imaginable, however, had never been inevitable: limiting the horizons of colonial journalists to the borders of the nation—whether French or Algerian—risks not only denying the creativity of these writers but also foreclosing the many possibilities still present in our reading of the past.

NOTES

INTRODUCTION

1. *Le Progrès algérien*, March 12, 1900. All translations are my own.
2. *Le Progrès algérien*, March 12, 1900.
3. *L'Algérie française* (Algiers), February 21, 1909.
4. Habermas, *Structural Transformation*; Anderson, *Imagined Communities*.
5. Kaul, *Media and the British Empire*; Potter, *Newspapers and Empire*.
6. *L'Estafette d'Alger*, June 25, 1830.
7. Ageron, *Les Algériens musulmans*, 427; Maison, "La population de l'Algérie," 1082; McDougall, *History of Algeria*, 89–90; Maison, "La population de l'Algérie," 1079; Zimmerman, "Le recensement de 1911," 185.
8. Sers-Gal, "La presse algérienne"; Sers-Gal, "Le régime de la presse."
9. Ihaddaden, "L'histoire de la presse indigène," 70–71.
10. French minister of justice Jules Cazot, quoted in Briselainne, *La loi du 29 juillet*, ii, 2.
11. Based on statistics from the 1886 census given in Vignon, *La France dans L'Afrique du Nord*, 15.
12. The child was automatically naturalized if one parent had also been born on French soil. If both parents were foreign and born outside of France, the child became French at the age of majority unless he formally rejected French citizenship. See Le Sueur and Dreyfus, *La nationalité (droit interne)*.
13. Guignard, *L'abus de pouvoir*, 311.
14. Guignard, *L'abus de pouvoir*, 311.
15. Guignard, *L'abus de pouvoir*, 311.
16. Rector to Governor General, Algiers, August 28, 1912, and November 14, 1913, ANA, IBA/INS-033 no. 1869.
17. Asseraf, *Electric News*.
18. Ballantyne, "Reading the Newspaper," 49.

19. Montoy, "La presse dans le département"; Bouaboud, "L'Echo d'Alger."

20. Habermas, *Structural Transformation*; Anderson, *Imagined Communities*; Kalifa et al., *La civilisation du journal*; de la Motte and Pryzblyski, *Making the News*.

21. Anderson, *Imagined Communities*.

22. Chatterjee, *Nation and Its Fragments*, 3–13; Burton, *After the Imperial Turn*; McClintock, *Imperial Leather*, 352–89; Prakash, *Another Reason*.

23. Kalifa and Régnier, "Homogénéiser le corps national," 1411–28. See also Martin, "La presse départementale," 595–13; Venayre, "Identités nationales, altérités culturelles," 1381–1410; Zessin, "Presse et journalistes 'indigènes,'" 35–46; Merdaci, "Journalisme et littérature au XIXe siècle," 97–117.

24. Kalifa et al., *La civilisation du journal*.

25. Esclangon-Morin, *Les rapatriés d'Afrique du Nord*; Weil, *La république et sa diversité*; Silverman, *Deconstructing the Nation*.

26. See Cooper-Richet, "Aux marges de l'histoire," 175–87.

27. Gosnell, *Politics of Frenchness*, 79.

28. Smith, *Colonial Memory*; Vermeren, *Les Italiens à Bône*; Asseraf, *Electric News*.

29. Lorcin and Shepard, *French Mediterraneans*; Lewis, *Divided Rule*; Clancy-Smith, *Mediterraneans*.

30. Choi, *Decolonization and the French of Algeria*, 3.

31. Eldridge, *From Empire to Exile*, 259. The term *francisation* is used in Crespo and Jordi, *Les Espagnols dans l'algérois*, 160.

32. Vilar, "Argelia en las relaciones hispano-francesas," 323–43; Vermeren, *Les Italiens à Bône*.

33. Prochaska, *Making Algeria French*. See also Dine, "Shaping the Colonial Body," 33–48.

34. Clancy-Smith, *Rebel and Saint*.

35. McDougall, *History of Algeria*.

36. Asseraf, *Electric News*.

37. Asseraf, *Electric News*, 191, 19, 193.

38. Veracini, *Settler Colonialism*, 16–18.

39. McDougall, *History of Algeria*, examines the precolonial, colonial, and postindependence history of Algeria in detail.

40. The presence of settlers must therefore be added to the "tensions" recognized in the seminal work on colonial power edited by Cooper and Stoler, *Tensions of Empire*. For comparative studies, see Cavanagh and Veracini, *Routledge Handbook*; Michel, *Colonies de peuplement*.

41. Conklin, *Mission to Civilize*.

42. Sessions, *By Sword and Plow*, examines the context of this indecision. See also Sessions, "'L'Algérie devenue française,'" 165–77.

43. Durieu, *Les juifs algériens*, 46.

44. Politican Gustave Rouanet quoted in Durieu, *Les juifs algériens*, 42.

45. Bouveresse, *Un parlement colonial?*

46. Documents relating to the "contrôle des étrangers suspects du point de vue de la défense nationale," ANOM, 91 1F 21.

47. For a study of this discourse, see Davis, *Resurrecting the Granary of Rome*.

48. The French national dimension of Latin identification is examined in Lorcin, "Rome and France in Africa," 295–329; Lorcin, *Imperial Identities*.

49. Amster, *Medicine and the Saints*.

50. Ricoux, *La population européenne en Algérie (1873–1881)*, 47, 92.

51. Ricoux, *Contribution à l'étude*, 105.

52. On Maltese settlers, see Smith, *Colonial Memory*.

53. Hall, *White, Male and Middle Class*, 205–95; Mangan, *"Manufactured" Masculinity*; Schwarz, *White Man's World*, 85.

54. Nye, *Masculinity and Male Codes of Honor*.

55. Evans, "Towards an Emotional History," 213.

56. Vergès, *Monsters and Revolutionaries*.

1. THE NEW WHITE RACE

1. *El Patuet*, August 30, 1883.

2. *La Croix de l'Algérie et de la Tunisie*, January 2, 1908.

3. *Le Sans-culotte*, March 4, 1888.

4. *L'Algérie, journal du soir*, December 16, 1894.

5. *Le Progrès algérien*, March 12, 1890.

6. *Annuaires de la presse*, Paris, 1884–1901.

7. *La Joven España*, November 22, 1888.

8. *La France algérienne* (Bône [Annaba]), April 14, 1907.

9. *Le Sémaphore*, November 1, 1915.

10. Roberts, *Disruptive Acts*.

11. *Le Petit fanal oranais*, January 1, 1900.

12. *L'Union latine*, May 13, 1903, March 20, 1904; *La France algérienne* (Bône [Annaba]), May 5, 1907; *La Guerre aux Abus*, November 23, 1891; *Le Sans-culotte*, October 30, 1887; *Le Progrès algérien*, March 21, 1900; *Le Petit fanal*, January 5, 1900.

13. *Le Petit fanal oranais*, January 1, 1900.

14. *Le Progrès algérien*, March 15, 20, 1900.

15. Pick, *Faces of Degeneration*.

16. Jennings, *Curing the Colonizers*.

17. Legg, "Medical Press," 105–24.

18. *Bulletin médical de l'Algérie*, April 10, 1911.

19. *La Kabylie*, July 10, 1910; *Oran journal*, December 2, 1900.

20. *Le Réveil des colons*, August 9, 1896.

21. *L'Indépendant*, February 5, 1885.

22. Ricoux, *Contribution à l'étude*, 2.

23. Ricoux, *Contribution à l'étude*, 105.

24. *L'Algérie, journal du soir*, December 16, 1894.

25. See Corbin, *Foul and the Fragrant*.

26. *L'Algérie, journal du soir*, December 21, 1894.

27. *L'Algérie, journal du soir*, January 24, 1895.

28. Hunt, "Many Bodies of Marie-Antoinette," 268–84; Andress, "Living the Revolutionary Melodrama," 103–28.

29. Scott, *La citoyenne paradoxale*.

30. *Le Petit fanal oranais*, January 1, 1900.

31. Nye, *Masculinity and Male Codes of Honor*.

32. Forth, *Dreyfus Affair*.

33. McLaren, *Trials of Masculinity*; Berenson, *Trial of Madame Caillaux*.

34. *Bulletin médical de l'Algérie*, April 10, 1911.

35. *La France algérienne* (Bône [Annaba]), April 7, 1907.

36. ANOM, 91 1F 44.

37. *Algérie-Sports*, April 29, 1905.

38. Surkis, *Sexing the Citizen*.

39. *La Bataille*, March 4–June 20, 1897; *La Voix des jeunes*, May 15–29, 1904. A similar publication, *La Jeune France*, limited its readership to the descendants of French settlers and promoted French cultural assimilation; see *La Jeune France*, November 21–December 19, 1907.

40. *La Bataille*, March 11, 1897.

41. *L'Algérie nouvelle*, August 6, 1893.

42. *L'Algérie, journal du soir*, March 10, 1895.

43. Sessions, *By Sword and Plow*.

44. *La France africaine*, April 10, 1892.

45. *La France africaine*, April 1, 1894.

46. *L'Algérie, journal du soir*, December 16, 1894.

47. See plans for the urban development of Bône and Oran in *La France algérienne* (Bône [Annaba]), April 21, 1907; *La France africaine*, August 4–8, 1893.

48. *La Nouvelle France* (Algiers), September 11–October 16, 1886; *La France africaine*, December 10, 1892.

49. *La France africaine*, December 10, 1892; emphasis added.

50. *La France africaine*, December 10, 1892.

51. *L'Algérie française* (Constantine), July 2, 1897.

52. *L'Indépendant*, January 17, 1885.

53. *Le Peuple algérien*, December 2, 1910.

54. *L'Union latine*, May 17, 1903.

55. See *Le Zéramna*, January 23, 1883; *L'Indépendant*, February 1, 1885; *La France africaine*, September 19, 1893.

56. *L'Ami du peuple*, November 5, 1896.

57. *Le Sans-culotte*, October 23, 1887–August 20, 1893; *La Guerre aux Abus*, July/August–November 23, 1891; *Mon journal*, July 10, 1907.

58. *La Guerre aux Abus*, July/August 1891.

59. Martin, *La presse écrite en France*, 47.

60. *Le Progrès*, August 17, 1895.

61. *L'Africain*, March 22, 1882.

62. *Le Progrès*, August 19, 1905, July 21, 1906; *L'Illustration algérienne, tunisienne et marocaine*, December 25, 1906, May 18, 1907.

63. *L'Illustration algérienne, tunisienne et marocaine*, May 18, 1907.

64. Chopin, "Embodying 'the New White Race,'" 1–20.

65. Roberts, *Disruptive Acts*.

66. Sinha, "Britishness, Clubbability," 489–521.

67. *L'Algérie, journal du soir*, January 2–3, 1895.

68. *L'Algérie, journal du soir*, December 21, 1894, January 10, 1895; *Le Républicain*, December 22, 1901.

69. *L'Algérie, journal du soir*, December 21, 1894.

70. *L'Algérie, journal du soir*, January 23, 1895. See also E. Guerin in *L'Union latine*, April 5, 1903.

71. Lorcin, *Imperial Identities*.

72. *La Nouvelle France* (Algiers), October 2, 1886.

73. *La France africaine*, November 18, 1891.

74. *La Nouvelle France* (Algiers), October 2, 1886.

75. *Le Petit fanal*, January 10, 1900; *La France africaine*, January 1, 1882.

76. *La Lanterne de Cagayous*, no. 1, 1901

77. *Le Petit fanal*, April 11, 1900.

78. *La Nouvelle France* (Algiers), September 11, 1886.

79. *La Nouvelle France* (Algiers), September 11, 1886.

80. *Fémitania* [*Fémina journal*], June 25, 1911.

81. *Fémina journal*, June 25, 1911.

82. Roberts, *Disruptive Acts*.

83. *Fémina journal*, June 4, 1911.

84. *Fémitania* [*Fémina journal*], June 25, 1911.

85. *L'Egalité*, October 1, 1892.

86. *Fémina journal*, June 4, 1911.

87. *Fémitania* [*Fémina journal*], June 25, 1911.

88. *La Jeune France antijuive*, May 6, March 28, 1900.

89. *La Jeune France antijuive*, March 21, 1900.

90. *La Jeune France antijuive*, March 31, 1900. Writing under a pseudonym, Anza gave no further clues to her identity.

91. *La Jeune France antijuive*, March 28, 1900.

92. Assan, *Les consistoires israélites d'Algérie*, 209.

93. *L'Israélite algérien*, July 23, 1870.

94. Assan, *Les consistoires israélites d'Algérie*, 86.

95. *L'Israélite algérien*, August 12, 1870.

96. *La Jeunesse israélite*, from May 2, 1890; *L'Israélite algérien*, from January 15, 1900; *Le Nouvelliste oranais*, from December 5, 1902.

97. *Le Nouvelliste oranais*, December 5, 1902.

98. *Le Nouvelliste oranais*, December 5, 1902.

99. *La Jeunesse israélite*, June 20, 1890.

100. *La Jeunesse israélite*, June 6, 1890. See also *Le Radical algérien*, May 30, 1883.

101. Assan, *Les consistoires israélites d'Algérie*, 208.

102. *La Gazette de l'Algérie*, July 11, 1884.

103. *La Gazette de l'Algérie*, July 11, 1884.

104. *La Gazette de l'Algérie*, July 11, 20, 1884.

105. *La Gazette de l'Algérie*, August 3, 1884.

106. Zessin, "Presse et journalistes 'indigènes,'" 35–46.

107. *Le Siècle*, August 31, September 21, October 5, 12, 20, 26, November 2, 23, December 2, 1863.

108. Levallois, *Ismaÿl Urbain*, 431–32.

109. *L'Echo d'Oran*, December 24, 1863.

110. *El Montakheb*, April 23, 1882.

111. *El Montakheb*, June 4, 1882.

112. *El Montakheb*, July 2, 1882.

113. *L'Echo d'Oran* quoted in *L'Akhbar*, May 23, 1865.

114. *La Lanterne de Mohamed Biskri*, April 28–June 2, 1898.

115. *La Lanterne de Mohamed Biskri*, April 28, 1898.

116. *La Lanterne de Mohamed Biskri*, April 28, 1898.

117. See chapter 4.

118. *L'Indépendant*, May 2, 5, 1865.

119. *La Kabylie*, July 10, 1910.

120. *Fraternidad obrera*, November 1, 1883.

121. Article 5 of the law of July 29, 1881.

122. *El Hack* (Bône [Annaba]), from July 30, 1893; Merdaci, "Journalisme et littérature au XIXe siècle," 97; *El Misbah*, from June 3, 1904.

123. Ihaddaden, "L'histoire de la presse indigène," 201.

124. *Le Croissant*, December 1, 1906; *L'Echo d'Alger*, January 23, 1914.

125. Ihaddaden, "L'histoire de la presse indigène," 79.

126. Colonna, "Educating Conformity," 346–70.

127. *El Misbah*, from June 3, 1904; *L'Algérie franco-arabe*, from August 25–26, 1898; *L'Islam*, from January 7, 1912 (launched in 1910); *Le Rachidi*, from June 28, 1912 (launched in 1911); *El Hack* (Bône [Annaba]), from July 30, 1893; *L'Eclair*, from March 24, 1895; *Le Croissant*, from October 22, 1906; *El Hack* (Oran), from October 15–21, 1911.

128. Merdaci, "Journalisme et littérature au XIXe siècle," 103.

129. Ihaddaden, "L'Histoire de la presse indigène en Algérie"; Zessin, "Presse et journalistes 'indigènes,'" 35–46; Asseraf, *Electric News*. For the increase in Algerian Muslim use of the press and also the airwaves in the interwar era, see Scales, *Radio and the Politics of Sound*.

130. Aissaoui, "'For Progress and Civilization,'" 483.

131. *El Hack* (Bône [Annaba]), July 30, 1893.

132. *El Misbah*, June 3, 1904; *El Hack* (Oran), October 15–21, 1911.

133. *El Misbah*, June 10, 1904.

134. *L'Algérie franco-arabe*, August 25–26, 1898.

135. *El Hack* (Bône [Annaba]), July 29, 1893.

136. *L'Eclair*, March 24, 1895.

137. Ageron, "Une politique algérienne libérale," 126.

138. *Dou-el-fakar*, October 5, 1913–June 28, 1914.

139. *Dou-el-fakar*, October 20, 1913.

140. *Dou-el-fakar*, October 5, 1913.

141. *Tout ou Rien*, June 1912–June 1913.

142. *Tout ou Rien*, September 6, 1912.

143. *Tout ou Rien*, September 6, 1912.

144. *Tout ou Rien*, October 4, 1912.

145. *Tout ou Rien*, June 1912.

146. *Tout ou Rien*, July 1912.

147. *Tout ou Rien*, January and June 1913.

148. *Tout ou Rien*, June 1913.

149. *Tout ou Rien*, July 1912.

150. *Tout ou Rien,* June 1913.

151. Auclert, *Les femmes arabes en Algérie.*

2. SETTLER COLONIAL FAMILY ROMANCE

1. *Le Voyage de leurs majestés en Algérie,* 18.

2. *Le Voyage de leurs majestés en Algérie,* 19.

3. *Le Voyage de leurs majestés en Algérie,* 20.

4. Oulebsir, *Les usages du patrimoine,* 115–17.

5. *L'Akhbar,* May 4, 1865.

6. *L'Indépendant,* May 12, 1865.

7. Ageron, *Histoire de l'Algérie contemporaine,* 14.

8. *L'Akhbar,* May 18, 1865.

9. *Le Tell,* April 25, 1903.

10. Graebner, "'Unknown and Unloved,'" 51.

11. Vergès, *Monsters and Revolutionaries.*

12. Vergès, *Monsters and Revolutionaries.*

13. Barclay, "*Pied-Noir* Colonial Family Romance," 67–78.

14. Hunt, *Family Romance,* 53.

15. Best, "Une statue monumentale," 303–22; Forth, *Dreyfus Affair.*

16. Vergès, *Monsters and Revolutionaries.*

17. Nandy, *Intimate Enemy.*

18. Sessions, *By Sword and Plow.*

19. Arsan, "'There Is, in the Heart of Asia,'" 79.

20. Georgel, Vergès, and Vivien, *L'abolition de l'esclavage.* For an artistic depiction, see Alphonse Garreau, *Allégorie de l'abolition de l'esclavage à la Réunion, 20 décembre 1848,* 1849, oil on canvas, 129.5x108 cm, Musée du Quai Branly, Paris, http://www.quaibranly.fr/fr/explorer-les-collections/base/Work/action/show/notice/373950-allegorie-de-labolition-de-lesclavage-a-la-reunion-20-decembre-1848/.

21. On the development of the "civilizing mission," see Conklin, *Mission to Civilize.* On the representation of this mission in the press and the gendered dimension of these representations, see Berenson, *Heroes of Empire;* Katz, *Murder in Marrakesh.*

22. *La France algérienne* (Bône [Annaba]), April 7, 1907.

23. Vergès, *Monsters and Revolutionaries,* 4.

24. Settlers' attitudes conform to the "French declensionist environmental narrative" described in Davis, *Resurrecting the Granary of Rome.*

25. Veracini, *Settler Colonialism,* 34.

26. *L'Echo d'Oran* in *L'Indépendant,* May 5, 1865.

27. Oulebsir, *Les usages du patrimoine.*

28. Guignard, "Conservatoire ou révolutionnaire?," 81–95.

29. *L'Indépendant*, May 9, 1865.

30. *L'Indépendant*, May 9, 1865; *L'Akhbar*, May 19, 1865.

31. *L'Indépendant*, May 9, 1865.

32. *L'Akhbur*, May 1, 1865.

33. *L'Indépendant*, May 9, 1865.

34. *L'Akhbar*, May 1, 1865.

35. *L'Indépendant*, May 16, 1865.

36. *L'Echo d'Oran* in *L'Akhbar*, May 25, 1865.

37. Adresse de la municipalité de Cheragar à Sa Majesté l'Empereur, May 25, 1865, ANOM, GGA 6G 1.

38. Ageron, *Histoire de l'Algérie contemporaine*, 33–34.

39. *Voyage de leurs majestés en Algérie*.

40. *Voyage de leurs majestés en Algérie*, 39.

41. *Voyage de leurs majestés en Algérie*, 22.

42. *Voyage de leurs majestés en Algérie*, 27.

43. Secrétaire General to S. Ex. le Gouvr. Gnl., July 6, 1865, ANOM, GGA 6G 1.

44. *L'Akhbar*, May 16, 1865.

45. *L'Indépendant*, May 31, 1865.

46. *L'Akhbar*, June 4, 1865; *L'Indépendant*, June 2, 9, 1865.

47. *L'Akhbar*, May 28, 1865.

48. *L'Indépendant*, May 5, 1865.

49. *L'Indépendant*, May 9, 1865.

50. *Le Sémaphore* in *L'Indépendant*, May 19, 1865.

51. *L'Akbhar*, May 4, 1865.

52. *L'Akbhar*, May 11, 1865

53. *L'Indépendant*, June 6, 1865

54. *Le Sémaphore* quoted in *L'Indépendant*, May 23, 1865.

55. *Le Sémaphore* quoted in *L'Indépendant*, May 23, 1865.

56. *Le Siècle*, July 2, August 24, 31, September 21, October 5, 12, 20, 26, November 2, 23, December 2, 1863; *La Presse*, March 5, 1863.

57. *Le Siècle*, August 31, September 21, October 5, 12, 20, 26, November 2, 23, December 2, 1863; Levallois, *Ismaÿl Urbain*, 431–32.

58. *Le Siècle*, November 23, 1863; also quoted in *L'Echo d'Oran*, December 24, 1863.

59. *L'Echo d'Oran*, December 24, 1863.

60. *L'Akhbar*, May 19, 1865.

61. *L'Akhbar*, June 4, 1865. In the original article, the neologism *arabolâtre*—which fuses the two words *arabe* (Arab) and *idolâtre* (idolatrous)—was used in the place of the suggested translation, *arabophile*.

62. *L'Illustration*, May 13, 1865.

63. *L'Akhbar*, May 19, 1865.

64. *L'Akhbar*, May 19, June 4, 1865; *L'Indépendant*, May 23, 1865.

65. *L'Akhbar*, May 19, 1865.

66. *L'Akhbar*, May 19, June 4, 1865.

67. Sessions, "'L'Algerie devenue française,'" 172.

68. *L'Indépendant*, May 19, 1865.

69. *L'Indépendant*, May 23, 1865.

70. *L'Indépendant*, May 19, 1865.

71. *L'Indépendant*, May 19, 1865.

72. *L'Indépendant*, May 16, 1865.

73. *L'Indépendant*, May 23, 1865.

74. *L'Akhbar*, May 1, 1865.

75. *L'Akhbar*, May 14, 1865.

76. *L'Indépendant*, May 16, 1865.

77. Membres du conseil municipal de Ténès to Sa Majesté l'Empereur Napoléon III, Ténès, May 9, 1865; *Préfet d'Alger* to Governor General, Algiers, May 17, 1865, ANOM, GGA 6G 1.

78. Shepard, *Invention of Decolonization*, 26.

79. Administrator's note on "M.Mohammed-ben-Driss" [1903], ANOM, GGA 6G 1.

80. Taithe, "La famine de 1866–1868," 113–27.

81. Sers-Gal, "Le régime de la presse."

82. Extrait du registre des délibérations du conseil municipal, Algiers, May 16, 1870, ANOM, GGA 6G 2.

83. *La France algérienne* (Oran), October 29, 1871.

84. *La France algérienne* (Algiers), October 29, 1871.

85. Ageron, *Histoire de l'Algérie contemporaine*, 49.

86. *Le Sans-culotte*, May 17, 1891.

87. Ricoux, *Contribution à l'étude*; Ricoux, *La démographie figurée*; Ricoux, *La Population européenne en Algérie (1873–1881)*; Ricoux, *La Population européenne en Algérie pendant l'année 1886*; Mandeville and Demontès, *Etudes de démographie algérienne*; *L'Indépendant*, February 5, 1885.

88. Mandeville and Demontès, *Etudes de démographie algérienne*, 6–7.

89. *L'Algérie, journal du soir*, March 16, 1895.

90. See chapter 3.

91. *L'Antijuif algérien*, May 18, 1898.

92. *L'Avenir de Tebessa*, April 26, 1903.

93. *Le Tell*, April 22, 1903.

94. Ihl, "Sous le regard de l'indigène," 216.

95. Ihl, "Sous le regard de l'indigène," 216.

96. The prevalent myths of French historiography are criticized in Meynier, *L'Algérie et la France*, 10–17. That the colonial regime was itself structured by violence was observed in Fanon, *Les damnés de la Terre*.

97. *La Dépêche algérienne*, March 30, 1903.

98. "Voyage de Monsieur le Président en Algérie et Tunisie. Avril 1903," ANOM, GGA 6G 1.

99. Inspecteur Général Chef du Service des Postes, des Télégraphes et des Téléphones de l'Algérie to Monsieur le Directeur des Postes et des Télégraphes Alger/Constantine/Oran, Algiers, March 31, 1903, ANOM, GGA 6G 1.

100. ANOM, GGA 6G 1.

101. "Le port de Bône," March 28, 1903; "Notice sur Philippeville," [1903], ANOM, GGA 6G 1.

102. "Notice sur la ville de Bône ainsi que sur les grands travaux, exploitations et monuments qui pourraient être visités par Monsieur le Président de la République," [1903], ANOM, GGA 6G 1.

103. "Notice sur Philippeville," ANOM, GGA 6G 1.

104. "Notice sur le développement de la colonisation dans la plaine de Bône," [1903]; "Notice sur Biskra," [1903], ANOM, GGA 6G 1.

105. "Notice sur Bou-Medine," [1903], ANOM, GGA 6G 1.

106. "Notice sur la mosquée de Sidi-bel-hassen," [1903], ANOM, GGA 6G 1.

107. *Le Réveil de Bougie*, April 26, 1903.

108. *L'Impartial*, April 26, 1903.

109. *La Dépêche algérienne*, April 16, 1903.

110. *Le Tell*, April 22, 1903; *L'Impartial*, March 29, 1903; *L'Avenir de Tebessa*, April 26, 1903.

111. *La Dépêche algérienne*, April 3, 8, 1903.

112. *Le Petit oranais*, March 23, 1903; *Le Tell*, March 14, 21, 1903.

113. *Le Tell*, March 14, April 8, 1903.

114. *Le Tell*, April 11, 1903.

115. The uprising and its aftermath is examined in detail in Phéline, *L'aube d'une révolution*.

116. Prochaska, *Making Algeria French*.

117. Phéline, *L'aube d'une révolution*, 73–90. On land requisition and its role in the debates surrounding the Margueritte uprising, see Sessions, "Débattre la licitation," 60–76.

118. *Le Tell*, March 4, 1903.

119. *Le Tell*, April 11, 1903.

120. *Le Réveil de Bougie*, March 26, 29, 1903.

121. *La Revue nord-africaine*, March 5, 1903.

122. *Le Tell*, April 5, 1903; *Le Réveil de Bougie*, March 26, 1903.

123. *L'Avenir de Tebessa*, April 26, 1903.

124. *Le Tell*, April 22, 1903.

125. *Le Tell*, April 15, 18, 1903.

126. *Le Petit oranais*, April 17, 1903

127. *La Revue nord-africaine*, April 15, 1903.

128. Surkis, *Sexing the Citizen*.

129. *La Dépêche algérienne*, April 16, 1903.

130. *Le Tell*, April 25, 1903.

131. *La Dépêche algérienne*, April 16, 1903.

132. *Le Tell*, April 25, 1903.

133. *Le Tell*, April 22, 1903.

134. *Le Tell*, April 25, 1903.

135. *L'Union latine*, April 12, 1903.

136. *Le Petit oranais*, April 17, 1903.

137. Révoil's uncle, Pierre Baragnon, was director of *Le Petit dauphinois,* a paper that had criticized Combes for his involvement in the expulsion of the Chartreux religious order. See *Le Journal du Loiret*, April 14, 15, 1903.

138. Phéline, *L'aube d'une révolution*, 177.

139. *La Défense*, April 11, 1903; *L'Impartial*, April 12, 1903.

140. *La Dépêche algérienne*, April 13, 14, 1903.

141. *Le Réveil de Bougie*, April 16, 1903; *Le Tell*, April 15, 18, 22, 1903.

142. *La Dépêche algérienne*, April 13, 14, 15, 1903.

143. Phéline, *L'aube d'une révolution*, 86.

144. *La Dépêche algérienne*, October 19, 1901.

145. *La Dépêche algérienne*, April 14, 1903.

146. *La Dépêche algérienne*, April 15, 1903.

147. *Le Tell*, April 18, 1903; *La Dépêche algérienne*, April 15, 1903.

148. Bouveresse, *Un parlement colonial?*

149. *Le Réveil de Bougie*, March 27, 1902.

150. *Le Réveil de Bougie*, April 23, 1903; *Le Tell*, May 6, 1903.

151. *Le Tell*, May 6, 1903.

152. Note, "M. Beun," ANOM, GGA 6G 1.

153. Note, "Dr. Sanrey," ANOM, GGA 6G 1.

154. *Le Tell*, February 28, 1903.

155. *Le Petit oranais*, March 2, 1903.

156. *Le Petit oranais*, March 2, 1903; *La Dépêche algérienne*, April 16, 1903.

157. *Le Tell*, April 25, 1903.

158. Spivak, "Can the Subaltern Speak?," 271–313; McClintock, *Imperial Leather*; Sinha, *Specters of Mother India*; Stoler, *Carnal Knowledge and Imperial Power*.

159. Fanon, *Dying Colonialism*, 5; Vince, *Our Fighting Sisters*.

160. Taraud, *La prostitution coloniale*. The experience of Dr. Dorothée Chellier is instructive in this regard. See Fredj, *Femme médecin en Algérie*.

161. Dubarry, *Les déséquilibrés de l'amour*.

162. Vince, *Our Fighting Sisters*; Sinha, *Specters of Mother India*.

163. *La Dépêche algérienne*, March 28, 1903.

164. *Le Tell*, April 18, 1903.

165. *L'Union latine*, May 3, 1903.

166. Général de division commandant le province d'Oran to the Governor General, Oran, April 28, 1865, ANOM, GGA 6G 1.

167. *La Dépêche algérienne*, April 15, 1903.

168. *L'Union latine*, April 5, 1903. See chapter 5 for a study of bilingual and multilingual publications.

169. *L'Union latine*, April 15, 19, 1903.

170. *Pro-patria*, June 16, 1910.

171. *El Misbah*, June 3, 1904.

172. *El Misbah*, June 3, 10, 1904.

173. *El Misbah*, June 10, 1904.

174. *El Misbah*, October 4, 1904.

175. *El Misbah*, June 17, July 29, August 12, September 2, 1904.

176. *El Hack* (Oran), October 15–21, October 29–November 4, December 23–30, 1911.

177. *El Hack* (Oran), December 9–16, 1911.

3. FOREIGNERS INTO FRENCHMEN?

1. Castéran, *L'Algérie française*, 114.

2. Obituary in *Le Sémaphore algérien*, November 1, 1915.

3. Castéran, *L'Algérie française*, 69.

4. *L'Antijuif*, from August 1898.

5. Castéran, *Les troubles d'Alger*, iii.

6. Castéran, *Les troubles d'Alger*, 9.

7. Castéran, *Les troubles d'Alger*, 7.

8. Castéran, *Les troubles d'Alger*, 135.

9. Wilson, "Anti-Semitic Riots," 803.

10. Friedman, *Colonialism and After*, xii. Benjamin Stora and Pierre Darmon have advanced similar arguments, interpreting settler anti-Jewish prejudice as a displaced reaction against Arabs. Stora, *Histoire de l'Algérie coloniale*, 39; Darmon, *Un siècle de passion algériennes*, 560.

11. Friedman, *Colonialism and After*.

12. The links made by journalists between local and national concerns at the time of the Dreyfus Affair in rural areas in France have been examined in Fitch, "Mass Culture," 55–95.

13. Wilson, *Ideology and Experience*, 232; emphasis added.

14. Hebey, *Alger, 1898*, 292.

15. Zack, "French and Algerian Identity Formation," 115–43.

16. Castéran, *Les troubles d'Alger*, 1.

17. Hassett, "Proud *Colons*," 195–212.

18. *Le Combat*, March 16, 1893.

19. See chapter 2.

20. Pick, *Faces of Degeneration*; Barrows, *Distorting Mirrors*.

21. Winock, "Les Affaires Dreyfus," 19–37.

22. Forth, *Dreyfus Affair*.

23. *L'Antijuif algérien*, January 20, 1898.

24. Dermenjian, "Les Juifs d'Algérie," 106.

25. The French term used by journalists was *judaïsant*.

26. Hebey, *Alger, 1898*, 56.

27. Bessis, *Maghreb, questions d'histoire*, 57; Dermenjian, "Les Juifs d'Algérie," 109.

28. *Le Combat*, March 9, 1893; Bonnenfant, *La Ligue antijuive*; *La Lutte antijuive*, May 11, 1898.

29. *Le Combat*, March 2, 1893.

30. *Le Combat*, March 9, 1893.

31. *Le Combat*, March 2, 1893.

32. Dermenjian, "Les Juifs d'Algérie," 111.

33. See chapter 5.

34. *La Lutte antijuive*, February 25, 1898.

35. Darmon, *Un siècle de passions algériennes*, 558.

36. For the period from 1870 to 1943, Geneviève Dermenjian estimates at least thirty colonial publications featured the term *Antijuif* in the title or subtitle, and "several dozen" more diffused anti-Jewish content without advertising the fact in the title. "La presse antijuive," 136.

37. *Le Colon antijuif algérien*, September 14, 1898.

38. *Le Combat socialiste antijuif*, March 15–29, 1895; *La Guerre aux Abus*, July/August–November 23, 1891.

39. See, for example, *Le Patriote*, July 7, 1895–March 29, 1896; *Le Progrès algérien*, March 12–31, 1900; *La Bataille*, March 4–June 20, 1897; *L'Algérie française* (Constantine), June 11–25, 1897; *Le Pauvre colon*, August 31, 1895–June 6, 1896; *La France africaine*, November 18, 1891–April 1, 1894; *La Nouvelle France*

(Algiers), August 28–October 23, 1886; *Le Radical algérien*, May 30, 1883; *Le Sans-culotte*, October 23, 1887–August 30, 1893.

40. *La Lanterne de Mohamed Biskri*, May 8, 1898.
41. *Le Combat*, March 2, 1893.
42. *Le Combat*, March 9, 1893.
43. *Le Combat*, March 2, 1893.
44. *L'Antijuif algérien*, February 27, 1898.
45. *L'Antijuif algérien*, March 20, 1898.
46. *L'Antijuif algérien*, February 13, 27, 1898.
47. *L'Antijuif algérien*, February 13, 27, 1898.
48. Drumont, *La France juive*; *La Libre parole*, from April 20, 1892.
49. *L'Antijuif algérien*, February 27, 1898.
50. *La Lutte antijuive*, May 8, 1898.
51. "After the vote," *Le Supplément illustré de l'Antijuif algérien*, May 8, 1898.
52. *Le Combat*, March 2, 1893.
53. *L'Antijuif algérien*, August 1, 1897.
54. *Le Radical algérien*, May 30, 1883.
55. *La Guerre aux Abus*, nos. 10 and 11, October 1891.
56. *L'Antijuif algérien*, February 27, 1898.
57. Nye, *Masculinity and Male Codes of Honor*; Surkis, *Sexing the Citizen*; McLaren, *Trials of Masculinity*.
58. Forth, *Dreyfus Affair*.
59. Castéran, *Les troubles d'Alger*, 1.
60. *Le Radical algérien*, May 30, 1883.
61. Castéran, *L'Algérie française*, 32–40.
62. Castéran, *L'Algérie française*, 40.
63. *L'Antijuif algérien*, August 1, 1897.
64. *Le Progrès algérien*, March 12, 1900.
65. *Le Radical algérien*, May 30, 1883.
66. *Le Sans-culotte*, May 13, 1888.
67. *Le Pauvre colon*, February 1, 1896.
68. *Le Pauvre colon*, May 1, 1896.
69. *Le Supplément illustré de l'Antijuif algérien*, December 19, 1899.
70. *Le Supplément illustré de l'Antijuif algérien*, August 6, 1899.
71. See Parisian publications *La Libre parole*, *L'Antijuif*, and *L'Antijuif français illustré* from the same period for examples of similar themes in metropolitan antisemitism.
72. *La France africaine*, July 21, 1893.
73. *La France africaine*, July 21, 1893.

74. *L'Algérie française* (Constantine), June 11, 1897.

75. *Mon journal*, July 10, 1907; *La Guerre aux Abus*, from July–August 1891.

76. *La Guerre aux Abus*, July–August 1891.

77. *Le Supplément illustré de l'Antijuif algérien*, September 18, 1898.

78. *Le Combat*, March 15, 1895.

79. Berenson, *Heroes of Empire*, 5.

80. Berenson, *Heroes of Empire*, 12.

81. *L'Antijuif algérien*, November 17, 1897, March 23, 24, 1898.

82. *L'Antijuif algérien*, March 24, 1898.

83. Castéran, *Les troubles d'Alger*, 14–18.

84. *Le Progrès algérien*, March 12, 1900; *L'Algérie française* (Constantine), June 15, 1897.

85. Castéran, *L'Algérie française*, 58.

86. *L'Antijuif algérien*, January 27, 1898.

87. *L'Antijuif algérien*, January 30, 1904.

88. *La Lutte antijuive*, March 30, May 11, 1898; *Le Progrès algérien*, March 24, 1900; *La Jeune France antijuive*, March 28, 1900; *Le Colon antijuif algérien*, October 12, 1898; *L'Antijuif algérien*, October 14, 1897; *Le Combat*, March 2, 1893.

89. *L'Antijuif algérien*, October 14, 1897; *Le Colon antijuif algérien*, October 12, 1898.

90. *Le Colon antijuif algérien*, October 12, 1898.

91. *L'Antijuif algérien*, January 25, 1900.

92. *La Lutte antijuive*, May 11, 1898.

93. *La Jeune France antijuive*, March 18, 1900.

94. Article in response to *Le Tirailleur* in *La Jeune France antijuive*, March 28, 1900.

95. *La Jeune France antijuive*, March 31, 1900.

96. *La Jeune France antijuive*, March 31, 1900. See also Anza's article "Dévouement entre femmes" in the April 11, 1900, issue.

97. *La Jeune France antijuive*, July 14, 1900.

98. *Le Colon antijuif algérien*, October 5, 1898.

99. *Le Radical algérien*, May 30, 1883.

100. *Le Combat*, March 9, 1893.

101. *Le Colon antijuif algérien*, September 14, 1898.

102. *Le Colon antijuif algérien*, October 16, 1898. At the time, these representatives were nominated by the governor general.

103. *La France africaine*, November 18, 1891.

104. *L'Antijuif algérien*, August 1, 1897.

105. Dermenjian-Hannequart, "La Crise antijuive à Oran," 316.

106. *Le Progrès algérien*, March 12, 1900; *L'Argus algérien*, April 12, 1895.

107. *Le Républicain*, January 2 and 5, 1902.

108. *La Bataille,* June 17, 1897.

109. *L'Algérie, journal du soir,* January 16, 1895.

110. Garrot, *Les juifs algériens,* 49–50.

111. Garrot, *Les juifs algériens,* 50.

112. *L'Algérie, journal du soir,* January 10, 1895.

113. *Le Progrès algérien,* March 12, 1900.

114. *Le Supplément illustré de l'Antijuif algérien,* March 27, 1898.

115. *La Lutte antijuive,* May 11, 1898.

116. "Préfecture d'Alger. Commissariat Spécial de la sureté des chemins de fer et du port. No 4216. La journée des Antijuifs. Rapport spécial du 2 mai 1901," ANOM, 91 1F 14. The nationalist allegiance of the Jeunesse Antisémite Nationaliste was ambiguous—the colonial movement was led by Lionne, a supporter of Max Régis and his proclamations concerning Algerian independence.

117. "Préfet d'Alger, sureté, no 4480," ANOM, 91 1F 14.

118. "Préfet d'Alger, sureté, no 4480," ANOM, 91 1F 14.

119. See, for example, *Le Châtiment,* December 8, 1895; *Le Supplément illustré de l'Antijuif algérien,* May 15, 22, July 28, 1901.

120. "Lionne, by Bazitche," *Le Supplément illustré de l'Antijuif algérien,* July 22, 1901.

121. "Four Outlaws," *Le Supplément illustré de l'Antijuif algérien,* March 3, 1898.

122. *Le Supplément illustré de l'Antijuif algérien,* March 27, 1898.

123. *L'Antijuif algérien,* June 15, 1904.

124. "Préfecture d'Alger. Commissariat Spécial de la sureté des chemins de fer et du port. No 4216. La journée des Antijuifs. Rapport spécial du 2 mai 1901," ANOM, 91 1F 14.

125. For example, *L'Israélite algérien,* from July 23, 1870; *La Jeunesse israélite,* from May 2, 1890; *Le Nouvelliste oranais,* from December 5, 1902.

126. *La Jeunesse israélite,* May 2, 1890.

127. *La Jeunesse israélite,* November 22–29, 1890.

128. *La Jeunesse israélite,* May 2, 1890.

129. Incidents involving the mistreatment of Algerian Jews by the police are reported in *La Jeunesse israélite,* June 6, 27, 1890; habitual attacks against Jews perpetrated by Zouaves are mentioned in the May 30, 1890, issue; the neglect of the Jewish community by the prefecture of Oran is noted in October 11–18, 1890.

130. *La Jeunesse israélite,* May 2, 1890.

131. Quoted in Durieu, *Les juifs algériens,* 45.

132. Dermenjian-Hannequart, "La crise antijuive à Oran," 315–18; Hebey, *Alger, 1898,* 218; Darmon, *Un siècle de passions algériennes,* 540.

133. *La Jeunesse israélite,* May 25, 1890.

134. *La Bataille*, May 30, 1897.

135. *La Bataille*, April 22, 1897.

136. *La Bataille*, April 1, 1897.

137. *La Bataille*, March 4, 1897.

138. "Antisémitisme, Ville d'Alger. Police. Commissariat Central. Copie," report by Bigot, commissioner of police, 1901, ANOM, 91 1F 14.

139. "Gouvernement Général de l'Algérie. Sureté Générale. Commissariat de Police. M. J. Bigot, Commissaire de Police," Algiers, July 10, 1901, ANOM, 91 1F 13.

140. Préfet du département d'Alger to Monsieur le Président du conseil ministre de l'intérieur et des cultes, Algiers, May 1901, ANOM, 91 1F 13. The central commissioner was less anxious, however, reporting to the prefect a few months later that "educated indigenous Muslims seldom read the *Antijuif*." Le commissaire central d'Alger to Monsieur le Préfet d'Alger, Algiers, July 12, 1901, ANOM, 91 1F 13.

141. "Gouvernement Général de l'Algérie. Sureté Générale. Commissariat de Police. M. J. Bigot, Commissaire de Police," Algiers, July 10, 1901, ANOM, 91 1F 13. The *préfet* of Algiers expressed similar anxieties. See Préfet du département de l'Alger to Monsieur le Président du conseil ministère de l'intérieur et des cultes, Algiers, May 1901, ANOM, 91 1F 13.

142. As noted in Lorcin, *Imperial Identities*, the attitudes of administrators and settlers differed toward Arabs and Berbers, yet converged in their suspicion of Islam.

143. Durieu, *Les juifs algériens*, 53.

144. Castéran, *L'Algérie française*, 260.

145. Durieu, *Les juifs algériens*, 52.

146. Durieu, *Les juifs algériens*, 44.

147. Durieu, *Les juifs algériens*, 41–42.

148. Durieu, *Les juifs algériens*, 42.

149. Durieu, *Les juifs algériens*, 46.

150. Quoted in Durieu, *Les juifs algériens*, xv.

151. *La Lanterne de Mohamed Biskri*, May 26, 1898.

152. Castéran, *L'Algérie française*, 131.

153. *La Lanterne de Mohamed Biskri*, May 26, 1898.

154. *Le Petit fanal oranais*, October 3, 1900.

155. Berenson, *Heroes of Empire*, 12–13.

156. *L'Union Antijuive*, December 23, 1903.

157. *La Jeune France antijuive*, March 18, 1900; *Le Républicain*, May 22, 1902.

158. Castéran, *L'Algérie française*, 133. Castéran did, however, support financial autonomy.

159. Castéran, *L'Algérie française*, 272; *Le Petit fanal oranais*, October 8, 1900.

160. *La Jeune France*, November 21, 1907. The Oranais paper shared the same title as the contemporaneous publication from Algiers yet advocated the cultural assimilation of foreign settlers instead of their cultural and political exclusion.

161. *Le Trait d'union*, May 17, 1903.

162. Anonymous "old Algerian" journalist quoted in Durieu, *Les juifs algériens*, 43.

163. *Le Républicain*, January 26, 1902.

164. Ricoux dedicated his first work on acclimatization and demography in Algeria to his wife, referencing their common interest in the topic as "children of this land," born in Algeria and founding their own family in the colony. Ricoux, *Contribution à l'étude*. See also Ricoux, *La population européenne en Algérie (1873–1881)*.

165. *Le Bulletin médical de l'Algérie*, April 10, 1911.

166. Paul Leroy-Beaulieu quoted in *L'Union latine*, May 17, 1903.

167. *Le Progrès*, July 24, 1910.

168. *L'Africa*, May 21, 1911.

169. See chapters 1 and 5.

170. *L'Union latine*, May 3, 1903.

171. Bouveresse, *Un parlement colonial?*

172. *Le Petit oranais*, December 1, 1902.

173. *L'Union latine*, May 17, 1903.

174. *Le Trait d'union*, May 17, 1903.

175. *L'Union latine*, May 24, 1903.

176. Hassett, "Proud *Colons*."

177. Ricoux, *Contribution à l'étude*, 109–13.

4. PAGES WITHOUT BORDERS

1. Acknowledgment: This chapter is derived in part from Chopin, "Pages without Borders," 152–74. *La Revue algérienne et tunisienne*, from January 31, 1891; *Le Turco*, from March 3, 1895; *Annales africaines*, from September 1904.

2. Mallebay, *Cinquante ans de journalisme*, 218.

3. Mallebay, *Cinquante ans de journalisme*, 219.

4. Wenzlhuemer, "Dematerialization of Telecommunication," 345–72.

5. Bouaboud, "L'Echo d'Alger"; Montoy, "La presse dans le département."

6. Mallebay, *Cinquante ans de journalisme*, 218.

7. Wenzlhuemer, "Dematerialization of Telecommunication," 365.

8. Wenzlhuemer, "Dematerialization of Telecommunication," 362.

9. Lester, "British Settler Discourse," 24–48.

10. Asseraf, *Electric News*, 68.

11. Asseraf, *Electric News*, 66.

12. Asseraf, *Electric News*, 18.

13. Habermas, *Structural Transformation*; Anderson, *Imagined Communities*.

14. Asseraf, *Electric News*; Bouaboud, "L'Echo d'Alger"; Montoy, "La presse dans le département."

15. Montoy, "La presse dans le département," 47–50.

16. Mallebay, *Cinquante ans de journalisme*, 219.

17. Mallebay, *Cinquante ans de journalisme*, 271.

18. Hourant, "Ernest Mallebay, journaliste algérien."

19. Ballantyne, "Reading the Newspaper," 49.

20. Bouaboud, "L'Echo d'Alger"; Montoy, "La presse dans le département."

21. Ballantyne, "Reading the Newspaper," 50.

22. Rantanen, "New Sense of Place," 438.

23. Bielsa, "News Translation," 196–211.

24. Potter, *News and the British World*; Lambert, "'Thinking Is Done in London'"; Lester, "British Settler Discourse."

25. Burton, "Getting outside the Global," 199–216.

26. Potter, *News and the British World*, 13.

27. Veracini, *Settler Colonialism*, 29.

28. Bouaboud, "L'Echo d'Alger"; Montoy, "La presse dans le département."

29. Bouaboud, "L'Echo d'Alger," 30.

30. Mallebay, *Cinquante ans de journalisme*.

31. Mallebay, *Cinquante ans de journalisme*, 14.

32. Mallebay, *Cinquante ans de journalisme*, 303.

33. Daniel Nadeau has identified similar conditions of production within the ethnically and culturally diverse settler population of Sherbrooke, Quebec. Nadeau, "Identité nationale ou identités nationales," 307–19.

34. Mallebay, *Cinquante ans de journalisme*, 322.

35. Mallebay, *Cinquante ans de journalisme*, 313.

36. *Le Petit fanal oranais*, January 5, 1900.

37. *Le Petit fanal oranais*, October 1, 1897.

38. Griset, *Entreprise, technologie et souveraineté*; Potter, *News and the British World*.

39. *Le Trait d'union*, May 17, 1903; *L'Union latine*, November 14, 1907. *L'Union latine* was a multilingual paper but did not adhere to a strict correspondence of national language and national news. The three articles from *L'Union latine* were all printed in French.

40. Bouaboud, "L'Echo d'Alger," 33.

41. *La Dépêche algérienne*. The column "Spanish Affairs" appeared regularly from January 1, 1898, and the column "Italian News" from March 25, 1898.

42. Ballantyne, "Reading the Newspaper," 55.

43. *La Revue algérienne et tunisienne*, January 31, 1891; *La Lega franco-italiana*, from December 10, 1896.

44. *Fraternidad obrera*, January 6, 24, 1884; *L'Union latine*, August 24, 1907; *Pro-patria*, June 23, 1910.

45. *Fraternidad obrera*, January 24, 1884.

46. *L'Africa*, May 21, 1911.

47. *Le Trait d'union*, May 17, 1903.

48. *L'Union latine*, April 5, 1903.

49. *Le Trait d'union*, May 17, 1903; *Journal général de l'Algérie et de la Tunisie*, September 12, 1909.

50. Mallebay, *Cinquante ans de journalisme*, 219.

51. Durieu, *Les juifs algériens*, 41.

52. Wilson, "Anti-Semitic Riots," 803.

53. Darmon, *Un siècle de passions algériennes*, 256–62.

54. *La France algérienne* (Oran), October 29, 1871.

55. *El Mosquito español*, November 16, 1884.

56. *El Patuet*, July 14, 1883.

57. *El Patuet*, September 23, 1883.

58. *Le Sans-culotte*, April 22, 1888.

59. Jansen, "Celebrating the 'Nation,'" 36–68.

60. *La Lanterne de Mohamed Biskri*, May 26, 1898.

61. *L'Algérie, journal du soir*, February 6, 1895.

62. *La Lanterne de Mohamed Biskri*, May 26, 1898.

63. *L'Algérie, journal du soir*, January 2–3, 1895.

64. *Le Sans-culotte*, 1887–91; *Le Bonnet phrygien*, 1901–8.

65. *La France africaine*, November 11, 1892. See also *La Nouvelle France* (Algiers), September 18, 1886; *Fraternidad obrera*, January 24, 1884; *La France algérienne* (Oran), October 31, 1871; *L'Union latine*, April 5, 1903.

66. *La France africaine*, November 11, 1892.

67. *Fraternidad obrera*, January 24, 1884.

68. *La France africaine*, November 11, 1892; *La Nouvelle France* (Algiers), September 18, 1886; *La France algérienne* (Oran), October 31, 1871; *Fraternidad obrera*, January 24 and 31, 1884.

69. *Fraternidad obrera*, April 6, 1884; *L'Union latine*, April 5, 1903.

70. *La France africaine*, April 10, 1892; *L'Union latine*, May 24, 1903.

71. *L'Algérie, journal du soir*, March 16, 1895.

72. *La France africaine*, April 10, 1892.

73. *La Kabylie*, August 7, 1910.

74. Evans, *Algeria*, 291.

75. Cambon, *Le gouvernement général de l'Algérie*, xv.

76. Beaumont, "Making of a War Correspondent," 124–37; Morgan, "Boer War and the Media," 1–16.

77. *La Dépêche algérienne*, January 1–June 12, 1900.

78. *La Dépêche algérienne*, February 25, 1900. Viator was the pseudonym of M. Meton-Cressent.

79. *Le Petit journal*, January 28, 1900.

80. *La Dépêche algérienne*, January 2, 1900.

81. *La Dépêche algérienne*, January 2, 12, 17, 1900; *Le Progrès de Bel Abbès*, May 16, 1900.

82. *La Dépêche algérienne*, January 12, 1900.

83. *Le Bulletin municipal officiel de la ville d'Alger*, December 20, 1899.

84. *Le Petit mascaréen*, November 11, December 2, 16, 1900; *L'Illustration*, December 1, 1900; *Le Petit journal*, December 2, 9, 16, 1900; *Le Petit parisien*, December 2, 9, 1900.

85. *La Dépêche algérienne*, February 25, 1900.

86. *L'Algérie, journal du soir*, December 16, 1894.

87. *La Croix de l'Algérie et de la Tunisie*, November 4, 1900.

88. *L'Union latine*, May 3, 1903.

89. *Le Petit fanal*, October 10, 1900. This rumor appears to have been unfounded.

90. *Le Républicain*, December 26, 29, 1901.

91. Castéran, *L'Algérie française*, 255.

92. Castéran, *L'Algérie française*, 133.

93. *L'Union latine*, May 3, 1903.

94. *L'Union latine*, May 3, April 5, 1903.

95. *El Patuet*, July 29, 1883; *Fraternidad obrera*, May 4, 1884.

96. *El Correo español*, January 5, 12, 16, 30, 1897; *La Dépêche algérienne*, January 30, March 4, 1898.

97. *El Mosquito español*, November 30, 1884; *El Patuet*, July 29, 1883.

98. *El Correo español*, January 5, 1897; *L'Ami du peuple*, May 1, 1898.

99. Schmidt-Nowara, *Conquest of History*.

100. *Fraternidad obrera*, April 20, November 6, 1884.

101. *El Correo español*, January 12, 16, 1897; *La Dépêche algérienne*, January 30, 1898.

102. *El Correo español*, January 16, 1897.

103. *Fraternidad obrera*, April 20, 1884.

104. *El Correo español*, January 30, 1897.

105. *L'Union latine*, May 3, 1903.

106. *L'Ami du peuple*, June 9–23, 1898.

107. *L'Ami du peuple*, June 9, 1898.

108. Ricoux, *Contribution à l'étude*, 105.

109. *L'Union latine*, May 17, 1903.

110. *L'Union latine*, April 5, 1903.

111. *La Dépêche algérienne*, March 3, 1898.

112. *Le Progrès algérien*, March 18, 1900; *L'Algérie, journal du soir*, March 12, 1895; *L'Impartial oranais*, September 27, 1895.

113. *Le Progrès algérien*, March 18, 1900.

114. Bouveresse, *Un parlement colonial?*

115. *Le Tell*, March 8, 14, 1903.

116. *Le Petit oranais*, December 1, 1902. See also *Le Républicain*, December 22, 1901; *Le Réveil de Bougie*, April 30, 1903.

117. *L'Algérie, journal du soir*, March 12, 1895.

118. *Oran journal*, December 2, 1900.

5. ALGERIANS OF ANY NATIONALITY

1. *L'Union latine*, April 5, 1903.

2. *El Hack* (Oran), October 22–28, 1911.

3. These included at least nine Franco-Arabic newspapers, one Franco-Hebraic newspaper, two Franco-Judeo-Arabic newspapers, five Franco-Spanish newspapers, two Franco-Italian newspapers, and two trilingual newspapers in French, Spanish, and Italian. A number of untraceable additional bi- and multilingual papers are advertised in other local publications.

4. Bhabha, *Location of Culture*.

5. For a detailed analysis of the various linguistic phenomena associated with language contact, see Matras, *Language Contact*. For the history of language contact in precolonial Algeria, see Dakhlia, *Trames de langues*; Benrabah, *Language Conflict in Algeria*, 22–23. For observations concerning bi- and multilingualism among settlers, see Vilar, "La presse espagnole en Algérie," 53–64; Flores, *Le voleur d'huile*, 95.

6. Vilar, "La presse espagnole en Algérie," 54.

7. Gosnell, *Politics of Frenchness*, 48.

8. Ageron, *Histoire de l'Algérie contemporaine*, 67.

9. Ihaddaden, "L'histoire de la presse indigène," 157. The figure of three hundred was attained by *Le Croissant*, and the exceptional figure of three thousand by *L'Akhbar*.

10. For example, the column "Orthographe simplifiée" in *La Défense*, April 4, 11, 1902; "Lettre sabir" in *Le Sans-culotte*, November 20, 1887; "Condolences" from *El Correo español*, in *L'Union républicaine d'Oran*, January 10, 1905.

11. For the development of romantic thought concerning language, see Eymar, *La langue plurielle*, 25–26.

12. Dakhlia, "L'histoire parle-t-elle en langues?," 11–18
13. Benrabah, *Language Conflict in Algeria*, 4; Krishnaswamy and Burde, *Politics of Indians' English*.
14. Benrabah, *Language Conflict in Algeria*, 4.
15. See Lorcin, *Imperial Identities*.
16. Benrabah, *Language Conflict in Algeria*; Quitout, *Paysage linguistique*.
17. Veracini, *Settler Colonialism*, 4.
18. Bridge and Fedorowich, *British World*; Fedorowich and Thompson, *Empire, Migration and Identity*; Belich, *Replenishing the Earth*, 36.
19. Smith, *Colonial Memory*, 47.
20. Flores, *Le voleur d'huile*, 91.
21. For studies of language contact in other settler colonial contexts, see Ó Ciosain, "Old Languages in a New Country," 58–72; O'Connor, *Translation and Language*.
22. Thiesse, "Rôles de la presse," 127–37; Martin, "La presse départementale," 495–513; Venayre, "Identités nationales, altérités culturelles," 1381–1410.
23. Cooper-Richet, "Aux marges de l'histoire," 175. For discussion of international transfer in the press in France, see Thérenty and Vaillant, *Presse, nations et mondialisation*; Gumarães, *Les transferts culturels*; Cooper-Richet, Mollier, and Silem, *Passeurs culturels*; Mollier, Régnier, and Vaillant, *La production de l'immatériel*.
24. Cooper-Richet, "La diffusion du modèle victorien," 30. See also Cooper-Richet, "La presse en langue étrangère," 583–604.
25. Coski, *From Barbarism to Universality*.
26. *El Montakheb*, July 23, 1882; *El Misbah*, June 3, 10, 1904; *El Hack* (Oran), October 14, 1911, April 13, 1912.
27. Betts, *Assimilation and Association*.
28. This law was applied to the Algerian provinces from September 27, 1907. The general government retained the option of providing financial support to religious institutions for ten years following the application of the law.
29. Prochaska, *Making Algeria French*, 224; Prochaska, "History as Literature," 670–711. For an analysis of the linguistic traits of *pataouète*, see Flores, *Le voleur d'huile*.
30. *Le Petit oranais*, March 2, 1903; *Le Tell*, March 7, 1903.
31. Ihaddaden, "L'histoire de la presse indigène," 75–77.
32. *Le Moniteur algérien*, from January 27, 1832. See also Souriau-Hoebrechts, *La presse maghrébine*, 68–69.
33. Behagel, *La liberté de la presse*, 14.
34. *Le Mobacher*, from February 15, 1849.

35. Turin, "L'instruction sans l'école?," 367.

36. Souriau-Hoebrechts, *La presse maghrébine*, 70.

37. Ihaddaden, "L'histoire de la presse indigène," 46.

38. Ihaddaden, "L'histoire de la presse indigène," 162.

39. Dubois, *Colony of Citizens*, describes a similar appropriation of the language of French nationhood among *gens libres de couleur* and slaves during the French Revolution.

40. *El Montakheb*, July 2, 1882.

41. *El Montakheb*, August 20, 1882.

42. *El Montakheb*, August 20, 1882.

43. *El Montakheb*, April 30, 1882.

44. *El Montakheb*, April 23, 1882.

45. *El Montakheb.*, August 20, 1882.

46. Souriau-Hoebrechts, *La presse maghrébine*.

47. *El Hack* (Bône [Annaba]), July 30, 1893.

48. *El Hack* (Oran), March 16–23, April 6–13, 13–20, 1912.

49. Both versions of *El Hack* began as French-language publications before adopting a bilingual format.

50. Weil, *Qu'est-ce qu'un Français?*, 338.

51. Weil, *Qu'est-ce qu'un Français?*, 341.

52. Weil, *Qu'est-ce qu'un Français?*, 349–52.

53. *El Montakheb*, April 30, 1882.

54. *Le Croissant*, December 1, 1906.

55. *El Hack* (Oran), October 23–November 4, 1911.

56. *El Montakheb*, April 23, September 24, 1882; *El Hack* (Bône [Annaba]), August 6, 1893; *Le Croissant*, November 1, 22, 1906.

57. *Le Croissant*, November 22, 1906.

58. *Le Croissant*, October 22, 1906; *El Hack* (Oran), December 30, 1911.

59. *El Hack* (Oran), December 23–30, 1911.

60. *El Montakheb*, April 30, 1882.

61. *El Hack* (Oran), January 27–February 3, 1912.

62. *El Hack* (Oran), June 8–15, 1912.

63. *El Montakheb*, January 21, 1883.

64. *Le Croissant*, October 22, 1906.

65. *Le Croissant*, December 1, 1906, January 11, 22, 1907.

66. *Le Croissant*, December 1, 1906.

67. *El Montakheb*, June 18, 1882.

68. *El Hack* (Bône [Annaba]), July 30, 1893; *Le Croissant*, November 22, 1906; *El Hack* (Oran), November 4, 1911.

69. *El Hack* (Oran), March 2, 1912.

70. *Dou-el-fakar*, from October 5, 1913.

71. *El Hack* (Oran), May 11–18, 1912.

72. *Dou-el-fakar*, from October 5, 1913.

73. Ihaddaden, "L'histoire de la presse indigène," 290.

74. Ihaddaden, "L'histoire de la presse indigène," 85.

75. *L'Algérie franco-arabe*, August 25–26, 1898.

76. *El Misbah*, June 4, 1904.

77. *El Misbah*, June 10, 1904.

78. *El Misbah*, October 21, 1904.

79. *El Misbah*, June 10, 1904.

80. *El Misbah*, October 21, 1904.

81. *El Misbah*, August 5, 1904.

82. *El Misbah*, July 1, 1904.

83. *El Misbah*, November 25, 1904.

84. *El Misbah*, June 24, October 14, 21, 1904.

85. *El Misbah*, October 14, 1904.

86. *El Misbah*, November 25, 1904.

87. *El Misbah*, January 6, 1905.

88. *El Misbah*, June 3, 1904.

89. *L'Israélite algérien*, July 23, 1870.

90. *L'Israélite algérien*, July 23, 1870.

91. *La Jeunesse israélite*, May 2, 1890.

92. *Le Nouvelliste oranais*, December 5, 1902.

93. *La Jeunesse israélite*, May 2, 1890.

94. *Le Nouvelliste oranais*, December 5, 1902.

95. Benbassa, *Jews of France*, 90–92.

96. Allouche-Benayoun and Bensimon, *Les Juifs d'Algérie*, 37–39; Assan, "Les rabbins de France," 63–73.

97. *La Jeunesse israélite*, May 9, 1890.

98. *L'Israélite algérien*, August 26, 1870.

99. *Le Nouvelliste oranais*, January 16, 1903.

100. *L'Israélite algérien*, August 12, 1870.

101. *L'Israélite algérien*, July 29, 1870.

102. Vilar, "La presse espagnole en Algérie," 55.

103. Vilar, "La presse espagnole en Algérie," 55; Vilar, *La emigración española*; Yacine, "La communauté espagnole en Algérie," 41–52; Yacine, "Un journaliste espagnol en Algérie," 127–31.

104. *El Patuet*, from July 14, 1883; *La Fraternidad obrera*, from November 1, 1883.

105. *Lanterne des Issers*, November 7, 1884; *La Fraternidad obrera*, October 9, 1884.

106. *El Patuet*, September 27, 1883.

107. Vilar, "Argelia en las relaciones hispano-francesas," 325.

108. Vilar, *La emigración española*, 45.

109. *La Fraternidad obrera*, November 15, 1883.

110. *El Patuet*, September 27, 1883.

111. *La Fraternidad obrera*, January 16, 1887.

112. *La Fraternidad obrera*, November 11, 1883.

113. *La Fraternidad obrera*, August 31, 1884.

114. Schmidt-Nowara, *Conquest of History*, 10.

115. *La Fraternidad obrera*, January 17, 1884.

116. *La Fraternidad obrera*, December 9, 1883; *El Patuet*, September 6, 1883.

117. *La Fraternidad obrera*, December 9, 1883.

118. *La Fraternidad obrera*, November 1, 1883.

119. *El Patuet*, September 9, 1883.

120. Carden, *German Policy toward Neutral Spain*, 13.

121. *La Fraternidad obrera*, January 24, 1884.

122. *El Patuet*, September 23, 1883.

123. "We Will See Who Prevails," *El Patuet*, September 23, 1883.

124. *El Patuet*, September 23, 1883.

125. *El Patuet*, September 9, 1883.

126. *El Patuet*, August 18, 1883.

127. Friedman, *Colonialism and After*, xii.

128. *El Patuet*, August 18, 1883.

129. *La Fraternidad obrera*, January 16, 1887.

130. *La Fraternidad obrera*, December 9, 1883.

131. Renan, *Qu'est-ce qu'une nation?*

132. *La Fraternidad obrera*, January 16, 1887.

133. *La Fraternidad obrera*, December 9, 1883.

134. *Fraternidad obrera*, January 24, August 19, September 25, 1884.

135. See Matras, *Language Contact*, 101.

136. *La Fraternidad obrera*, November 18, 1883.

137. *La Fraternidad obrera*, November 18, 1883.

138. *La Fraternidad obrera*, November 11, 1883.

139. Flores, *Le voleur d'huile*, 95.

140. *La Fraternidad obrera*, March 30, 1884.

141. Bernard, "Le recensement de 1906," 27.

142. *Le Tonnerre*, from January 15, 1892; *La Mekerra*, from February 5, 1892; *Le Trait d'union*, from March 5, 1891; *La Lega franco-italiana*, from December 10, 1896.

143. *Le Tonnerre*, January 15, 22, 29, 1892.

144. Choate, "Identity Politics," 97–109.

145. *Le Trait d'union*, March 5, 1891.

146. *La Lega franco-italiana*, December 10, 1896.

147. *La Lega franco-italiana*, December 10, 13, 25, 31, 1896; *Le Trait d'Union*, March 5, 1891.

148. *Le Trait d'union*, March 19, 1891, April 23, 1891.

149. *La Lega franco-italiana*, 1896–97; *Le Tonnerre*, 1892.

150. *Le Trait d'union*, March 5, 1891.

151. *La Lega franco-italiana*, December 10, 1896.

152. *L'Africa*, May 21, 1911.

153. *La Lega franco-italiana*, December 20, 1896.

154. *Le Trait d'union*, September 27, 1891.

155. *Le Trait d'union*, March 5, April 23, September 27, 1891.

156. *L'Union latine*, from April 5, 1903; *Pro-patria*, from June 16, 1910.

157. *Pro-patria*, June 16, 1910.

158. *L'Union latine*, April 5, 1903.

159. *L'Union latine*, April 5, 1903.

160. *L'Union latine*, May 3, 1903

161. *L'Union latine*, May 3, 17, 24, 1903, January 17, 1904, April 15, 1906.

162. Reclus, *France, Algérie et colonies* ; *L'Union latine*, April 5, 1903.

163. Reclus, *France, Algérie et colonies*, 424–25.

164. Reclus quoted in *L'Union latine*, April 5, 1903.

165. *Pro-patria*, July 14, 1910.

166. Vilar, "La presse espagnole en Algérie," 59.

167. *L'Union latine*, October 11, 18, 25, November 1, 15, 22, 29, 1903, August 24, 1907.

168. *Pro-patria*, July 14, 1910.

169. *La Croix de l'Algérie et de la Tunisie*, August 20, 1905, October 31, 1907, January 2, 5, 1908; *La Semaine religieuse d'Oran* quoted in *La Croix de l'Algérie et de la Tunisie*, October 31, 1907.

170. *La Croix de l'Algérie et de la Tunisie*, January 5, 1908.

171. *L'Union latine*, September 7, 1907.

172. Randau, *Les Colons*, ii; Randau, *Les Algérianistes*.

CONCLUSION

1. Kalifa and Régnier, "Homogénéiser le corps national," 1411–28.

2. Anderson, *Cultivation of Whiteness*.

3. Levine, *Gender and Empire*; McClintock, *Imperial Leather*; Mangan, *"Manufactured" Masculinity*; Hall, *White, Male and Middle Class*.

4. Ageron, *Histoire de l'Algérie contemporaine*, 69.

5. McDougall, *History of Algeria*, 15.

6. McDougall, *History of Algeria*, 154–66.

7. Kaddache, *L'Etoile Nord-Africaine*.

8. Asseraf, *Electric News*.

9. Hassett, *Mobilizing Memory*.

10. Cummings, "Civilizing the Settler," 175–94; Hassett, "Proud *Colons*," 195–212.

11. Gosnell, *Politics of Frenchness*.

12. On the centennial celebrations and settlers' desire to use them to reaffirm belonging to the French nation, see Jansen, "Fête et ordre colonial," 64.

13. Eldridge, *From Empire to Exile*; Barclay, "Remembering Algeria," 244–61.

BIBLIOGRAPHY

Newspapers and journals used as primary sources are listed separately, given that they form the principal primary corpus of the work. This is intended to facilitate readers' evaluation of the use of sources.

ARCHIVES

ANA   Archives Nationales de l'Algérie, Birkhadem, Algeria
ANOM   Archives Nationales d'Outre-mer, Aix-en-Provence, France

NEWSPAPERS AND JOURNALS

Africa (Algiers)
Algérie-Sports (Algiers)
Annales africaines (Algiers)
Bulletin médical de l'Algérie (Algiers)
Dou-el-fakar (Algiers)
El Correo español (Oran)
El Hack (Bône [Annaba])
El Hack (Oran)
El Misbah (Oran)
El Montakheb (Constantine)
El Mosquito español (Oran)
El Patuet (Algiers)
Fémina journal (Algiers)
Fémitania [*Fémina journal*] *(Algiers)*
Fraternidad obrera (Algiers, then Oran)
Journal général de l'Algérie et de la Tunisie (Algiers)
La Bataille, Organe de la jeunesse algérienne (Constantine)
La Croix de l'Algérie et de la Tunisie (Algiers)
La Défense (Sétif)
La Dépêche algérienne (Algiers)
La France africaine (Oran)
La France algérienne (Algiers)
La France algérienne (Bône [Annaba])
La France algérienne (Oran)
La Gazette de l'Algérie (Algiers)
La Guerre aux Abus (Djidjeli [Jijel] then Bougie [Béjaïa])
La Jeune France (Oran)
La Jeune France antijuive (Algiers)
La Jeunesse israélite (Oran)
La Joven España (Oran)
La Kabylie (Bougie [Béjaïa])
L'Akhbar (Algiers)
La Lanterne de Mohamed Biskri (Algiers)

La Lanterne des Issers (Bordj-Menaïel)

La Lega franco-italiana (Bône [Annaba])

L'Algérie française (Algiers)

L'Algérie française (Constantine)

L'Algérie franco-arabe (Constantine)

L'Algérie, journal du soir (Algiers)

L'Algérie nouvelle (Oran)

La Libre parole (Paris)

La Lutte antijuive (Algiers)

La Mekerra (Bel Abbès)

L'Ami du peuple (Oran)

La Nouvelle France (Algiers)

La Nouvelle France (Oran)

L'Antijuif (Paris)

L'Antijuif algérien (Mustapha-Algiers)

L'Antijuif français illustré (Paris)

La Presse (Paris)

La Revue algérienne et tunisienne (Algiers)

La Revue nord-africaine (Algiers)

L'Argus algérien (Algiers)

L'Avenir de Tebessa (Constantine)

La Voix des jeunes (Algiers)

Le Bulletin municipal officiel de la ville d'Alger (Algiers)

Le Châtiment (Constantine)

L'Echo d'Oran (Oran)

L'Eclair (Bône [Annaba])

Le Colon antijuif algérien (Algiers)

Le Combat socialiste antijuif (Algiers)

Le Croissant (Algiers)

L'Egalité, Organe de la société civile pour la défense des droits des femmes (Algiers)

Le Journal du Loiret (Orléans)

Le Moniteur algérien (Algiers)

Le Nouvelliste oranais (Oran)

Le Patriote (Djidjeli [Jijel])

Le Pauvre colon (Bouira)

Le Petit fanal (Algiers)

Le Petit fanal oranais (Oran)

Le Petit journal (Paris)

Le Petit mascaréen (Mascara)

Le Petit oranais (Oran)

Le Petit parisien (Paris)

Le Peuple algérien (Algiers)

Le Progrès (Mascara)

Le Progrès algérien (Algiers)

Le Progrès de Bel-Abbès (Bel Abbès)

Le Rachidi (Djidjeli [Jijel])

Le Radical algérien (Algiers)

Le Républicain (Mascara)

Le Réveil de Bougie (Bougie [Béjaïa])

Le Réveil des colons (Algiers)

Le Sans-culotte (Oran)

Le Sémaphore (Algiers)

Le Siècle (Paris)

L'Estafette d'Alger (Algiers)

Le Supplément illustré de l'Antijuif algérien (Algiers)

Le Tell (Blida)

Le Tonnerre (Bel Abbès)

Le Trait d'union (Agha-Mustapha)

Le Trait d'union (Algiers)

Le Turco (Algiers)

Le Zéramna (Philippeville [Skikda])

L'Illustration (Paris)

L'Impartial (Djidjeli [Jijel])

L'Impartial oranais (Oran)

L'Indépendant (Constantine)

L'Islam (Algiers)

L'Israélite algérien (Algiers)

L'Union latine (Algiers)

L'Union républicaine d'Oran (Oran)

Mon journal (Tlemcen)

Oran journal (Oran)

Pro-patria (Algiers)

Tout ou Rien (Oran)

Ageron, Charles-Robert. *Histoire de l'Algérie contemporaine*. 1964. Reprint, Paris: Presses Universitaires de France, 1999.

———. *Les Algériens musulmans et la France 1871–1919. Tome premier*. 1968. Reprint, Paris: Editions Bouchene, 2005.

———. "Une politique algérienne libérale sous la III République (1912–1919)." *Revue d'histoire moderne et contemporaine* 6, no. 2 (1959): 121–51.

Aissaoui, Rabah. "'For Progress and Civilization': History, Memory and Alterity in Nineteenth-Century Colonial Algeria." *French History* 31, no. 4 (2017): 470–94.

Allouche-Benayoun, Joëlle, and Doris Bensimon. *Les Juifs d'Algérie: Mémoires et identités plurielles*. Paris: Editions Stavit, 1998.

Allouche-Benayoun, Joëlle, and Geneviève Dermenjian, eds. *Les Juifs d'Algérie: Une histoire des ruptures*. Aix-en-Provence: Presses universitaires de Provence, 2015.

Ameline de la Briselainne, Henri. *La loi du 29 juillet sur la liberté de la presse*. Paris: P. Dupont, 1881.

Amster, Ellen J. *Medicine and the Saints: Science, Islam and the Colonial Encounter in Morocco, 1877–1956*. Austin: University of Texas Press, 2013.

Anderson, Benedict. *Imagined Communities: Reflections on the Origins and Spread of Nationalism*. 1983. Reprint, New York: Verso, 2006.

Anderson, Warwick. *The Cultivation of Whiteness: Science, Health and Racial Destiny in Australia*. Durham NC: Duke University Press, 2006.

Andress, David. "Living the Revolutionary Melodrama: Robespierre's Sensibility and the Construction of Commitment in the French Revolution." *Representations* 114, no. 1 (2011): 103–28.

Annuaires de la presse. Paris, 1884–1901.

Arsan, Andrew. "'There Is, in the Heart of Asia, . . . an Entirely French Population': France, Mount Lebanon, and the Workings of Affective Empire in the Mediterranean, 1830–1920." In *French Mediterraneans. Transnational and Imperial Histories*, edited by Patricia M. E. Lorcin and Todd Shepard, 76–100. Lincoln: University of Nebraska Press, 2016.

Assan, Valérie. *Les consistoires israélites d'Algérie au XIXe siècle: "L'alliance de la civilisation et de la religion."* Paris: Armand Colin, 2012.

———. "Les rabbins de France et d'Algérie face à la 'mission civilisatrice.'" In Allouche-Benayoun and Dermenjian, *Les Juifs d'Algérie*, 63–73.

Asseraf, Arthur. *Electric News in Colonial Algeria*. Oxford: Oxford University Press, 2019.

Auclert, Hubertine. *Les femmes arabes en Algérie*. Paris: Société d'éditons littéraires, 1900.

Ballantyne, Tony. "Reading the Newspaper in Colonial Otago." *Journal of New Zealand Studies* 12 (2011): 47–64.

Barclay, Fiona. "The *Pied-Noir* Colonial Family Romance in André Téchiné's *Les Roseaux sauvages.*" *Expressions maghrébines* 12, no. 2 (2013): 67–78.

———. "Remembering Algeria: Melancholy, Depression and the Colonizing of the Pieds-Noirs." *Settler Colonial Studies* 8, no. 2 (2018): 244–61.

Barrows, Susanna. *Distorting Mirrors: Visions of the Crowd in Late Nineteenth-Century.* London: Yale University Press, 1981.

Beaumont, Jacqueline. "The Making of a War Correspondent: Lionel James of the *Times.*" in *The Impact of the South African War*, edited by David E. Omissi and Andrew S. Thompson, 124–37. Basingstoke: Palgrave Macmillan, 2002.

Behagel, Arthur-Alexandre. *La liberté de la presse, ce qu'elle est en Algérie, lettre à M. le baron David, député au corps législatif.* Paris: E. Dentu, 1863.

Belich, James. *Replenishing the Earth: The Settler Revolution and the Rise of the Anglo-World, 1783–1939.* Oxford: Oxford University Press, 2009.

Benbassa, Esther. *The Jews of France: A History from Antiquity to the Present.* Translated by M. B. DeBevoise. Princeton NJ: Princeton University Press, 1999.

Benrabah, Mohamed. *Language Conflict in Algeria from Colonialism to Independence.* Bristol: Multilingual Matters, 2013.

Berenson, Edward. *Heroes of Empire: Five Charismatic Men and the Conquest of Africa.* Berkeley: University of California Press, 2011.

———. *The Trial of Madame Caillaux.* Berkeley: University of California Press, 1993.

Bernard, Augustin. "Le recensement de 1906 en Algérie et en Tunisie." *Annales de géographie* 91 (1908): 24–33.

Bessis, Juliette. *Maghreb, questions d'histoire.* Paris: Editions l'Harmattan, 2003.

Best, Janice. "Une statue monumentale de la République." *Nineteenth-Century French Studies*, 34, 3&4 (2006): 303–22.

Betts, Raymond F. *Assimilation and Association in French Colonial Theory, 1890–1914.* 1961. Reprint, Lincoln: University of Nebraska Press, 2005.

Bhabha, Homi K. *The Location of Culture.* London: Routledge, 1994.

Bielsa, Esperanza. "News Translation: Global or Cosmopolitan Connections?" *Media, Culture and Society* 38, no. 2 (2016): 196–211.

Bonnenfant, Léon. *La ligue antijuive de Bougie.* Bougie: Imprimerie de Bonnenfant, [1892?].

Bouaboud, Idir. "L'Echo d'Alger, cinquante ans de vie politique française en Algérie, 1912–1961." PhD diss., Université Paris XII, 1998.

Bouveresse, Jacques. *Un parlement colonial? Les Délégations financières algériennes 1898–1945. Le déséquilibre des réalisations.* Paris: Publications des Universités de Rouen et du Havre, 2010.

Bridge, Carl, and Kent Fedorowich, eds. *The British World: Diaspora, Culture and Identity.* London: Frank Cass, 2003.

Burton, Antoinette, ed. *After the Imperial Turn: Thinking With and Through the Nation.* Durham NC: Duke University Press, 2003.

———. "Getting outside the Global: Repositioning British Imperialism in World History." In *Race, Nation and Empire: Making Histories, 1750 to the Present,* edited by Catherine Hall and Keith McClelland, 199–216. Manchester: Manchester University Press, 2010.

Cambon, Jules. *Le gouvernement général de l'Algérie (1891–1897).* Paris: E. Champion, 1918.

Carden, Ron M. *German Policy toward Neutral Spain, 1914–1918.* 1987. Reprint, London: Routledge, 2014.

Castéran, Augustin. *L'Algérie française. De 1884 à nos jours. Péril juif, péril étranger, péril arabe, procès d'un agitateur, reformes algériennes.* Paris: Ernest Flammarion, 1900.

———. *Les troubles d'Alger.* Algiers: Imprimerie Charles Zamith, 1898.

Cavanagh, Edward, and Lorenzo Veracini, eds. *The Routledge Handbook of the History of Settler Colonialism.* Oxon: Routledge, 2017.

Chatterjee, Partha. *The Nation and Its Fragments: Colonial and Postcolonial Histories.* Princeton NJ: Princeton University Press, 1993.

Choate, Mark. "Identity Politics and Political Perception in the European Settlement of Tunisia: The French Colony vs. the Italian Colony." *French Colonial History* 8 (2007): 97–109.

Choi, Sung-Eun. *Decolonization and the French of Algeria: Bringing the Settler Colony Home.* Basingstoke: Palgrave Macmillan, 2016.

Chopin, Charlotte Ann. "Embodying 'the New White Race': Colonial Doctors and Settler Society in Algeria, 1878–1914." *Social History of Medicine* 29, no. 1 (2016): 1–20.

———. "Pages without Borders: Global Networks and the Settler Press in Algeria, 1881–1914." *Settler Colonial Studies* 8 (2018): 152–74. http://www.tandfonline.com/doi/full/10.1080/2201473x.2016.1273868.

Clancy-Smith, Julia Ann. *Mediterraneans: North Africa and Europe in an Age of Migration, c. 1800–1900.* Berkeley: University of California Press, 2011.

———. *Rebel and Saint: Muslim Notables, Populist Protest, Colonial Encounters (Algeria and Tunisia, 1800–1904).* Berkeley: University of California Press, 1994.

Colonna, Fanny. "Educating Conformity in French Colonial Algeria." In *Tensions of Empire: Colonial Cultures in a Bourgeois World*, edited by Frederick Cooper and Ann Laura Stoler, 346–70. Berkeley: University of California Press, 1997.

Conklin, Alice L. *A Mission to Civilize: The Republican Idea of Empire in France and West Africa, 1895–1930*. Stanford CA: Stanford University Press, 1997.

Cooper, Frederick, and Ann Laura Stoler, eds. *Tensions of Empire: Colonial Cultures in a Bourgeois World*. Berkeley: University of California Press, 1997.

Cooper-Richet, Diana. "Aux marges de l'histoire de la presse nationale: Les périodiques en langue étrangère en France (XIXe-XXe siècles)." *Le Temps des médias* 16 (2011): 175–87.

———. "La diffusion du modèle victorien à travers le monde. Le rôle de la presse en anglais publiée en France au XIXe siecle." In Thérenty and Vaillant, *Presse, nations et mondialisation*, 17–32.

———. "La presse en langue étrangère." In Kalifa et al., *La civilisation du journal*, 583–604.

Cooper-Richet, Diana, Jean-Yves Mollier, and Ahmed Silem, eds. *Passeurs culturels dans le monde des médias et de l'édition en Europe (XIXe et XXe siècles)*. Villeurbanne: Presses de l'ENSSIB, 2005.

Corbin, Alain. *The Foul and the Fragrant*. Cambridge MA: Harvard University Press, 1986.

Coski, Christopher. *From Barbarism to Universality: Language and Identity in Early Modern France*. Columbia: University of South Carolina Press, 2011.

Crespo, Gérard, and Jean-Jacques Jordi. *Les Espagnols dans l'algérois, 1830–1914: Histoire d'une immigration*. Versailles: Editions de l'Atlanthrope, 1991.

Cummings, David. "Civilizing the Settler: Unstable Representations of French Settler Colonialism in Algeria." *Settler Colonial Studies* 8, no. 2 (2018): 175–94.

Dakhlia, Jocelyne. "L'histoire parle-t-elle en langues?" In Dakhlia, *Trames de langues*, 11–18.

———, ed. *Trames de langues: Usages et métissages linguistiques dans l'histoire du Maghreb*. Tunis: Institut de recherche sur le Maghreb contemporain, 2004. http://books.openedition.org/irmc/1446.

Darmon, Pierre. *Un siècle de passions algériennes: Une histoire de l'Algérie coloniale, 1830–1940*. Paris: Fayard, 2009.

Davis, Diana K. *Resurrecting the Granary of Rome: Environmental History and French Colonial Expansion in North Africa*. Athens: Ohio University Press, 2007.

Déjeux, Jean, and D.-H. Pageaux, eds. *Espagne et Algérie au Xxe siècle: Contacts culturels et création littéraire*. Paris: L'Harmattan, 1985.

de la Motte, Dean, and Jennene M. Pryzblyski, eds. *Making the News: Modernity and the Mass Press in Nineteenth-Century France*. Boston: University of Massachusetts Press, 1999.

Dermenjian, Geneviève. "La presse antijuive (1870–1940)." In Allouche-Benayoun and Dermenjian, *Les Juifs d'Algérie*, 135–51.

———. "Les Juifs d'Algérie entre deux hostilités (1830–1943)." In Allouche-Benayoun and Dermenjian, *Les Juifs d'Algérie*, 105–33.

Dermenjian-Hannequart, Geneviève. "La crise antijuive à Oran (1895–1905)." PhD diss., Université de Nice, 1979.

Dine, Philip. "Shaping the Colonial Body. Sport and Society in Algeria, 1870–1962." In Lorcin, *Algeria & France*, 33–48.

Drumont, Édouard. *La France juive: Essai d'histoire contemporaine*. Paris: C. Marpon et E. Flammarion, 1886.

Dubarry, Armand. *Les déséquilibrés de l'amour. Les femmes eunuques*. Paris: Chamuel, 1898–1902.

Dubois, Laurent. *A Colony of Citizens: Revolution and Slave Emancipation in the French Caribbean, 1787–1804*. Chapel Hill: University of North Carolina Press, 2004.

Durieu, Louis. *Les juifs algériens, 1870–1901*. Paris: Cerf, 1902.

Eldridge, Claire. *From Empire to Exile: History and Memory within the Pied-Noir and Harki Communities, 1962–2012*. Manchester: Manchester University Press, 2016.

Esclangon-Morin, Valérie. *Les rapatriés d'Afrique du Nord de 1956 à nos jours*. Paris: L'Harmattan, 2007.

Evans, Martin. *Algeria: France's Undeclared War*. Oxford: Oxford University Press, 2012.

———. "Towards an Emotional History of Settler Decolonisation: De Gaulle, Political Masculinity and the End of French Algeria 1958–1962." *Settler Colonial Studies* 8 (2018): 213–43.

Eymar, Marco. *La langue plurielle: Le bilinguisme franco-espagnol dans la littérature hispano-américaine (1890–1950)*. Paris: L'Harmattan, 2011.

Fanon, Frantz. *A Dying Colonialism*. New York: Grove Press, 1967.

———. *Les damnés de la Terre*. 1961. Reprint, Paris: Maspero, 2002.

Fedorowich, Kent, and Andrew S. Thompson, eds. *Empire, Migration and Identity in the British World*. Manchester: Manchester University Press, 2013.

Fitch, Nancy. "Mass Culture, Mass Parliamentary Politics, and Modern Anti-Semitism: The Dreyfus Affair in Rural France." *American Historical Review* 97, no. 1 (1992): 55–95.

Flores, Christian. *Le voleur d'huile: L'Espagne dans l'Oranie française (1830–1962)*. Montpellier: Collection Français d'Ailleurs, 1988.

Forth, Christopher E. *The Dreyfus Affair and the Crisis of French Manhood*. Baltimore: Johns Hopkins University Press, 2004.

Fredj, Claire, ed. *Femme médecin en Algérie: Journal de Dorothée Chellier, 1895–1899*. Paris: Belin, 2015.

Friedman, Elizabeth. *Colonialism and After: An Algerian Jewish Community*. South Hadley MA: Bergin and Garvey Publishers, 1988.

Garrot, Henri. *Les juifs algériens; Leurs origines*. Algiers: Librairie Louis Relin, 1898.

Georgel, Chantal, Françoise Vergès, and Alain Vivien, eds. *L'abolition de l'esclavage: Un combat pour les droits de l'homme*. Brussels: Editions Complexe, 1998.

Gosnell, Jonathan K. *The Politics of Frenchness in Colonial Algeria, 1930–1954*. Rochester NY: University of Rochester Press, 2002.

Graebner, Seth. "'Unknown and Unloved': The Politics of French Ignorance in Algeria, 1860–1930." In Lorcin, *Algeria & France*, 49–62.

Griset, Pascal. *Entreprise, technologie et souveraineté: Les télécommunications transatlantiques de la France (XIXe–XXe siècles)*. Paris: Editions rive droite, 1996.

Guignard, Didier. "Conservatoire ou révolutionnaire? Le sénatus-consulte de 1863 appliqué au régime foncier d'Algérie." *Revue d'histoire du XIXe siècle* 41 (2010): 81–95.

———. *L'abus de pouvoir dans l'Algérie coloniale (1880–1914): Visibilité et singularité*. Presses universitaires de Paris Ouest, 2014.

———, ed. *Propriété et société en Algérie contemporaine: Quelles approches?* Aix-en-Provence: Institut de recherches et d'études sur le monde arabe et musulman, 2017. http://books.openedition.org/iremam/3648.

Gumarães, Valéria. *Les transferts culturels: L'exemple de la presse en France et au Brésil*. Paris: L'Harmattan, 2011.

Habermas, Jürgen. *The Structural Transformation of the Public Sphere: An Inquiry into a Category of Bourgeois Society*. Translated by Thomas Burger with the assistance of Frederick Lawrence. 1989. Reprint, Cambridge MA: MIT Press, 1992.

Hall, Catherine. *White, Male and Middle Class: Explorations in Feminism and History*. Cambridge: Polity, 1992.

Hassett, Dónal. *Mobilizing Memory: The Great War and the Language of Politics in Colonial Algeria, 1918–1939*. Oxford: Oxford University Press, 2019.

———. "Proud *Colons*, Proud Frenchmen: Settler Colonialism and the Extreme Right in Interwar Algeria." *Settler Colonial Studies* 8, no. 2 (2018): 195–212.

Hebey, Pierre. *Alger, 1898: La grande vague antijuive.* Paris: NiL Editions, 1996.

Hourant, Georges-Pierre. "Ernest Mallebay, journaliste algérien." *L'Algérianiste* 132 (2010). http://alger-roi.fr/Alger/presse/textes/2_ernest_mallebay _algerianiste_132.htm.

Hunt, Lynn. *The Family Romance of the French Revolution.* Berkeley: University of California Press, 1992.

———. "The Many Bodies of Marie-Antoinette: Political Pornography and the Problem of the Feminine in the French Revolution." In *The French Revolution in Social and Political Perspective,* edited by Peter Jones, 268–84. London: Arnold, 1996.

Ihaddaden, Zahir. "L'histoire de la presse indigène en Algérie, des origines jusqu'en 1930." PhD diss., Université de droit, d'économie et de sciences sociales de Paris (Paris 2), 1978.

Ihl, Olivier. "Sous le regard de l'indigène: Le voyage du Président Loubet en Algérie." In *Un cérémonial politique: Les voyages officiels des chefs d'état,* edited by Jean-William Dereymez, Olivier Ihl, and Gérard Sabatier, 215–42. Paris: L'Harmattan, 1998.

Jansen, Jan C. "Celebrating the 'Nation' in a Colonial Context: 'Bastille Day' and the Contested Public Space in Algeria, 1880–1939." *Journal of Modern History* 85, no. 1 (2013): 36–68.

———. "Fête et ordre colonial: Centenaires et résistance anticolonialiste en Algérie pendant les années 1930." *Vingtième siècle: Revue d'histoire* 1, no. 121 (2014): 61–76.

Jennings, Eric T. *Curing the Colonizers: Hydrotherapy, Climatology and French Colonial Spas.* Durham NC: Duke University Press, 2006.

Kaddache, Mahfoud. *L'Etoile Nord-Africaine, 1926–1937.* Algiers: Office des publications universitaires, 1984.

Kalifa, Dominique, and Philippe Régnier. "Homogénéiser le corps national." In Kalifa et al., *La civilisation du journal,* 1411–28.

Kalifa, Dominique, Philippe Régnier, Marie-Ève Thérenty, and Alain Vaillant, eds. *La civilisation du journal: Histoire culturelle et littéraire de la presse française au XIXe siècle.* Paris: Nouveau Monde éditions, 2011.

Katz, Jonathan G. *Murder in Marrakesh: Emile Mauchamp and the French Colonial Adventure.* Bloomington: Indiana University Press, 2006.

Kaul, Chandrika, ed. *Media and the British Empire.* 2006. Reprint, Basingstoke: Palgrave Macmillan, 2013.

Krishnaswamy, N., and Archana S. Burde. *The Politics of Indians' English: Linguistic Colonialism and the Expanding English Empire.* Delhi: Oxford University Press, 1998.

Lambert, John. "'The Thinking Is Done in London': South Africa's English Language Press and Imperialism." In *Media and the British Empire*, edited by Chandrika Kaul, 37–54. 2006. Reprint, Basingstoke: Palgrave Macmillan, 2013.

Legg, Charlotte Ann. "The Medical Press and the Settler Colonial Politics of Persuasion in French Algeria, 1850–1914." *History* 104, no. 359 (2019): 105–24.

Lester, Alan. "British Settler Discourse and the Circuits of Empire." *History Workshop Journal* 54 (2002): 24–48.

Le Sueur, Louis, and Eugène Dreyfus. *La nationalité (droit interne): Commentaire de la loi du 26 juin 1889.* Paris: G. Pedone-Lauriel, 1890.

Levallois, Michel. *Ismaÿl Urbain: Royaume arabe ou Algérie franco-musulmane? 1848–1870.* Paris: Riveneuve, 2012.

Levine, Pippa, ed. *Gender and Empire.* Oxford: Oxford University Press, 2004.

Le Voyage de leurs majestés en Algérie: Septembre 1860. Paris: Bureau de l'Illustration, 1860.

Lewis, Mary Dewhurst. *Divided Rule: Sovereignty and Empire in French Tunisia, 1881–1938.* Berkeley: University of California Press, 2013.

Lorcin, Patricia M. E., ed. *Algeria & France, 1800–2000: Identity, Memory, Nostalgia.* New York: Syracuse University Press, 2006.

———. *Imperial Identities: Stereotyping, Prejudice and Race in Colonial Algeria.* New York: I. B. Tauris, 1995.

———. "Rome and France in Africa: Recovering Colonial Algeria's Latin Past." *French Historical Studies* 25, no. 2 (2002): 295–329.

Lorcin, Patricia M. E., and Todd Shepard, eds. *French Mediterraneans: Transnational and Imperial Histories.* Lincoln: University of Nebraska Press, 2016.

Maison, Dominique. "La population de l'Algérie." *Population* 28, no. 6 (1973): 1079–1107.

Mallebay, Ernest. *Cinquante ans de journalisme.* Algiers: Edition F. Fontana, 1937.

Mandeville, G., and V. Demontès. *Etudes de démographie algérienne: Les populations européennes, leur accroissement, leur densité et leurs origines.* Paris: Bureaux de la Revue des questions diplomatiques et coloniales, 1900.

Mangan, J. A. *"Manufactured" Masculinity: Making Imperial Manliness, Morality and Militarism.* London: Routledge, 2012.

Martin, Laurent. *La presse écrite en France au XIXe siècle.* Paris: Librairie générale française, 2005.

Martin, Marc. "La presse départementale." In Kalifa et al., *La civilisation du journal,* 595–13.

Matras, Yaron. *Language Contact.* Cambridge: Cambridge University Press, 2009.

McClintock, Anne. *Imperial Leather: Race, Gender and Sexuality in the Colonial Contest.* New York: Routledge, 1995.

McDougall, James. *A History of Algeria*. Cambridge: Cambridge University Press, 2017.

McLaren, Angus. *The Trials of Masculinity: Policing Sexual Boundaries, 1870–1930*. Chicago: University of Chicago Press, 1999.

Merdaci, Samir. "Journalisme et littérature au XIXe siècle: Le cas Omar Samar." *Champs* 11, no. 21–22 (2015): 97–117.

Meynier, Gilbert. *L'Algérie et la France: Deux siècles d'histoire croisée*. Paris: L'Harmattan, 2017.

Michel, Joël. *Colonies de peuplement: Afrique, XIXe–XXe siècles*. Paris: CNRS Editions, 2018.

Mollier, Jean-Yves, Philippe Regnier, and Alain Vaillant, eds. *La production de l'immatériel: Théories, représentations et pratiques de la culture au XIXe siècle*. Saint-Etienne: Publications de l'Université de Saint-Etienne, 2008.

Montoy, Louis Pierre. "La presse dans le département de Constantine (1870–1918)." PhD diss., Université de Provence, 1982.

Morgan, Kenneth O. "The Boer War and the Media (1899–1902)." *Twentieth Century British History* 13, no. 1 (2002): 1–16.

Nadeau, Daniel. "Identité nationale ou identités nationales: L'opinion publique canadienne tronquée." In Thérenty and Vaillant, *Presse, nations et mondialisation*, 307–19.

Nandy, Ashis. *The Intimate Enemy: Loss and Recovery of Self under Colonialism*. 1983. Reprint, Delhi: Oxford University Press, 1990.

Nye, Robert A. *Masculinity and Male Codes of Honor in Modern France*. New York: Oxford University Press, 1993.

Ó Ciosain, Niall. "Old Languages in a New Country: Publishing and Reading in the Celtic Languages in Nineteenth-Century Australia." *Australian Journal of Irish Studies* 11 (2011): 58–72.

O'Connor, Anne. *Translation and Language in Nineteenth-Century Ireland: A European Perspective*. London: Palgrave Macmillan, 2017.

Omissi, David E., and Andrew S. Thompson, eds. *The Impact of the South African War*. Basingstoke: Palgrave Macmillan, 2002.

Oulebsir, Nabila. *Les usages du patrimoine: Monuments, musées et politique coloniale en Algérie 1830–1930*. Paris: Les Editions de la MSH, 2004.

Phéline, Christian. *L'aube d'une révolution: Margueritte, Algérie, 26 avril 1901*. Toulouse: Editions Privat, 2012.

Pick, Daniel. *Faces of Degeneration: A European Disorder, c. 1848–c. 1918*. Cambridge: Cambridge University Press, 1989.

Potter, Simon J., ed. *News and the British World: The Emergence of an Imperial Press System, 1876–1922*. Oxford: Oxford University Press, 2003.

————. *Newspapers and Empire in Ireland and Britain: Reporting the British Empire, c. 1857–1921.* Dublin: Four Courts, 2004.

Prakash, Gyan. *Another Reason: Science and the Imagination of Modern India.* Princeton NJ: Princeton University Press, 1999.

Prochaska, David. "History as Literature, Literature as History: Cagayous of Algiers." *American Historical Review* 101, no. 3 (1996): 670–711.

————. *Making Algeria French: Colonialism in Bône, 1870–1920.* Cambridge: Cambridge University Press, 2004.

Quitout, Michel. *Paysage linguistique et enseignements des langages au Maghreb des origines à nos jours.* Paris: L'Harmattan, 2007.

Randau, Robert. *Les Algérianistes.* Paris: E. Sansot, 1911.

————. *Les Colons: Roman de la patrie algérienne.* Paris: E. Sansot, 1907.

Rantanen, Terhi. "The New Sense of Place in Nineteenth-Century News." *Media, Culture and Society* 25 (2003): 435–49.

Reclus, Onésime. *France, Algérie et colonies.* Paris: Hachette, 1886.

Renan, Ernest. *Qu'est-ce qu'une nation?* Paris: C. Lévy, 1882.

Ricoux, René. *Contribution à l'étude de l'acclimatement des Français en Algérie.* Paris: G Masson, 1874.

————. *La démographie figurée de l'Algérie.* Paris: G. Masson, 1880.

————. *La population européenne en Algérie (1873–1881).* Algiers: Imprimerie administrative Gojosso et cie., 1883.

————. *La population européenne en Algérie pendant l'année 1886.* Philippeville: Imprimerie administrative et commerciale B. Feuille, 1887.

Roberts, Mary Louise. *Disruptive Acts: The New Woman in Fin-de-Siècle France.* Chicago: University of Chicago Press, 2002.Scales, Rebecca P. *Radio and the Politics of Sound in Interwar France, 1921–1939.* Cambridge: Cambridge University Press, 2016.

Schmidt-Nowara, Christopher. *The Conquest of History: Spanish Colonialism and National Histories in the Nineteenth Century.* Pittsburgh: University of Pittsburgh Press, 2006.

Schwarz, Bill. *The White Man's World.* Oxford: Oxford University Press, 2011.

Scott, Joan W. *La citoyenne paradoxale: Les féministes françaises et les droits de l'homme.* Paris: Bibliothèque Albin Michel, 1998.

Sers-Gal, G. "La presse algérienne de 1830 à 1852." *Documents algériens. Service d'information du cabinet du gouverneur général de l'Algérie. Série politique,* no. 21 (1948).

————. "Le régime de la presse en Algérie sous le Second Empire." *Documents algériens. Service d'information du cabinet du gouverneur général de l'Algérie. Série politique,* no. 22 (1948).

Sessions, Jennifer E. *By Sword and Plow: France and the Conquest of Algeria.* Ithaca NY: Cornell University Press, 2011.

———. "Débattre la licitation comme stratégie de réquisition des terres à la fin du xixe siècle." In *Propriété et société en Algérie contemporaine. Quelles approches?*, edited by Didier Guignard. Aix-en-Provence: Institut de recherches et d'études sur le monde arabe et musulman, 2017. http://books.openedition.org/iremam/3648.

———. "'L'Algérie devenue française': The Naturalization of Non-French Colonists in French Algeria, 1830–1849." *Proceedings of the Western Society for French History* 30 (2002): 165–77.

Shepard, Todd. *The Invention of Decolonization: The Algerian War and the Remaking of France.* Ithaca NY: Cornell University Press, 2006.

Silverman, Maxim. *Deconstructing the Nation: Immigration, Racism and Citizenship in Modern France.* London: Routledge, 1992.

Sinha, Mrinalini. "Britishness, Clubbability and the Colonial Public Sphere: The Genealogy of an Imperial Institution in Colonial India." *Journal of British Studies* 40, no. 4 (2001): 489–521.

———. *Specters of Mother India: The Global Restructuring of an Empire.* Durham NC: Duke University Press, 2006.

Smith, Andrea L. *Colonial Memory and Postcolonial Europe: Maltese Settlers in Algeria and France.* Bloomington: Indiana University Press, 2006.

Souriau-Hoebrechts, Christiane. *La presse maghrébine: Libye, Tunisie, Maroc, Algérie.* Paris: Editions du Centre National de la Recherche Scientifique, 1969.

Spivak, Gayatri Chakravorty. "Can the Subaltern Speak?" In *Marxism and the Interpretation of Culture*, edited by Cary Nelson and Lawrence Grossberg, 271–313. Chicago: University of Illinois Press, 1988.

Stoler, Ann Laura. *Carnal Knowledge and Imperial Power: Race and the Intimate in Colonial Rule.* Berkeley: University of California Press, 2002.

Stora, Benjamin. *Histoire de l'Algérie coloniale.* Paris: La Découverte, 1991.

Surkis, Judith. *Sexing the Citizen: Morality and Masculinity in France, 1870–1920.* Ithaca NY: Cornell University Press, 2006.

Taithe, Bertrand. "La famine de 1866–1868: Anatomie d'une catastrophe et construction médiatique d'un événement." *Revue d'histoire du XIXe siècle* 41 (2010): 113–27.

Taraud, Christelle. *La prostitution coloniale: Algérie, Tunisie, Maroc, 1830–1962.* Paris: Payot, 2003.

Thérenty, Marie-Eve, and Alain Vaillant, eds. *Presse, nations et mondialisation au XIXe siècle.* Paris: Nouveau Monde Editions, 2010.

Thiesse, Anne-Marie. "Rôles de la presse dans la formation des identités natio-nales." In Thérenty and Vaillant, *Presse, nations et mondialisation*, 127–37.

Turin, Yvonne. "L'instruction sans l'école? Les débuts du Mobacher, d'après une correspondance inédite d'Ismaïl Urbain." *Revue de l'occident musulman et de la Méditerrané* 15–16 (1973): 367–74.

Venayre, Sylvain. "Identités nationales, altérités culturelles." In Kalifa et al., *La civilisation du journal*, 1381–1410.

Veracini, Lorenzo. *Settler Colonialism: A Theoretical Overview*. Basingstoke: Palgrave Macmillan, 2010.

Vergès, Françoise. *Monsters and Revolutionaries: Colonial Family Romance and Métissage*. Durham NC: Duke University Press, 1999.

Vermeren, Hugo. *Les Italiens à Bône (1865–1940): Migrations méditerranéennes et colonisation de peuplement en Algérie*. Rome: Ecole française de Rome, 2017.

Vignon, Louis. *La France dans L'Afrique du Nord, Algérie et Tunisie*. Paris: Guillaumin, 1887.

Vilar, Juan Bautista. "Argelia en las relaciones hispano-francesas (1898–1914)." In *Españoles y franceses en la primera mitad del siglo XX*, edited by Consejo superior de investigaciones científicas, Centro de estudios históricos, Departamento de historia contemporánea, 323–43. Madrid: CSIC, 1986.

———. *La emigración española al Norte de África (1830–1999)*. Madrid: Arco Libros, 1999.

———. "La presse espagnole en Algérie (1880–1931)." In Déjeux and Pageaux, *Espagne et Algérie*, 53–64.

Vince, Natalya. *Our Fighting Sisters: Nation, Memory and Gender in Algeria, 1954–2012*. Manchester: Manchester University Press, 2015.

Weil, Patrick. *La république et sa diversité: Migrations, intégration, discrimination*. Paris: Seuil, 2005.

———. *Qu'est-ce qu'un Français?* 2002. Reprint, Paris: Gallimard, 2005.

Wenzlhuemer, Roland. "The Dematerialization of Telecommunication: Communication Centres and Peripheries in Europe and the World, 1850–1920." *Journal of Global History* 2 (2007): 345–72.

Wilson, Stephen. "The Anti-Semitic Riots of 1898 in France." *Comparative Studies in Society and History* 16, no. 4 (1973): 789–806.

———. *Ideology and Experience: Anti-Semitism in France at the Time of the Dreyfus Affair*. London: Associated University Press, 1982.

Winock, Michel. "Les Affaires Dreyfus." *Vingtième siècle: Revue d'histoire* 5 (1985): 19–37.

Yacine, Tassadit. "La communauté espagnole en Algérie à la veille du XXe siècle." In Déjeux and Pageaux, *Espagne et Algérie*, 41–52.

———. "Un journaliste espagnol en Algérie à la fin du XIXe siècle, défenseur de sa communauté." *Revue d'histoire maghrébine* 17 (1980): 127–31.

Zack, Lizabeth. "French and Algerian Identity Formation in 1890s Algiers." *French Colonial History* 2 (2002): 115 43.

Zessin, Philipp. "Presse et journalistes 'indigènes' en Algérie coloniale (années 1890–années 1950)." *Le mouvement social* 236 (2011): 35–46.

Zimmerman, Maurice. "Le recensement de 1911 en Algérie." *Annales de géographie* 116 (1912): 184–85.

INDEX

Page numbers in italics indicate illustrations

South African Republic, 171. *See also* Transvaal

South African War, 168, 172, 179

Spain, 159–61, 163, 213–14; and Cuban rebellion, 173–75; and Latin community, 177, 222; and Morocco, 210; news from, 155, 207–8

sports, 27, 43

suffering (as journalistic ideal), 31; and anti-Jewish movement, 110, *124, 126,* 130–31, 137, 142, 149; and femininity, 45; and masculinity, 31–33, 60

surveillance, 4, 18, 54, 75

Syndicat de la presse algérienne, 33

Syndicat de la presse périodique, 33

système des rattachements, 29, 86. *See also* administrative integration; assimilation

telecommunications, 17, 90, 151–56, 169, 178

telegraph. *See* telecommunications

Third Republic, 36, 81, 85, 105, 163, 186, 230; and liberalization of press, 1, 33, 65; and masculinity, 96

Tonkin, 196

transnational Latin community, 70, 82, 149, 156, 168, 179, 188, 206, 211, 223. *See also* Latinism; Latinness; transnational Latin family

transnational Latin family, 67, 89, 102. *See also* Latinism; Latinness; transnational Latin community

Transvaal, 156, 168, 169–70. *See also* South African Republic

Treaty of Tafna, 65, 72

Triple Alliance, 179, 210, 211

Tubiana, Henry, 49

Tunisia, 89, 160–61, 177, 186, 195, 200, 216–17; and Muslim journalists, 104

UFF. *See* Union des femmes de France

ulama, 232

Union des femmes de France, 24, 39–41, *40*

United Kingdom, 169. *See also* England; Great Britain

United States, 17, 81, 87, 156, 166–68, 173, 176, 179, 184, 230

Urbain, Ismaÿl, 50–51, 79, 189. *See also* El Medani, Messaoud

Vidal, Edmond, 24, 40–41, *40,* 144–45

Villebois-Mareuil, Georges de, 170

women journalists, 43, 45. *See also* female journalists

xenophobia, 113, 130

youth (as journalistic ideal), 35, 60; and Algerian Jewish journalists, 46, 48; and anti-Jewish movement, 112, 122, 136; and masculinity, 26, 28; and Muslim journalists, 57; and women journalists, 45

Zavala, Francisco, 165, 206–8, 210–11, 213, 215

In the France Overseas series

Regeneration through Empire: French Pronatalists and Colonial Settlement in the Third Republic
Margaret Cook Andersen

To Hell and Back: The Life of Samira Bellil
Samira Bellil
Translated by Lucy R. McNair
Introduction by Alec G. Hargreaves

Colonial Metropolis: The Urban Grounds of Anti-Imperialism and Feminism in Interwar Paris
Jennifer Anne Boittin

Paradise Destroyed: Catastrophe and Citizenship in the French Caribbean
Christopher M. Church

Nomad's Land: Pastoralism and French Environmental Policy in the Nineteenth-Century Mediterranean World
Andrea E. Duffy

The French Navy and the Seven Years' War
Jonathan R. Dull

Hostages of Empire: Colonial Prisoners of War in Vichy France
Sarah Ann Frank
I, Nadia, Wife of a Terrorist
Baya Gacemi

Transnational Spaces and Identities in the Francophone World
Edited by Hafid Gafaïti, Patricia M. E. Lorcin, and David G. Troyansky

Contesting French West Africa: Battles over Schools and the Colonial Order, 1900–1950
Harry Gamble

Black French Women and the Struggle for Equality, 1848–2016
Edited and with an introduction by Félix Germain and Silyane Larcher

The French Army and Its African Soldiers: The Years of Decolonization
Ruth Ginio

French Colonialism Unmasked: The Vichy Years in French West Africa
Ruth Ginio

French St. Louis: Landscape, Contexts, and Legacy
Edited by Jay Gitlin, Robert Michael Morrissey, and Peter J. Kastor

Bourdieu in Algeria: Colonial Politics, Ethnographic Practices, Theoretical Developments
Edited and with an introduction by Jane E. Goodman and Paul A. Silverstein

Franco America in the Making: The Creole Nation Within
Jonathan K. Gosnell

Endgame 1758: The Promise, the Glory, and the Despair of Louisbourg's Last Decade
A. J. B. Johnston

The Albert Memmi Reader
Edited by Jonathan Judaken and Michael Lejman

To order or obtain more
information on these or other
University of Nebraska Press titles,
visit nebraskapress.unl.edu.